LANDSCAPE PLANNING

LANDSCAPE PLANNING

PRACTICAL TECHNIQUES FOR THE HOME GARDENER

JUDITH ADAM

FIREFLY BOOKS

A FIREFLY BOOK

Published by Firefly Books Ltd. 2002

First Printing

U.S. Cataloguing-in-Publication Data

Adam, Judith.
         Landscape planning : practical techniques for the home gardener
/ Judith Adam.—1st ed.
[224] p. : col. photos. ;   cm.
Includes index.
Summary: A hands-on guide to landscaping for homeowners. Includes all basics, projects,
more than 20 best-plants lists, irrigation and lawn tips.
ISBN 1-55209-620-3
ISBN 1-55209-618-1 (pbk.)
1. Landscape gardening. 2. Landscape design. 3. Ornamental trees. 4. Gardens—Design.
I. Title.
712./6   21   CIP   SB473.D45   2002

National Library of Canada Cataloguing in Publication Data

Adam, Judith
         Landscape planning : practical techniques for the home gardener
Includes index.
ISBN 1-55209-620-3 (bound)
ISBN 1-55209-618-1 (pbk.)
1. Landscape gardening. 2. Gardens—Design. I. Title.
SB473.A32 2002   712'.6   C2001-930411-0

Published in Canada in 2002 by
Firefly Books Ltd.
3680 Victoria Park Avenue
Toronto, Ontario, Canada   M2H 3K1

Published in United States in 2002 by
Firefly Books (U.S.) Inc.
P.O. Box 1338, Ellicott Station
Buffalo, New York, USA 14205

Design by Interrobang Graphic Design Inc.
Edited by Wendy Thomas
Production by Françoise Vulpé

Printed and bound in Canada by Friesens, Altona, Manitoba

*The Publisher acknowledges the financial support of the Government of Canada through
the Book Publishing Industry Development Program for its publishing activities.*

DEDICATION

To Frank and Dolores Del Vecchio –

Amici cari e generosi, rendete sempre bello il giardino.

(Dear and generous friends, you always make the garden beautiful.)

ACKNOWLEDGMENTS

Thanks to Lionel Koffler for having the idea

and Michael Worek for following through.

Special thanks to Françoise Vulpé and Wendy Thomas,

two hybrid editors with skills beyond their calling.

Much appreciation goes to Kathryn Riley and Vincent Summers for friendly support,

and to Marc, Brendan and Arden for being there, again.

CONTENTS

introduction

ALMOST every gardener understands how one thing leads to another. Buy a new shrub and a perennial plant bed needs to be moved. Change the house downspouts and a dry walkway becomes wet. Install a swimming pool and privacy fencing is necessary. As the garden ages, opportunities for development and renovation are always at hand. But how do you determine what's really needed? If an outdoor seating area is required, should it be a wood deck or a brick patio? To create dappled shade overhead, should you plant a locust tree or a Norway maple? And what about that steep slope in the lawn? Could it have a step, or should the grade be changed? Learning to think about landscape planning is what this book offers to home gardeners.

Landscaping is about making changes and choices in all the areas of your property—in the front lawn and entrance, the private spaces in the backyard, and the functional areas along the driveway and sides of the house. Increasing the beauty of the garden is an important goal of a landscape plan. But equally important is making sure that all the features of your lot are functional and work well. Every garden has its problems, and landscape planning always starts with an objective assessment of the site. This book will guide you through the process of evaluation, sorting out what should be kept or discarded, and helping to prioritize your lists of necessary improvements and discretionary changes. What comes first, a new set of front steps or a personal hot tub? Should the narrow front path be widened, or is in-ground irrigation more important? Learning to evaluate the need for change is just as important as getting the job done well.

Plants of every kind are the most prominent features in your garden, and also the most complex and diverse. As living components of the landscape, their

value is more than aesthetic—they create a healthy and rewarding context for your outdoor activities. It's important to understand the cultural needs of plants already in your garden, and also the features of plants you will add to the landscape. Understanding the conditions of soil quality, moisture, light and environmental exposure in your garden is an important key to plant selection. This book will show you how to match plant requirements to site conditions, so that new plant purchases will thrive and beautify the garden for many years to come. Making informed choices of plant material is the most crucial step toward successful landscape planning. The many plant lists in this book, with descriptions and photo illustrations, will guide you through a generous selection of plants for every kind of site and circumstance.

It's often the case that gardening careers begin in small ways, with planting a few flowers or vegetables just outside the back door. But as the garden grows, small gestures soon lead to larger efforts and increasing rewards. Landscape planning is the logical extension of gardening, and you're probably doing it already. Most imagined improvements and attempted changes reflect your interest in developing the garden landscape. This book is meant to encourage and support those interests, and show the way to effective decision-making. You may plan changes requiring professional skills, or perhaps your own hands can do the job. Whether the project is small or large, this book will provide information and alternatives for making the best landscape decisions.

Take a good look at your garden today, because it's going to change and grow with this book.

beyond gardening

What is the connection between gardening and landscaping? Most home gardeners puzzle over this as they search through weekend project books with directions for laying concrete patio stones and installing chain-link fencing, but with little to say to real gardeners. Is landscaping a professional discipline requiring consultants and construction trades, or can a home gardener develop a plan and make the leap from planting beds to landscape planning?

The simple answer is yes; with a bit of research and a lot of the meaningful contemplation gardeners are good at, you can make significant changes in backyards and front gardens. If the issue is whether to lay a lawn or pave a parking pad, ways to create privacy or how high to make raised beds, it all begins with understanding the essential differences in scale and concept between gardening and landscaping.

Home gardening skills are often handed down through families, and many people garden the way their parents did. Some gardeners, like myself, learn "how to" from books, along with supportive coaching from friends and neighbors. But almost all gardening activity begins with a love of plants or a particular kind of plant. The desire for luxuriant borders packed with peonies, roses and homegrown raspberries has countless times been the impetus for putting spade to soil and plunging in. Trial and error, along with patience and a strong back, are effective techniques for acquiring basic planting skills. But the leap from planting flowerbeds to making berms, gravel pathways and terraced slopes—that which gives a garden its "bones"—can be a mystifying stretch.

Painted fences are charming, but they will eventually need repainting.

A high retaining wall might have to be professionally installed.

Every planting bed needs an irrigation plan.

A tapestry of coniferous plants is consistent in all seasons.

opposite: Determining the need for hard surfaces and green space is your first big planning decision. Allow enough patio area for comfortable use and, if possible, leave two-thirds of the garden for planting and lawn. Setting a large natural boulder near a formal hard surface makes a good focal point and is an introduction to green areas.

what is landscaping?

In simple terms, gardening is what you do within a planting bed or area. Think of rose beds, alpine scree, the vegetable patch and a shrub border. Landscaping is a practical method of dividing your outdoor space, relating one area to another in a way that makes sense, and requires a broader look at the garden as a whole.

Landscape planning is like a wide-angle lens taking in all your territory and even the borrowed view beyond the hedge. Landscaping includes consideration for the ecology and topographical "lay of the land," the mechanical functions of air and water movement, the necessary conventions of boundaries, pathways and entrances. Lining a driveway with trees, lifting and relocating a lawn and adding steps to a slippery incline are some of the landscaping changes that can make the most of your garden.

Does this mean landscaping is garden design? No, in the sense of imposing on the garden themes like Victorian perennial borders or southwestern grasslands. Garden design is a process of imparting style and character to a landscape that reflects the interests, ideas and temperament of the gardener.

Landscaping is a realistic assessment of what you own and the practical methods to best develop it. Whether you do the work yourself, taking on one small project at a time, or accomplish big changes in short seasons with the help of hired professionals, the choice and pace of work are your own.

Almost every gardener experiences uncertainty over how to solve a structural problem or better use an important space. Landscaping solutions to these challenges lie just beyond the garden bed, but well within the home gardener's grasp.

Plants in a garden bed can be changed frequently, but renewing a worn pathway is more complex and permanent. Options include a stone curb with straight-cut slabs of flagstone for a formal style. Irregular random flagstone would require stone-cutting skills, while tumbled concrete cobblestones are simple to work with and durable. Hardened, non-shattering brick in a basketweave pattern might be the answer.

the ten elements of landscape design

All landscapes are defined by their natural settings and their histories. Where glaciers once roamed, expect erratic changes in levels and accumulations of large boulders. If the garden has previously been used as a car park, expect compacted soil and weed proliferation. Gardeners must play the hand they are dealt and make the most of their landscape.

Landscape design begins with an objective assessment of assets and debits inherent in the site, balanced against a realistic projection of how you would like to use the space. Resolving what you have with what you want is a giant leap toward designing a landscape to meet your needs. After that, following some traditional guidelines of style, structure, plant material and color selection will help to move you through each phase and project.

Above all, plan thoughtfully and don't rush. Sometimes the best landscaping results evolve gradually as you learn design and building techniques.

1. **Personal Style**   Despite what the latest design magazines tell us, we all know what we like and that's a good thing. Personal "style" is another way of saying personal "preference." Formal or informal; traditional or contemporary; controlled and full of careful details, or relaxed and unfinished around the edges; dense with flowering plants or subdued with green foliage textures. Personal preference will

A terra cotta pot of geraniums is a small gesture of style on a corner step in this formal garden.

influence your selection of plants, hard materials and building techniques. For instance, the patio in a formal garden could be made from straight-cut natural stone; in an informal setting cobblestones might be used. A controlled style would be reflected in a patterned brick patio, while a relaxed gardener might select a patio of "crazy paving" made from random-shaped flagstone with spaces left for moss and plants between the stones. A traditional patio would have stones running in straight and symmetrical courses, while a contemporary patio might have natural and prefabricated stone materials used together in a diagonal pattern.

2. **Planning**   Good planning is based on an objective assessment of the site conditions. Planting a dry hillside with moisture-loving roses, taking up the front lawn for a high-maintenance victory garden or fitting a hot tub on a narrow deck are interesting ideas, but what will it take to make them work? Large objects like a swimming pool or double garage are desirable, but do you have adequate space for them? When a pool fills most of the backyard, it's no longer a garden, it's a swimming hole. Identifying what

Select plants to match site conditions, such as dry under a tree.

is possible, reasonable and achievable will provide guidelines for a practical design plan. The amount of available light, wet or dry soil, flat tableland or inconsistent soil grades are all factors to be considered and weighed against the design features you hope for. Your plan should include a time schedule and sequence of events, materials and plants required, and a division of labor responsibilities—what work you can accomplish, and the tasks that require consultants, construction contractors and skilled artisans.

3. **Lines of Definition**   Private garden space looks more like a public area if you can't see where it begins and ends. Marking the perimeter will give it substance and cohesion, holding it together in your view. Fences and hedges are obvious devices for defining your space, but you can achieve the same effect more subtly with partial hedges of flowering shrubs, planting beds, tree alleys and architectural features such as low stone walls and curbs. Lines within the garden tell you where to go by indicating direction, and also emphasize the relationship of one area to another by connecting features. A path of large stepping stones draws a line from one place to another and shows you where to walk. A well-made mowing strip along the edge of the lawn separates turf from ornamental areas and can connect important features—a cluster of boulders at one end of a long planting bed to a bird bath at the other end. Every line adds character to the setting and contributes to style and design. Straight lines are suited to formal designs, curved lines are more flowing and relaxed, and staggered lines look and feel contemporary.

4. **Space Division**   Dividing space and separating areas in the garden is a way of recognizing its potential use. Planting beds are separated from turf grass, underlining the distinction between areas for growing and walking. Patios are separated from lawns, showing you where to sit and where to play soccer. Of course it's permissible to take your chair out onto the lawn, but it helps to

Shapes of green beds and lines of pathways define and divide space.

Green vines and trees overhead help to connect areas divided according to their use.

organize the garden by visually indicating how the space will be used. Large gardens are made more interesting and manageable by creating separate areas. Drift plantings of low shrubs and ground covers, island beds, berms, pathways and arbors can be used to make partial separations, block views, and encourage curiosity. Small gardens can be made to appear more spacious with subtle indications of division. A simple change in grade, raising a deck or stone patio by only a few inches (a few centimeters), will make a small garden seem larger.

5. **Scale and Balance**   Understanding the scale of the garden will ensure plants and trees appear nat-

Keep elements in scale: a small bench and a small shed for a small yard.

ural in their setting. A large garden can accommodate spreading trees and shrubs in mass plantings. Dwarf shrubs and pyramidal trees are more in scale for a small garden, with individual specimen plants for accent. The elements of the garden—vertical trees and shrubs, horizontal lawns and groundcovers, hard stone surfaces and architectural structures— should be in balance or "agreement" with the available space to appear comfortable. Too many arbors and archways in a limited space will appear contrived without enough horizontal areas to offset them. Too much stone in patio flooring and retaining walls can "outweigh" the green spaces of the garden.

6. **Garden Bones**   Prominent woody plants and architectural structures are the bones of the garden that form a permanent structure through the changing seasons. Imagine the garden as it will appear in the coldest part of the winter, and use that as a baseline for determining where to plant trees or evergreen shrubs, build a stone wall or place a bird bath. What you see in the winter are the garden bones that will support the display of spring and summer plants. Begin by selecting

Permanent structures and woody plants are a garden's bones in all seasons.

the largest trees and shrubs first. Other features should include woody plants with a minimum height of 36 inches (90 cm), and might be single specimens like a delicate Japanese maple, a cluster of flowering shrubs or dwarf conifers. All woody plants contribute to the permanent structure of the garden, but it's useful to select some with beautiful characteristics such as weeping form or ornamental bark. Architectural features include functional objects such as fences, gates and steps, and also ornamental structures like trellises, arbors, statuary and containers.

7. **Planting Style**   The preferred style of planting will influence the character of the garden. Plants can

be used in groups and clusters to effectively cover space in a mass, or with less density and more focus on detail and individual profile. English cottage gardens or woodland themes are based on massed plants that cover a lot of ground. Japanese and southwestern themes are more sparing in their use of plant material, with less density, and use more individual specimen plants that stand alone. It's not necessary to have a total theme concept throughout your garden, and planting styles can be adapted to suit the needs of each area. Massed plants can be used along a house foundation or to conceal equipment and rough ground. Weeping plants can be staggered

Natural rocks integrate easily in a relaxed garden style.

along an incline to accent the rising grade and use it as a design advantage. Or a single magnificent specimen tree could indicate the transition from front to rear gardens.

8. **Color Choices** Color is the most personal element of garden design, and can influence how the garden is used and enjoyed. The colors of perennial and annual plants and bulbs can change with the seasons by making selections for hot (deep jewel tones), cool (blues, mauves, whites) or green tapestry effects. Various areas of the garden can be planted with quite differing color schemes, all in the same season. A front garden might be devoted to hot colors like reds, and the backyard given a softer treatment with cool purples, blues and pale yellows. To build a strong color theme, at least four kinds of plants should fall into the selected color category. The color plan should also include enhancing colors that complement the central selection and make up approximately 25% of the flowering plants. If you're making a pink border, the enhancers might be mauve, gray and white. The colors of trees and shrubs also bring character to the garden. Woody plants with

Coniferous plants provide texture, form and year-round color.

purple leaves contribute a depth and richness to the landscape. Variegated plants with green and white or cream leaves bring light to shady areas, and gold or chartreuse foliage contribute interest and diversity. Conifers also come in colors such as blue-green, steel blue, gray and gold.

9. **Succession Planting** Flowering trees and shrubs and herbaceous perennial plants provide blossoms, texture and scent that are important features of each season. All too often the majority of floral display comes in spring and early summer. With planning, the garden can include plants that demonstrate their ornamental value throughout the growing season, including the later months,

when gardens can be exclusively green. Keeping an accurate record of when plants in the garden blossom will reveal the periods when blooms are abundant or scarce. Careful research in books and community gardens will help to identify perennial plants that bloom in mid to late summer and autumn frost, and these can be purchased and set in beds and borders. Late-flowering shrubs such as *Hydrangea tardiva*, Rose of Sharon, pink and white summersweet (*Clethra alnifolia*) and bluebeard (*Caryopteris* x *clandonensis*), and woody plants with ornamental fruit like the small species rose *R. pendulina* and the columnar Siberian crabapple, *Malus baccata*, are valuable in the

Plan for a succession of blooming plants from spring through summer and autumn.

autumn garden. Brilliant autumn coloring can also be factored into the plantings for successive waves of ornamental display with shrubs such as red chokeberry (*Aronia arbutifolia*), red-vein enkianthus (*E. campanulatus*) and lace-leaf Japanese maples (*Acer palmatum dissectum*).

10. **Architectural Features**   Almost any kind of hard construction has architectural value in the garden. The most familiar objects are walkways and benches, fences and

Fences, floors and seats are functional architectural objects.

gates, trellises and pergolas, arbors and ponds, and their design value is increased when they're crafted with skill from appropriate materials. Small objects such as bird baths and statuary are useful for

punctuating entrances and creating local interest within a planting bed. Gardens are enhanced when architectural accents are well placed where they will emphasize the purpose of an area or contribute to plant growth, and make garden use more comfortable or accessible. Using too many architectural objects can disrupt the flow of garden areas and confuse the design intent. The best guideline is to be sure that each object has functional or artistic merit. But architectural objects and features should never replace plant material, and gratuitous littering of the garden with gnomes, lanterns and windmills detracts from the intent of garden design.

the basis for change

Gardeners are quick to be critical of their home ground and that impetus, slowed down, can be useful in identifying the need for change. We sometimes get a bee in our bonnets over some small nuisance.

However it's best not to focus on aggravating details, but first take a broad view of the area and determine its character. Is this an old garden with accumulated artifacts from previous owners, or a new and barren land-scape? Does it appear empty or crowded, disorganized or messy, vacant or overwhelming in size and scale? Are structures tumbled down, in disrepair, antiquated? Or is there nothing but a new sod lawn and board fence?

This well-constructed garden is full of ideas. Steps and a low retaining wall, a formal walkway and relaxed stepping-stone path, a mowing strip, picket fencing and garden arbor are all useful hard features. Dwarf conifers are used in the foundation bed, with pyramidal trees at the corners. The lawn is contained by two hedges and enhanced with an ornamental weeping shrub and a cluster of birch trees with ground-cover plants beneath.

The gardener's eye is a tricky device. At first glance, we notice only the features that excite our interest. But it's smarter to spend some time sorting out the good, the bad and the useless. An objective evaluation always begins with identifying what can be eliminated from the scene. In one client's garden, I once found a small power mower rusted in place where it had sputtered to an end, as if the gardener had been called to the telephone and never returned. And it's not unusual for fifty-something empty nesters to have a sand pit and swing set taking pride of place out back. When these things are removed, the picture clarifies and changes. If your garden has been in the family for generations, you might not have noticed how run down and disorganized some areas have become. If you've recently moved in, now is when you catalogue what was purchased along with the house. Do you really want to keep an aboveground vinyl pool? Or an enormous satellite dish? And how about brick barbecues last used by the Romans? If you love it, it's a keeper; otherwise, it's for quick sale or demolition.

But don't be needlessly hasty. It's also important to judge the value of what you see and its possible use. I'm always on the lookout for potential treasures in my clients' gardens. I've found antique urns under mountains of bittersweet vines, an Art Deco fountain buried in a brick pile, and in one yard a stone patio was discovered under a lawn. (Given enough time, grass will creep over anything that stands in its way.) You may initially disregard a fine flagstone wall, just because it's half tumbled down. Is repair possible, can the entire wall be moved to a better location, or can some stones be salvaged and used for a patio or front entrance?

If your lot was developed before 1950, there may be a treasure trove of granite cobblestones used for pathways, now of considerable value and requiring only a stiff cleaning. Woody plants and trees that have weathered the ages can sometimes be cleaned up and pruned to display the character of their years. Are there desirable perennial plants that could be saved and relocated when changes take place? Can overgrown hedges and flowering shrubs be rejuvenated?

DESIGN TRUE TO ITS PLACE

EVERY home and garden has a sense of place, a feeling of character that defines how it fits into the neighborhood and universe at large. Whatever landscaping tactics are applied, they should always enhance that identity and be in sympathy with the setting. When inappropriate choices are made, like installing high-tech lighting fixtures in a country garden, we're left wondering what's wrong with the picture.

Getting a "feel" for the place has a lot to do with historical perspective. In contemporary homes and gardens, you'll often find materials like composed aggregate stone and precast concrete. But a century home deserves a gravel driveway that reflects its age and tradition. A Cape Cod cottage is most authentic when the front path is laid in a brick herringbone pattern. Using materials and techniques appropriately is one way of keeping the setting honest and true to its essential character.

why am I doing this?

You may see a lot of potential for garden development. And a lot of work, sweat and expense down the road. But good reasons exist for taking on landscaping renovations, whether small or large, and they all start with space and function. The essential question is: Does this space work, and does it suit my needs? Can I sit and eat pleasantly outdoors? Can I walk where I need to go without stepping in soil? Is the terrain safe or will I slip and stumble? Are the boundaries marked and contained? Is there a place for the special interests of family members and guests—kids, athletes, swimmers, gardeners?

Not all change is large. You may only want to make a mowing edge on the lawn, repair the cracked front walkway, or plant a handsome yew hedge. But whatever landscaping change you accomplish should add to the value of your property and bring the special satisfaction of accrued value. Good choices in landscape development always reveal the thoughtful intent of the gardener. You can see the unfortunate choices in work accomplished using inferior materials and "patch-up" methods. Temporary resolutions fail to enhance property value and demonstrate poor judgment and planning. Patching steps instead of rebuilding, propping up what needs to be torn down, and using boards to hold back a heavy bank of soil all detract from the pleasure and value of a garden.

When the initial investment figures go higher, be sure your landscaping improvements are likely to be saleable to a future buyer. The more expensive and permanent the landscaping development, the more necessary it is to ensure its lasting value and broad appeal. Swimming pools are the particular passion of many people, but some buyers will immediately discount the purchase of a home with a pool; removing the pool is seldom successful. As well, extensive paving for car parking can ruin soil conditions should a potential buyer want to lift the hard surfaces and plant an arboretum. Before you customize your garden and make it the fulfillment of personal dreams, be sure you intend to stick around and enjoy it for some time. Regardless of what your investment may be, you can expect the "curb appeal" of a well-landscaped garden to add seven to ten percent to the value of your property, provided the changes you make are reasonable, enhancing and appreciable by just about everyone on the road.

GETTING YOUR MONEY'S WORTH

THE cost of ambitious landscaping projects can make your bankbook twitch, so before making large-scale plans, consider how long you intend to live at the current address.

The simple ratio of one thousand dollars' worth of development for each year you expect to remain on the property works well for short-term planning. For five thousand dollars spent in the garden, you should hope to be enjoying the changes for five years to get your value from the investment. Ten thousand dollars' worth of landscaping investment should get you ten years of "payback" and you can feel the money was well spent.

All kinds of desirable projects, such as new decks and garden beds, irrigation systems and patios, could fall into this budget. Set a budget that reflects your financial comfort level—enough money to make a change you can appreciate in the immediate future, but not so much that you resent the cost of improvements.

moving mountains: who does the work?

Gardeners usually have a good sense of their own skill level. Digging a new bed, dividing perennial plants, lawn mowing and composting all require familiar skills. You may be proficient at one and more of an amateur at another, but these accomplishments are generally within most gardeners' abilities. Now you're considering new levels of achievement requiring tasks and skills you may have seen carried out but never attempted on your own. You might enjoy standing at the side of a construction site and watching the progress, but that doesn't qualify a gardener for construction work. Could you possibly figure out the basics of soil grading, understand how to fit interlock bricks together, select and install large-scale nursery plants? Or should you be looking for a professional service to carry out your plans?

Some skills are the specific domain of traditional trades like bricklayers and stonemasons, and with good reasons. Laying a dry brick pathway with sand in the joints requires more thought than skill, but building a mortared brick wall requires a depth of experience best left to professional bricklayers. Similarly, fitting together a patio of machine-cut, straight-edged flagstone is not very complicated, but making a patio of random flagstone with irregular shapes requires the stone-cutting skills of a professional mason. Taking on jobs like these that are beyond your possible abilities is a waste of time and costly materials.

right: A new driveway requires heavy equipment for excavation, a compacted foundation and a finished surface. Let a professional do the job.

WE often know more than we realize about landscaping skills, and that's because so much of it is common sense. It's obvious that soil will wash away from a raised planting bed, so a high curb or retaining wall must be built to hold soil and plants in place. If you understand the need for perennial plants to have sufficient good soil for strong root systems, you'll also see the point of providing 6 inches (15 cm) of quality loam under a new lawn.

Observation is also a useful educator. Every time you see an interlocking brick driveway with sunken areas, you know right away that it has an inadequate foundation. The lesson in making a strong foundation for heavy materials can be applied when you want to install a stepping-stone path through the grass in your yard. A strong foundation under each stepping stone ensures it won't heave with frost and will remain high and level (see page 79). Thorough research in libraries at building centers, and advice from friends who've "been there and done that," can provide enormous amounts of useful information. For every complex task there is a wealth of printed material, but the fine points come only with experience.

Courage, resourcefulness and street savvy have a place in home landscaping, so don't immediately panic. Every landscaping project requires a level of skill, knowledge, muscular strength and time. But don't assume inexperience and a slim build put you immediately out of the picture.

Take a good look at a construction site and you'll notice that not all the workers involved are built like Cro-Magnon Man. Size isn't always commensurate with strength, and brute strength isn't always a crucial factor. In fact, clever gardeners already know that well-chosen tools can often replace pumped-up muscles. A sharpened spade powered by a normal arm digs a hole quickly and efficiently; a dull spade requires a lot more muscle to accomplish the same job.

Special equipment can be rented for many kinds of laborious tasks—sod cutters, brick splitters, stone chisels, soil compactors, conveyor belts—and using these devices replaces the need for personal strength and endurance. If you're working with massive weights, you can usually arrange for small, truck-mounted cranes and forklifts along with the delivery of materials like brick, stone and lumber. The truck's machinery will be able to place the load to the side of your driveway, and your own heavy-duty wheelbarrow will let you break up and move the material to where you need it. If you've ordered several tons of ornamental boulders and the truck has no crane or lifting device, the rock will be unceremoniously tipped out on the driveway or lawn. Putting down some old blankets and car tires wherever the rocks are going to land will prevent injury to the surface below.

calling for help

Sometimes it's smart to divvy up the work, hiring professionals to get parts of the job done quickly and with expertise. If you're no longer on the sunny side of fifty you might want an instant garden effect with hefty trees up to 15 feet (4.5 m) in height, and nurseries will deliver just about anything you fancy. That much living wood arrives attached to a root ball 3 feet (90 cm) in diameter and weighing in excess of 600 pounds (270 kg). Just digging the hole is enough to evoke nightmares of cardiac arrest. This situation and others like it call for a bit of help from someone who has done the job before, has the right equipment and thinks your tree is beautiful. Local community newspapers list all kinds of hired help for lifting, carrying and digging, or you can ask a tree service or landscaper to supply and install the really big plant material. Save your own grunt power for the smaller stuff.

If you're working with a professional landscaper, it's a good idea to have a clear understanding of what's to be supplied and installed. Plants should be ordered by their Latin botanical names so that you get exactly what you want. Size should also be indicated, because plant size has a lot to do with price. For hard materials such as natural stone, precast concrete pavers and hardened or vitrified brick, be sure the landscaper specifies what kinds, sizes and quantity will be used. Product shortages often happen in a busy landscaping season and substitutions may be necessary, but you will want to be assured the substitutions meet the original specifications.

Hiring a Professional

Professional landscapers have a large fund of experience and information to share, and you should select one who is generous with his or her time. There's much to be gained by listening to their advice, as well as their cautions, and involving them in reaching final decisions. Landscape contractors want to give you a job that is well installed and lasting, for they rely on your satisfaction and referrals for future business.

You should receive a written cost estimate with details of how many plants will be supplied, their Latin botanical names, plant sizes and costs. Necessary amounts of soil, shredded bark and foundation materials should be specified in cubic yards. Sizes and kinds of stone and lumber should be noted. Start and completion dates should be agreed upon, although some delays may be unavoidable. The cost of "add-on" projects that arise while work is in progress should also be written up with cost estimates. Be clear on what guarantees come with the labor, building materials and plants. And expect the site to be cleaned at the end of each day, walkways swept and tools and materials put away. You should be prepared to pay a deposit up front before work begins, and provide washroom facilities for anyone working on your property.

If You Do It Yourself

Finding time is usually the most difficult requirement. Will you be working on your own, or is help at hand? Helpers will shorten the time needed, but won't cut it in half.

Start with a realistic appreciation for the time required to find and purchase materials, get set up on the site, carry out the project, clean up and return rental equipment. Is it an afternoon's work, have you got vacation time for this commitment, or must it be accomplished on weekends? Living with a messy on-going project won't endear you to friends and neighbors, so it's important to establish a completion date if you want the satisfaction of a job well done. If the spirit is willing but you just haven't got the time, that's one good reason to call in a professional landscaper.

BUYING TREES

Growers charge nurseries more for maintaining a plant until it reaches premium size, and that cost is passed on to consumers. Woody shrubs are measured in linear height, and there will be a big price difference between a small, 24-inch (60 cm) holly and an older, more mature specimen measuring 48 inches (1.2 m) high.

Trees are caliper-measured in centimeters or inches of trunk diameter. A tree may be less than 10 feet (3 m) in height, but if the diameter of the trunk is 28 inches (70 cm), you're buying a more mature tree and this will be reflected in the cost. A taller tree with a slimmer trunk could be cheaper, but it is younger, possibly slimmer than its stakes, and won't have the solid appearance of older wood. Of course there's nothing wrong with buying a younger tree and watching it grow—just be sure that's what you wanted.

BUYING HARD MATERIAL

Natural stone, such as flagstone and sandstone, will absorb water, and in cold climates this affects its strength over time. Stone that is 1½ inches (3.75 cm) thick or more has strength to withstand repeated winter frosts without shattering, but you can also expect the cost to increase proportionately.

Precast concrete pavers, manufactured cobblestones and bricks are uniform in size and competitive in price, but the underlying foundation preparation can make a difference in project cost. A quote that sounds like a bargain in interlock brick installation could reflect inadequate foundation excavation and materials.

The higher cost to install a minimum 10 inches (25 cm) of compacted crushed gravel, limestone screenings and sand will provide a foundation with the strength and durability to resist sinking and sagging. Unless you like that "puddling" effect in paved driveways, plan to spend a reasonable amount for a strong base.

One graceful tree like *Betula pendula*, European white birch, can transform the character of an ordinary front garden into something distinctive. Buying a larger specimen brings quicker satisfaction.

The cost of hard surfaces is expensive, but even small areas can be useful and add aesthetic appeal. Most important is a firm foundation under stone, brick or concrete pavers. Here, a round birdbath provided design inspiration.

paying for it

As in all matters of investment, let your purse be your guide to accomplishment. The work you can do yourself is a great dollar saving, but only if you have the skill and information to do it competently. Ruining expensive lumber or planting trees backwards (yes, there is a front and back to every plant) can punch quite a hole in your budget. Hiring a professional will cost two to three times more than doing the work yourself, but you'll get a job well done.

Nevertheless, you can learn lots of landscaping techniques with just a bit of time and research, so make a point of starting your planning process with a clear division of labor. Decide which techniques you need to master, and what kind of skilled professionals you want for the hard-and-heavy stuff.

Before you drag the bank manager into your backyard project, consider some traditional methods of fundraising. It's a fact that people will buy almost anything you put out on the lawn on a Saturday morning. So why not organize a garage sale, perhaps with surrounding neighbors? This will give you a quick infusion of cash for plants and materials. Or establish a landscaping fund and advertise it among the family for birthday and anniversary gifts, offering to dedicate trees, a sundial and a new bench to your Aunt Hattie. Even just saving the coins from your pocket each night over winter can add up to a new trellis by springtime.

Consider purchasing second-hand materials from older homes undergoing renovation. Dry-laid natural stone with sand between the joints is easily lifted for re-use. You might be able to purchase iron fences and gates from schools and churches in the process of upgrading, or lumber if it's in good condition and carefully deconstructed. Some wrecking companies will salvage materials and art items and offer them for sale from their work yards. Advertise your "wants list" in the community newspaper or library bulletin board. Ornamental items like fountains and garden statuary often turn up at local auction halls, and it's worth attending several over a period of time to catch some one-of-a-kind bargains. The best deals are often at the end of the auction, when fewer buyers are around.

The best financial strategy is to do what you can easily afford and feel gratified every time you see it. Any work you accomplish in the garden should give you only pleasure. Creating economic stress for the sake of landscaping defeats the purpose of having a garden retreat to call your own. Better to live in an apartment.

MANUFACTURING SOIL

THE best soil can be manufactured in your own garden in any season with materials that are easily obtained. The basic ingredients are equal proportions of small or shredded leaves, well-rotted manure and coarse builder's sand. The leaves can be saved in autumn (in a pile or in open plastic bags with many air holes) and will compost in the mix to produce humus and plant food minerals. Rotted manure (purchased in bags or delivered in cubic yards/meters) contributes humus, nutrients and essential micro-organisms for the biological life of the new soil. The coarse sand provides a drainage system for oxygen and moisture to move through the soil.

You can make this soil mixture in small or large amounts, and plant into it immediately. Expect the newly made soil to sink down by a third of its height over a period of 12 months. Watch for worms, the best indicators that your new soil is premium quality.

understanding the basics: grades, levels and drainage

Certain things gardeners know almost by instinct, or at least they think they do. Practical information like "green side up" and "water flows downhill" are so basic we consider them jokes. But it's no joke if water is flowing downhill right into your basement or turning the front lawn into a bog. Grading and drainage are basic factors in garden-making yet are seldom mentioned in traditional gardening books. They may seem like engineering mysteries, but every garden project is affected by the lay of the land and where the water flows, and gardeners can do something about this.

The naked eye is a good judge of levels when surveying an open soil surface before anything is growing. But even a planted surface covered with grass conceals many irregularities and requires a naked foot to judge where they are. Walking across the lawn without shoes will give you an indication of subtle slopes and valleys in the lawn as your ankle adjusts to the surface with each step. For broader areas, an initial appraisal can be had by lying full-length on your back in the grass and moving your position about the yard several times. You will feel the direction of slope just as you would know if your bed mattress was on a slant. Gardeners are not generally fastidious, but you can lie on a thin sheet if necessary.

Grading refers to elevations and how the earth is leveled, and it's important information in small and large garden projects. In a typical garden bed, a useful grade can be established by raking the soil slightly higher along the back of the bed, perhaps an elevation of only 8–10 inches (20–25 cm), and gradually leveling the soil as it reaches the front edge of the bed. This ensures water will drain forward toward the lawn and prevents puddling and swamping that could damage plants, such as delphiniums and yews, that can't tolerate excessive mois-

The truest aphorism is that water always travels downhill. It's important that the grade or level of soil is higher at the house wall and lower as you move away from the house. This ensures water will flow quickly away from your basement.

ture. Grading in this manner also has a design value and can make the bed appear deeper and the plants more mature.

A foundation bed should be graded in a similar manner, referred to as positive grading. The soil surrounding a house foundation is slanted higher against the house wall and sloped to a lower point in front to carry water away from the foundation. Of course, negative grading would be the opposite, and water trapped close to the wall would quickly find a way to the inside through cracks in the foundation.

The soil around a house foundation has a tendency to settle over time and the original positive grade can be lost. Installation of heavy equipment close to the foundation such as air conditioners and pool heaters can disturb the grade, resulting in a wet basement. The grade is also changed by the removal of large shrubs or trees and their roots from the foundation plantings. Remembering to re-establish the correct grade whenever soil is disturbed near the foundation walls will keep the basement dry and the situation positive in every respect.

Imagine a cartoon drawing of your house set on a hill and the garden surrounding it on land sloping down and away. That exaggerated picture shows you the ideal concept of how land should be rough-graded to ensure water

from rain and snowmelt runs away efficiently. In reality, the slope of the land is subtle and gradual, but effective in preventing pockets and troughs where water could be trapped.

Rough-grading is accomplished using heavy machinery like a skid loader or "Bobcat" to shift substantial amounts of soil and sculpt the configuration of the land. This procedure is always part of initial construction, but can also be used to make changes and corrections to grading and drainage problems that develop over time. Fine-grading is done with hand tools such as a stiff rake to finish the grade smoothly, breaking up clods of soil and making it ready for sod or other kinds of planting.

Grading is an important issue when preparing a foundation surface for hard materials like concrete, asphalt and brick. Hard surfaces efficiently direct water that falls on them, and you want to make sure it's going in the right direction. A pathway running beside the garage or a patio extending from the house should be pitched slightly higher where it meets the wall.

Allowing the grade to drop 1 inch (2.5 cm) every 4 feet (1.2 m) will create a two percent slope, sufficient to carry water away quickly. If you're living in a townhouse with an underground garage, the driveway grade will be pitched toward the house and downward. The builder will have installed a large catch-

ment drain across the front of the garage foundation where it meets the driveway, and this carries water away before it can enter the garage.

Older lawns with large trees can shift and heave inconsistently as roots move through the soil, creating a surface full of lumps and ridges. Grass growth may disguise the uneven surface to the eye, but your feet will feel the uncomfortable lumpiness below. If the problem is severe, you may need to strip the grass, re-grade with additional soil using a skid loader, and lay new sod. But if you're patient, the lumpiness can be evened out by top-dressing twice a year, applying a 1-inch (2.5 cm) layer of good soil over the lawn in spring and autumn. Be sure to cut the grass first, and then spread the soil evenly across the lawn with a soft leaf rake. A 1-inch (2.5 cm) covering won't suffocate the grass, and you will gradually build up the surface soil and soften the lumps.

Where telephone cables and utility service lines have been buried in a lawn, sunken troughs several inches deep may develop as the soil continues to settle. These visible depressions can cause you to stumble and will collect water and ice. To fill in a trough, leave the grass in place and pack the depression with soil. Spread grass seed over top, cover the seed with another inch of soil or peat moss, and water the area daily until the new grass is established.

Small gullies and larger swales can form at the base of a steep incline where runoff rainwater rapidly falls to the bottom, erodes a depression, and can't find a way out. Re-contouring the slope with additional soil and gravel will create a more gradual drop and spread the water over a broader area. In situations where extreme flooding occurs, the swale can be extended on a downward tilt to a street drain or low point away from the slope.

A constructed dry stream bed at the bottom of a slope is a clever way to catch runoff water and prevent puddling in the lawn. A line of drainage tile buried underneath will carry water away quickly.

HOW TO MEASURE THE POSITIVE GRADE

Ensuring that water runs away from a house foundation wall is the first and most important issue for a foundation planting bed. When soil is disturbed around a foundation wall, the grade (or level of earth) can be subtly changed and result in water flowing backward, toward the house. This can happen when a mature shrub or tree planted too close to the wall is removed. If puddling appear near the wall after the next big rain, the grade must be corrected to move water away from the foundation. You'll know there is a grade problem if the soil level is higher farther away from the wall than it is closer to the wall.

To establish efficient drainage of water away from a house foundation, the level of soil should drop 1 inch (2.5 cm) in every 6 linear inches (15 cm) for 3–4 feet (90–120 cm) extending away from the house. Beyond that point, the grade should drop 1 inch (2.5 cm) for every 12 inches (30 cm) for the next 5 feet (1.5 m).

1. Measuring the soil grade surrounding a foundation wall requires only a 6-foot (1.8 m) length of 2 x 4 lumber and a long carpenter's level.

2. Use a pencil and stiff metal tape measure to mark off 6-inch (15 cm) lengths along the 2 x 4. Tape the level to the 2 x 4 and place one end where the soil surface meets the foundation wall.

3. Hold the extended lumber and adjust its height until it's level.

4. Measure how much the grade drops or slants down every 6 inches (15 cm) for a distance of 4 feet (1.2 m) from the wall.

As an example, if the first grade measurement is an elevation of 8 inches (20 cm) and the second grade measurement, taken 6 inches (15 cm) farther out, is 9.5 inches (24 cm), the grade is rising. Two and a half inches of soil must be removed at the point of the second measurement to create a downward grade, changing the second measurement to 7 inches (17 cm) for a change of 1 inch (2.5 cm) for every 6 inches (15 cm). The grade at a further 6 inches (15 cm) away may also need adjusting, and so on.

Use a snub-nose spade to remove soil, starting where the grade first begins to rise, going as far as necessary to achieve a downward grade. Use a stiff rake to even out the newly lowered area. Then measure the grade again, to be sure the new contour drops down as you move away from the wall.

where the water goes

Like all important resources, water requires management. We try to keep track of it, predict when to expect it, anticipate how much the garden needs, and determine what happens to the excess—because too much water is too much of a good thing. Solving simple drainage problems is well within the grasp of home gardeners, if you understand where the water goes.

If you suspect drainage problems, it's best to get out and investigate the situation. That means getting hold of boots and an umbrella and venturing into the garden during a torrential downpour.

Over time the foundation under a pathway may sink and cause puddling or an ice hazard. The path needs to be remade, with a higher sloping grade (see page 29) to carry water away. Lawn puddles can be corrected gradually by spreading 1 inch (2.5 cm) of topsoil twice a year until the grade is sufficiently raised.

The neighbors have already seen you out lying on the lawn, so this walkabout in the rain won't draw too much comment. If it's really raining buckets, you should be able to see in which direction the water runs and where it accumulates.

If the lawn feels spongy and water spurts around every footstep, you'll know the compacted soil underneath is slow to absorb excessive moisture. It's not unusual for a lawn to drain unevenly, some sections absorbing rainwater while other areas flood. Drainage tiles made of perforated flexible plastic piping can be buried in a gravel bed under the turf to attract and carry away excess moisture. The tiles are easily installed without starting a full-scale lawn reno-vation, and provide a good solution when the problem is localized. They can be run alongside a planting bed, around a patio or in staggered lines through the lawn.

If water turns the lawn into a lake for three weeks in spring and after every summer cloudburst, more serious drainage solutions are required. A sys-tem of drainage tiles and dry wells can be installed to quickly collect water under-ground, allowing it to slowly drain away, or a plastic barrel or concrete catch basin with surface grate can be built into a low spot. You can be successful with most drainage improvements yourself, but concrete catch basins might require pro-fessionals who've done it before.

KEEPING THE FOUNDATION DRY

THE 18 inches (45 cm) of soil at the house foundation is a dry shade area and a no-man's-land for landscape plants. But rainwater and weeds do find their way into this strip of soil and sometimes cause problems. Water cascading from eavestrough exits can cause flash floods, eroding soil and seeping into foundation cracks. Adding on a long downspout extension to carry the water 2–4 feet (60–120 cm) away will help disperse it, and you can mask the extension with low evergreen shrubs.

It's also useful to make a shallow gravel bed around the entire house foundation, removing the soil 3 inches (7.5 cm) deep and 12 inches (30 cm) wide. Line the bed with heavy landscape fabric and fill the space with small-size pea gravel, banked slightly against the foundation wall. The pea gravel will stop mud from splashing against the house and prevents weeds from growing in this space. Don't skimp on the landscape fabric, as it keeps the gravel from sinking into the soil.

A flat grade with no slope is an invitation for flooding. Renovating the wide foundation bed and increasing the slope away from the wall will help keep the basement dry.

HOW DRAINAGE TILES WORK

FINDING SOLUTIONS TO WATER PROBLEMS

HEALTHY soil with good structure effectively drains excess moisture away. But compacted soil and dense clay are slower to drain. Water held in soil displaces oxygen and results in poor plant growth. It can also enter fine cracks in the house walls. Drainage tiles are a good solution for excess water problems such as puddling in grass, soil erosion and flooding at the bottom of a slope, or chronically saturated soil close to the house foundation wall.

When the spring melt or a summer cloudburst causes rapid accumulation of surface water, a swale can be installed to move water away quickly. A swale is a shallow depression that fills a low corner of a lot or can be extended to follow along a lot line. Excess water runs off into the swale and then slowly dissipates. Many swales are formed naturally by previous patterns of water erosion, and if not too unattractive, can be allowed to remain. If you're digging a shallow swale in an obscure corner, you can stabilize it by lining the bottom and sides with landscape fabric, and then covering the fabric with gravel or fist-sized landscape stones.

right: If flooding is a chronic problem and great amounts of water must be drained effectively, you might want to have more than one line of drainage tiles, and they each can culminate in a dry well. This is a hole 4–5 feet (1.2–1.5 m) deep and wide, filled with gravel and capped with landscape fabric, soil and sod.

left: A drainage tile is a flexible length of 6-inch (15 cm) wide vinyl pipe. It's perforated on all sides so that water can flow in and out, and it can be cut to whatever length is required. Sometimes it's sold with a mesh sheath to prevent soil from entering the pipe.

The pipe should be buried where excessive water is collected in the soil. Ideally it will follow a grade leading to lower ground where the water can slowly drain away through holes in the pipe. If no lower ground is accessible, the pipe is still a useful solution. Bury it where water accumulates and lead it to a concealed corner where it can be "daylighted"—with the end protruding slightly from the ground. The passage of air into the pipe will help to dissipate the water more quickly.

HOW TO INSTALL DRAINAGE TILES

Installing drainage tile requires no special tools and isn't difficult to do. The amount of digging isn't onerous and the work can be accomplished in a single day or spread over several days. One line of tile is often enough to improve water drainage in a small area, at the bottom of a hillside garden, for instance. But if several lines of tile are required for a larger area, it's not necessary to install them all at once. The work can be spread out over several weeks, or as your schedule allows. And the best thing about drainage tiles is that they work right away. No more flooding and puddles to contend with, and the oxygen content of the soil will be improved.

If there is grass over the area to be drained, use a sharp blunt-nosed spade to cut a slit in the turf along the length where the tile will be installed. Holding the spade horizontally, slide it under the turf on both sides of the slit, and fold the grass back to expose a 14-inch (35 cm) strip of soil.

1. Dig a trench 14 inches (35 cm) deep and 14 inches (35 cm) wide, and as long as necessary to move water away from the area. Line the trench bottom and sides with sturdy filter cloth, a type of landscape fabric purchased at garden centers. Leave enough filter cloth to also cover and enclose the top of the trench.

2. Put 4 inches (10 cm) of gravel in the bottom of the trench, lay the pipe on top and fill in the sides with gravel, allowing the gravel to cover the pipe by 2 inches (5 cm).

3. Cover the gravel with the filter cloth and then add soil on top of the cloth and up to the surrounding soil level. Push the grass back down over the trench and firm it in place with your hands.

planning a landscape

2

Gardeners know that one small project invariably leads to another, and the half-hour of weeding before breakfast can ultimately end at sundown. There is simply no end of work needing to be done and it's easier to motor through rather than attempt to prioritize. Everything is important. But when the projects are larger and more expensive, that's the time to shift gears and consider the choice of what to do first.

Before you make any decisions, it's important to understand the planning process. Planning has everything to do with prioritizing needs and little to do with satisfying wish-fulfillment. The chocoholic's dream of being set loose in the candy factory would not find a place in nutritional planning. And the desire for a personal theme park should not be included in a landscaping plan. A landscape plan is based on intelligent consideration of what is

Beauty may be in the eye of the beholder, but everyone recognizes the value of good planning and construction. Every garden has valuable assets, like a pleasant seat under a graceful tree. Good planning will integrate new ideas with existing features to make the space more useful.

opposite: Old features sometimes have great charm that can be improved with new materials and building techniques. Painted wood surfaces need periodic refinishing. A new fence and gate in identical style and finished with preservative stain require much less maintenance than paint.

necessary and useful in developing the potential of a garden. The functional qualities of the property and how you can be comfortable and "at home" in your own outdoors are paramount. Landscape planning isn't meant to produce a site worthy of a magazine illustration. Choices should enhance the value of your home and make the garden a place your family and friends can spend more time in.

Of course, we want the garden to be transformed yesterday. Soon isn't quick enough. But there's a case to be made for allowing landscape changes to evolve in a paced progression. If you understand the character of the garden and the changes you want to make, you need a time-line or strategic plan. It's sad to say, but contemporary culture often works against the appreciation of gardens and outdoor living. The necessary hours spent in offices and in front of computers, and the draw of television and big-screen entertainment, all take time away from outdoor activities. Living in a cold climate can discourage garden use for several months of every year. So when we think of landscape planning, we have an urge, before our attention is distracted or the season passes, to get it all down on paper, every architectural detail and plant set in place on a permanent document. It may be thorough, but does it work?

It's not unusual to see gardeners-of-a-certain-age wandering about with large and tattered sheets of graph paper bearing their original landscape plan, now a decade old. The dilemma is they're finally ready to plant a 'Selkirk' crabapple, prized for its large and shiny ornamental fruits, but the designated location is currently in deep shade. Ten years ago it was a sunny spot, but of course, things change. Neighboring buildings and trees expand and block light, soil moisture patterns are dis-

Replacing grass with a stone mulch is always an option, but carefully consider the type and color of material. White gravel is too bright, its uniform size and manufactured appearance better suited to a driveway. Gravel comes in many colors, including buff, gray and ocher, any of which would blend with this landscape.

rupted, and specimen crabapples suddenly become unavailable. And that's the point. Long-range planning is not entirely practical.

There's a great thrill to be had in seeing complex landscaping plans carried out in one season. But slower phases of development over two or three years provide you with time to evaluate your accomplishments and consider how to proceed. Gardeners can spend an inordinate number of hours in soulful contemplation of what they have wrought. It may seem nothing much is happening, but this is actually a valuable exercise in examining change and deciding what to do next. You might start out from a position of "wanting it all" only to find you are satisfied with slightly less, and that saves you money.

The key to working sequentially over a period of time is to make sure each phase has the look of being finished. You don't want any rough edges showing, or areas that end abruptly as if you'd run out of materials and left it at that. So if you're replacing the rotting deck as the first phase of a garden makeover, be sure to include the "apron" of hard stone or brick surface surrounding the bottom step as a transition into the lawn. This will give the new deck a finished and complete look, and you can take a breather while considering your next move.

A fallen tree trunk and irregular shapes of stone in natural gray tones complement plants and enhance the naturalism of a site. They might have been placed by a glacier . . . or perhaps the gardener.

ten-point assessment survey

If you're planning to landscape a new garden for the first time, or you are renovating an older property, these are the areas of critical assessment you should consider. Using the assessment questions you can identify the problems, determine the changes you want to make, and begin to order them in priority. Whether you plan to do all the work at once or in phases over several seasons, a step-by-step assessment will clarify what work needs to be done.

1. **Size and Shape**   What are the dimensions of the garden? Is it rectangular, square, pie-shaped, irregular? Does the garden have unusual proportions, is it long and narrow, wide and shallow, does it have sharp angles? If the size is too large, can it be divided; or if too small, can it be made to appear more spacious? Is the shape an asset, or will special consideration be needed to alter or disguise the proportions?

2. **Boundaries**   Is the perimeter defined with a low curb or wall, fence, hedge, informal row of shrubs or trees? How is the front garden separated from the public road? Is it visually clear where private property begins? How are the boundaries between neighbors indicated? How close are the neighbors on three sides? Is there any kind of privacy barrier or screening in place; is it needed? Are outdoor sitting and dining areas screened?

3. **Patios and Decks**   Is the patio level, does it shed water efficiently, are any bricks or stones heaved up? Are the patio edges stable

Shrubs and succession plantings would connect this garden's features and disjointed shapes while filling the obvious voids.

Marking private boundaries can be done with curbs, walls, fences or plants.

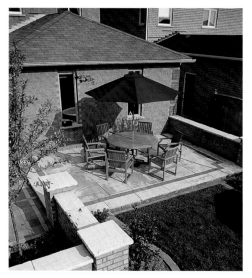

Hard surfaces separate formal and functional areas from relaxed green space.

and held in place by a concealed metal band? Are any boards in the deck split, bowed or rotting? Can animals get under the deck? Are the deck steps level and secure? Is the patio or deck large enough to accommodate your furniture?

4. **The Lawn** Is the grass healthy, thick and deep green? Does it grow vigorously? Does the lawn drain quickly after snow melts? How often has the lawn been aerated? Is the grass surrounding large lawn trees thin and weak? Do any areas have more weeds

If left too long, the chair will eventually cause the grass beneath to suffer.

than grass? Are there areas worn thin by constant foot traffic? Have furniture and sports or play equipment (trampolines, sand boxes, kiddy pools) damaged any areas of turf?

5. **Irrigation** How is the garden watered? By rain only? Is there an in-ground irrigation system, for the lawn only, for the planting

Irrigation in heavily planted small spaces is best done with a weeper hose.

beds? Do you water with a movable hose and sprinkler attachment? Is water distribution uneven; are there areas of excessive moisture or dryness? As a result of too much moisture, do perennial plants, shrubs and trees show symptoms of fungus diseases in spring or autumn? Does dry soil cause woody plants to suffer excessive twig dieback after winter?

6. **Entrance and Pathways** How many entrances are there to the garden? From the back door and side door of the house? Gate in back fence? Pathway alongside the garage? Are the entrances accented with arbors, vines and plant material alongside? Are any specimen plants used to enhance entrances and draw people into the garden? Are shrubs alongside

entrances too large or overwhelming? Do pathways lead to frequently used areas? How wide is the path? Are steps and paths

An insignificant side entrance can be elevated with a simple full-moon gate and trellis.

constructed with wood, concrete, paving bricks, natural stone? Are these access areas strictly functional or are they included in the character of the garden?

7. **Side Strips** Are there side strips of land alongside the house, driveway or garage walls? Are they surfaced with grass, concrete, stepping stones, paving bricks, natural stone? Is the strip of land level and clean to walk on? Can it be used in winter? Is there room for plants or groundcovers alongside or between stones? Do walls of the house or garage have room for

Wasted side space has been reclaimed using shade-tolerant evergreens and a formal walkway.

A garden bed creates a private seating area deep in the garden, and a welcome retreat.

vines? Does the side strip of land serve as a pathway entrance to the garden? Does it appear to be part of the garden?

8. **Growing Areas** Are beds placed where they can be appreciated from seating areas, entrances and doors, from inside through window views? Do planting areas drain well in early spring and after rain? Has the soil been frequently enriched with organic material and coarse sand? Are the beds wide enough to accommodate more than one row or tier of plants? Is edging the beds a part of regular garden maintenance? Is bare soil exposed between plants; are there weed problems; is organic mulch renewed annually?

9. **Trees and Shade** Do trees produce dense shade, filtered light or dappled light? All day, or how many hours? Have any roots risen out of the ground? Are massive trees such as maples and willow near to the house and growing beds? Are the larger trees high-pruned to increase light and air circulation? Are any trees growing on public property by the roadside? In your community are there bylaws governing pruning and removal of trees on private property?

10. **The Garage and Driveway** Is the garage a prominent feature of the property; is it softened by shrubs or vines? Does it have a window and a planted window box? If the driveway is asphalt, is it banded with cobblestones or another kind of ornamental stone? If the driveway is concrete or made from interlock bricks, is there any cracking or heaving and are there sunken areas? Is there staining from oil and tires?

Slender spring-blooming trees, such as dogwoods, are a seasonal greeting in the front yard.

Where large areas of driveway prevail, some patterning would help keep the surface in scale.

opposite: Consider how an older patio might change. Does outdoor cooking require a stone-constructed grill? Is wood furniture suited to the climate, or would other materials and styles better meet usage needs? Would a pergola or arbor provide some welcome shade?

putting it down on paper

The first step is a conceptual drawing (see next page), reflecting the current state of affairs in your garden. These drawings are most useful when firmly rooted in the present conditions, illustrating proposed changes to be made in the current season. Their value is to give you a basis of comparison for developing ideas and to help focus attention on decision-making. Drawings that include elaborate details of "wish list" items far in the future tend to diffuse the work at hand and drain vital impetus. The best advice is always to keep your plan fresh and in the present tense.

If you've made a plan for development of the garden in the near future,

you're undoubtedly anxious for something to happen. There you are, trembling on the brink of action and not sure what job to tackle first. It's common to focus on the most appealing task, but there are some protocols to follow. Professional landscape planners build gardens from the house outward into the landscape, beginning with hard-surface areas like paths, patios, decks and fences, then moving on to planting trees and shrubs, and finally establishing flowerbeds. Irrigation and lighting systems are the final phases of development, and that's when you might need to use sleeves that have already been laid under hard surfaces and pathways. Without planning ahead, you may well find yourself tearing up expensive work to install irrigation lines.

The dream scenario is to have enough time, help and funding to carry out the complete garden makeover in one season. But the reality is often that some part of the equation is in short supply and the project will be accomplished in phases of development over several seasons. This is not really a bad way to proceed, as you will have longer periods to evaluate your work and opportunities

to fine-tune the details as you proceed. You also have a more relaxed sense of ownership and control of the project when it's taken at a slower pace. However, a bit more thought is required to plan longer project phases in a logical sequence and avoid some common mistakes.

Selecting where to begin the first phase of work is always a tense moment. Some of us are easily drawn to items of personal interest, rather than the logistics of which comes first, the hot tub or the deck? There is no sense in purchasing a hot tub without a solid floor to put it on, so you need to focus first on building the foundation.

The textbook approach is to begin at the house walls and work outward and deeper into the yard. That means building the hard surfaces like decks, patios and pathways, and planting beds along the house foundations. But if you rush ahead to make and plant new beds deeper in the garden, you'll be in anguish when they're trampled by fence installers. Look carefully at what you want to accomplish and establish a logical sequence of events that maximizes all your resources.

WHY PLAN?

STARTING off with a plan for the near and foreseeable future not only makes better sense, it's often more economical in the end. Focusing on improvements you need and can appreciate in the next five years will allow you to develop a flexible approach to landscape planning. The top two-thirds of your priorities list are the items to consider most seriously. The remaining items might be flights of fancy. Don't be surprised if after the first improvements are made, some of your wants become less urgent, and possibly even easy to let go.

Do You Need to Paint a Picture?

We all see things in different ways, and some people have difficulty seeing them at all. If you're making modest changes, the circumstances will be clear, the details few, and a scale drawing of the property and its features isn't really necessary. But you may appreciate seeing the broad picture if your plan is for extensive planting, new pathways and changes in levels.

A drawing helps to organize information by presenting the current circumstances and proposed changes in one picture. It allows you to see the relationship of one area to another, and how that changes when you make additions like hedges, patios and ponds. And it helps you explain your plans to interested parties who might not see the point of what you're doing.

Making an overhead-view scale drawing isn't difficult. Use a long tape measure, graph paper and pencil to measure and record the boundary dimensions. Then measure the house, garage and any other buildings and place them on the drawing. Add prominent features such as trees, planting beds, patios and walkways that you intend to remain in place. If you've already designated plants and objects for removal, leave them off the drawing. You've now got the basic plan before any changes are made, and you can make photocopies of this to experiment with. You can sketch in a possible dog run, a new play area for preschoolers or the proposed terracing of a steep bank.

below: A scale drawing is a practical planning tool and reference, and clearly illustrates how each element fits in the available space.

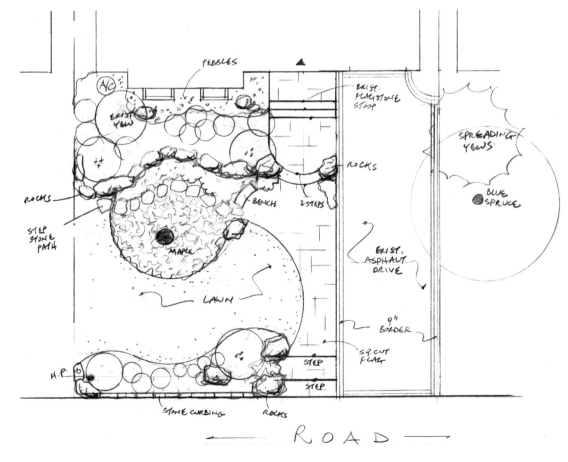

controlling the landscaping urge

There is little bloodshed in land-scaping, but sweat and tears are possibilities. Some folks just don't look forward to the experience, but others outnumber them whose enthusiasm leaps to zeal as the earth trembles with heavy equipment. These energies need to be constructively har-nessed, and starting off with a statement of purpose and limits is a good exercise in selecting priorities. It also aids the cause of democratic garden develop-ment, acknowledging the interests of all parties and users.

Your statement can be as simple as "The front yard is looking kind of tired. The gate is broken and the concrete walkway is badly cracked. Let's put $3,000 toward a contract for a new gate with an overhead arbor for climbing roses, and a front path made of cobble-stones." This is a good statement because it says why the changes are nec-essary, how much money is available for the work, and which items require pro-fessional skills. It pointedly leaves out other front yard improvements like ren-ovating the lawn, installing new founda-tion plantings, and selecting roses for the arbor, all tasks the gardeners can do themselves following the contractor's work.

Selecting priorities doesn't need to be painful, but it does require a bit of dis-ciplined soul-searching. It's always easier to go straight to the "gimme list" and reveal our secret obsession for a hot tub and personal putting green. We don't often make hard choices between neces-sities and wants, but it's a useful exercise in controlling self-interest.

1. First, begin by identifying what is necessary—that is, items needing repair or replacement to bring the garden up to an acceptable stan-dard. This could include solving the problems of eroding soil, lean-ing fences and crumbling retain-ing walls. Concrete steps and surfaces that are pitted, cracked and shattered, as well as split and heaved asphalt driveways, will need to be assessed. Major trees and plants that are storm dam-aged, diseased or deep into natural decline should be included as nec-essary items for consideration. Serious flooding and drainage problems are important candi-dates for correction, as well as property boundaries that have suf-fered neglect or vandalism. These items are the first priorities to be considered for attention.

The initial phase of a good landscaping plan is dedicated to repair or replacement of necessary garden apparatus. It's worth pay-ing attention to safety hazards—your insurance agent will agree with this. If the deck is so weath-ered you can easily put your foot through the boards, that item gets pushed to the top of the list. Any slippery-when-wet locations also need immediate attention. A fence that leans into a low curtsy or a driveway with cracks wide enough to grow cabbages in might be your first candidates for help. After you've planned for repair and replacement, you can turn your attention to projects of substance: the realization of new ideas like a privacy berm, a full-moon gate at the garden entrance, or an orna-mental pond with a water cascade.

2. Next focus on what you need—changes that could improve the use of the garden and encourage every-one to spend more time outdoors. You will want to be completely equitable and consider the interests of all garden users. Look for worthwhile improvements to seat-ing and outdoor dining locations,

play equipment and athletic recreation areas. Evaluate the need for additional privacy screening, adequate shade from hot sun, ornamental plantings and ground covers, storage for the lawnmower and other gardening tools, handicap ramps and extra parking space for vehicles and campers.

Some small changes can make large improvements, like widening a path, high-pruning trees, putting a gate in a fence and installing drainage tiles. This is the time to give serious thought to basketball hoops and sand boxes, badminton nets and vegetable patches— whether it's to add them or get rid of them. And don't forget a calm and quiet place to sit with a drink and contemplate personal desires as yet unrealized.

3. After sorting out the critical necessities and needs for landscape development, what's left is what you want. These are the objects of desire, perhaps extravagant or unreasonable, or even impossible on your site, but nevertheless, it's your personal wish list. There's no shame in saying you want a black-bottomed gunite pool with inset boulders and a waterfall. It's all right to express an interest in a cabana with wet bar, sauna and cable television. But the scale of your landscape should weight your decision of which personal luxury items to include.

THE accumulation of large-scale garden amenities can quickly overload a pleasant backyard.

Small city gardens given over totally to a swimming pool result in a bizarre imbalance with the stingy skirt of remaining space. Even generous suburban gardens begin to look overcrowded when they contain pool, cabana, towering play equipment, seating areas, decks and hot tubs. "Having it all" sometimes means losing a sense of proportion or forgetting what is comfortably appropriate in a garden.

It's best to keep in mind the basic premise of a garden as a space for the enjoyment of trees and plants. Overloading the landscape with objects of hard construction nullifies the natural landscape and leads in the direction of theme parks.

If your purse is big enough you may be able to include a wish-list item in planned improvements. Or you could be in for the long haul on a targeted savings plan. Just be sure to get your budget and priorities straight.

left: Mediterranean style might be what you want, but with three children and a dog, is it what you need? Sorting out practical change versus wish fulfillment is difficult work.

a sample four-year plan

A four-year plan to renovate a backyard might look something like this:

YEAR ONE

Repair items worth keeping and begin adding "bones." Build a cedar deck and a pathway of precast concrete cobblestones leading from the new deck to the side of the house. Build in sleeves you think are necessary for future water and electrical lines during path construction. Apply wood preservative to the deck. Establish foundation beds five feet (1.5 m) wide, with an 18-inch (45 cm) strip of landscape fabric covered with gravel at the back along the foundation wall. Purchase and install dwarf plants in the beds.

YEAR TWO

More "bones" and some architecture. Build a fence on three sides of the garden before making flower borders (to avoid construction damage to plants and soil). Build a gate with an arbor top opening onto the driveway. Plant major trees, and vines over the arbor.

YEAR THREE

Improve lawn and install flowering plants. Remove patchy grass, improve the soil with organic amendments and lay a new sod lawn. Water the sod daily. Shape and dig new flowerbeds, improving the soil. Purchase and install flowering shrubs and perennial plants.

YEAR FOUR

Add irrigation and lighting. Install in-ground irrigation for the lawn, with drip emitters for trees and raised emitters to deliver water from overhead for flowerbeds. Install low-voltage wiring and light fixtures.

Year 1 Repair hard features like steps, walkways and fences to prevent further damage.

Year 2 Install new structures that add style and character.

Year 3 Renovate lawns and flowerbeds, install important new shrubs and trees.

Year 4 Complete new plantings, and install irrigation and lighting systems.

a landscaping plan step-by-step

Use this example to help you plan. Many small projects are less intimidating—and more achievable—than a complete, all-or-nothing "makeover."

1. Determine your priorities for work to be accomplished this season. Include necessary repairs, improvements and upgrades to make the garden more useable, and special wish-list items.

2. Prepare a full plan statement listing the changes you intend to make, the work you will do yourself and the special tasks that will require professional contractors.

3. Prepare a scale drawing of the garden as it is and indicate the changes you want to make.

4. Make a time-line plan indicating start and completion dates for each phase of the project, and showing where some tasks might overlap to save time.

5. Apply for building permits if necessary.

6. Establish a budget for the entire project, and also for each phase.

7. Research and locate building materials and plants.

8. Find contractors for special skill requirements like brick laying, asphalt installation, irrigation and lighting.

9. Call utility companies to locate and mark buried service lines.

10. Notify neighbors of the work schedule.

11. Order building materials for delivery a week before your start date.

12. Clear the site of anything marked for sale, gift giving, recycling or disposal.

13. Salvage any materials like stone, pavers or plants that can be used in the new plan.

14. Establish a storage area for building materials and new plants.

15. Protect permanent plants like trees, shrubs, perennials and groundcovers from construction damage.

16. Reserve rental tools and equipment for the time they are needed.

17. Arrange for a dumpster bin if necessary.

18. Begin removal of plants in poor condition. Lift plants to be saved or moved and wrap their root balls in landscape fabric or put them in containers. Place them in a shady spot.

19. Correct grades where necessary.

20. Lay out hard-surface areas like patios, decks and pathways using stakes and string, and begin to excavate for foundation materials.

21. Lay sleeves (empty PVC piping) across pathways at 10-foot (3 m) intervals, buried in the foundation materials, and stuff each end of the pipes with a rag to keep soil out.

22. Finish hard surfaces with stone, brick, precast concrete blocks or wood.

23. Dig and install ornamental pond.

24. Build fences and gates.

25. Purchase new plants and store on site.

26. Outline the shape of new planting beds and prepare soil with organic materials.

27. Lift grass using sod cutter.

28. Lay electrical and irrigation lines.

29. Plant trees, shrubs, hedges and perennials.

30. Mulch soil around woody plants and perennials with shredded bark.

31. Install lighting fixtures and raised irrigation emitters in planting beds.

32. Install new sod lawn.

creating your own four-year landscaping plan

This exercise will reconcile your immediate needs with your dreams, while helping you work within your financial limits.

"What is essential" and "what you need" may appear redundant, but we know the difference, as we all have non-essential "needs" that we consider necessary to our enjoyment of life. There is nothing wrong with giving them a reasonable place of priority in your plan.

WHAT IS ESSENTIAL

1. List any items, from the house exterior to the front and back yards, that are in need of immediate repair for safety, insurance or property line reasons, or that you use regularly. This may include drainage problems, broken steps, lack of lighting, or fencing for security or privacy.

2. List any items that contribute to a shabby, unkempt or distasteful appearance. These are the items that need to be done to bring the property up to personal (and neighborhood) standards, such as foundation plantings, a perennial flowerbed, ground cover to replace a shabby lawn, or perhaps a new driveway.

WHAT YOU NEED

3. List any items or changes that would allow or encourage more frequent and more pleasurable use of your property. This may include repairing or installing a deck or patio area, creating garden "rooms", building a shed and utility area, or renovating the front entrance to welcome guests.

4. List any items or areas that are unused or so out of repair as to be unusable and indicate how you would like to use them. Perhaps there is a children's play area no longer used that would make a great patio or perennial bed.

5. List any areas, front or back, that require more shade or more sun. Often moving a tree or that metal shed is all that's needed to help your cut-flower bed flourish.

WHAT YOU WANT

6. List all those items you desire for your landscape, however small or extravagant. Across from each item, write down any limits to obtaining this item. For example, you want a pool but your lot is just too small and your neighbors are not going anywhere. Or perhaps all you've ever wanted for your hot, sun-drenched yard is a shady glade where you can read a favorite author's latest.

Item	*Limits*

7. Budget. Write down your available landscaping budget for this year, for two years off, and within four years. Realistic expectations will prevent disappointment.

This year: $ _____

Two years: $ _____

Four years: $ _____

CREATING YOUR PLAN

Now spend some time contemplating your lists. From the "What is essential" list, itemize that which must be done as soon as possible. Allocate their costs within your budget for this year and, if necessary, the next two and four years.

Once these essentials have been done, you can move to the "What you need" list. Using the same process, plan those items within your budget and over the next four years.

Finally, you get to look at your "What you want" list. You should have eliminated those items clearly not possible by virtue of their limits. For those items left over, determine approximate costs for each and consider its place within your budget and your two- and four-year plans. Keep in mind that as you actually make these changes, your property will have evolved, as will have you, and you may find that the orna-mental pond you so desperately wanted is no longer as desirable or no longer possible. Keep an open mind, remembering that a landscape changes, as will your needs and desires. Your four-year plan should be re-addressed frequently, and by year four, it should be redone in full. (Return to the Ten-Point Assessment Survey on page 38 and the Ten Elements of Landscaping Design on page 13 as needed.)

But for now, this exercise will create a list of priorities and possibilities from which you can create your own Four-Year Landscaping Plan.

FOUR-YEAR LANDSCAPING PLAN

This year: _____

_____

_____

_____

_____

_____

_____

_____

_____

_____

_____

_____

Within 2 years: _____

_____

_____

_____

_____

_____

_____

_____

_____

_____

_____

_____

Within 4 years: _____

_____

_____

_____

_____

_____

_____

_____

_____

_____

_____

_____

before you begin

Anyone who bakes from scratch knows preparation takes as much time—and is as important—as mixing and constructing the cake. Before you call for earthmovers, try to organize each step of the project and get your ducks all in line. Even if you're only going to reshape the lawn, you've got to find the crescent-shaped edger, or substitute a blunt-nosed spade borrowed from neighbors, and sharpen it with a mill file. You'll need a wheelbarrow to collect the trimmings and a place to pile them for composting. Grass along the new edge will be tall and ragged, so you'll need hand clippers or a powered string edge cutter. Nothing is simple, but planning makes the work go smoothly. What's required is the mindset of a bird building a nest in a storm. Get it organized right the first time and it won't fall out of the tree.

1. **BEGIN BIG PROJECTS BY MAKING COURTESY CALLS,** letting neighbors know your plans if the work will be disruptive to the road. Landscaping in a front yard falls under everyone's scrutiny and neighbors can be generous with their opinions. When you've heard enough, hand them a shovel and that will end the dialogue. If you're going to have a dumpster bin and make a mess on the boulevard, you'll need the friendly indulgence of anyone forced to walk through it. Let them know what to expect, how long the chaos will last and that you're on the case, making sure their driveways will never be blocked. During the progress of work, be sure to end each day with a cleanup of the street and sidewalk. Sweep the sidewalk and use a flat shovel to clear soil from the street where car tires can pick it up and carry the mud onto driveways. At the height of the mess everyone will want it all to go away quickly, but you must persevere in a tidy and determined manner. When work is finally complete, deliver flowers to neighbors on both sides and accept their admiration.

2. **CONSIDER PERMISSIONS, PERMITS AND CLEARANCES** your work might require. If you want to replace a fence on a lot line, you'll have to negotiate this with the neighbor or build on your own side within the line. Some cities and regions have few restrictions on landscaping, while others will be sending inspectors round with regularity. Building permits may be required for structural work like parking pads, decks and patios. If you want to plant a front hedge, you'll need to check how close it can be to the public pavement. Any landscaping plans involving a swimming pool will certainly have regulations attached, and some municipalities also require clearances for ornamental ponds, particularly if they're in front yards. If you know the guidelines you'll be able to adjust your project to fall within them.

3. **SIMPLE SITE PREPARATIONS WILL SAVE YOU TIME** and frustration. Be sure to call all utility services to have underground lines located. It's entirely possible that previous owners of your property buried telephone and television cables. You'll also need to locate gas lines, and newer subdivisions may also have buried electrical power lines. If the garden has an in-ground sprinkler system, get a map of the water lines. The soft vinyl pipes will be only 6–8 inches (15–20 cm) deep and are frequently cut or

opposite: Architectural objects are permanent fixtures that satisfy both ornamental and functional requirements. This relatively inexpensive obelisk lends strong character to a bed and supports plant growth, and the fence is attractive and provides privacy. Let your purse be your guide, but get the best you can afford.

nicked with a shovel during construction. Although they are easily mended (if you have metal clamps handy), the immediate gushing effect can be messy and alarming and is sure to draw critical remarks. Just what you don't need.

4. **THOROUGHLY CLEAN AND ORGANIZE THE SITE** before you begin, removing extraneous debris, old wood and abandoned dog houses, broken toys and anything else that isn't going to remain permanently in the garden. If large features like bird baths or benches are in the way, it's better to temporarily shift them aside so your work is unobstructed. Designate an area for storage of the tools and materials you'll need for the duration of the job, and get a large tarp for covering them at night and during rain.

5. **PROTECT VALUABLE PLANTS** while work is going on. Herbaceous perennials like peonies, daylilies and irises can be carefully lifted and set into plastic bags with drainage holes poked in the bottom. Give them a little water in the bag to keep the soil moist, and store the plants in a shady location, never in direct sun. Plants can stay in the bags as long as a month if you monitor them carefully, keep them upright in shade and supply water when necessary. When you return them to their place in the garden, water them in with transplant solution and they'll quickly readjust.

Grade changes can kill trees. A simple tree well, made from irregular rocks, prevents soil from piling up against a tree trunk and smothering its roots.

6. **PROTECT HARD SURFACES,** such as stone and interlock brick, from scratching and excessive mud by laying a heavy tarp over them until construction is finished.

Considerable changes to the grade can also be hazardous to trees if they're too big to be lifted and re-set at the new level. If you anticipate raising the grade where an established tree is growing, a tree well will need to be constructed. The well is formed by creating a retaining wall that holds back the newly raised soil and protects the tree's trunk and roots from being smothered. The well ensures that oxygen and water will continue to reach the bark and roots. The well walls hold back a great deal of pressure from soil that heaves and expands with frost, and their construction must include drainage materials and a solid foundation, so you might want to call in a professional for this important task.

7. **SPECIAL PREPARATIONS** may be needed for shrubs and trees. Large shrubs can be temporarily tied with cord to hold their branches in and away from the work area. Tie them round firmly, but not hard enough to snap twigs and branches. Carpeting ground-cover plants like sweet woodruff, ajuga and English ivy won't bear heavy foot traffic or wheelbarrows, but it may not be practical to lift them temporarily. Lay large sheets of plywood over the areas to distribute the weight passing over evenly. Although the plants will be pressed down, they'll recover within a few weeks when the boards are lifted and they've been given a good watering.

Trees already on the site require special protection to prevent injury to their bark and compression of soil in the root zone. If the tree's height is 20 feet (6 m) or less, its roots extend outward to the length of the longest branches at the drip line. If soil or other building materials are piled over the roots or against the trunk, their weight will compact the soil and cut off oxygen. If you're working alone it's easy to remember to keep materials away from the tree, but if you expect hired help, it's wise to put up a temporary snow fence or some kind of barrier at the drip line to prevent damage.

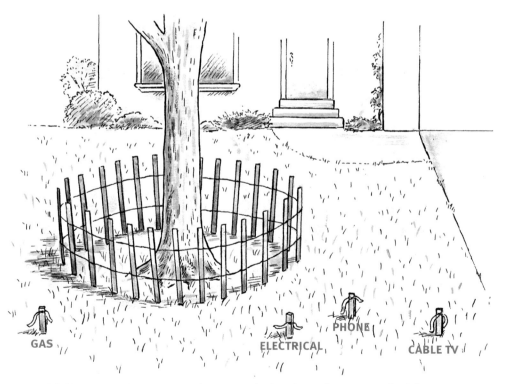

Establishing a protection zone around trees saves bark and roots from construction injury. Be sure to have the utility companies, such as gas, phone and TV cable, mark their buried lines.

making stone soup

New materials inspire excitement, but there's a special satisfaction in making something from nothing by re-using and recycling what's found on the site. Turning the soil and excavating new areas can unearth some interesting relics. If you're digging near the foundations of a century home, you might find construction parts such as ancient iron pulley wheels and vintage beer bottles from a tradesman's lunch. Digging around homes constructed in the 1950s often brings up lost toys and abandoned machine parts. But soils from every

Concrete rubble can be used to gain height, but try to conceal it with plant material.

decade contain treasure for gardeners in the form of natural rock minerals. Rocky soils may seem like a curse on the shovel, but they provide useful landscaping material.

Rural fieldstone walls are testament to a farmer's ability to make something from nothing by salvaging stone from the soil. Some regions have so much rock litter in the soil, they consider rocks a nuisance crop in the same category as weeds. Recognizing the potential value of seemingly worthless rocks is a useful way to reclaim your garden's natural resources. Smart gardeners know a beautiful rock when they see it, but it pays to save just about any stone you dig up. Landscapers grade natural rock sizes from gravel, the smallest, through pebbles, stones, rocks and boulders. If you are digging and encounter any size of stones, find a permanent place to accumulate them for future use. Your "rock department" will be an invaluable source of building material for propping things up, weighing things down and edging things round. And of course, with enough stones in varying sizes, you can make a naturalistic rock garden or an elaborate grotto.

Old flagstone is a wonderful material to save and recycle, providing it's free of mortar. If it's clean and smooth, you can use it for a dry-laid path with sand between the joints or as stepping stones. Cleaning mortar from flagstone is difficult and the results are seldom acceptable for re-laying as a patio, but the stone could be used to make a low retaining wall or for edging a raised bed. Smooth rounded pebbles or fist-sized stones have a use as separators between stepping stones, where they will fill in the gaps, hold the stones in place and keep down mud.

Interlock pavers can be re-used for many kinds of construction. If the bricks are stained or excessively dirty, try flipping them and using the other side up. Cleaned with a powered water jet or scrubbed with a wire brush, they're good for making all kinds of flat surfaces in small areas, such as a dry base for garbage cans or a firm and level pad under a gas barbecue; placed on end they're attractive for edging planting beds. The gravel and sand foundation under pavers can be stockpiled for future use. Lumber can be salvaged if it's in good condition—that is, without warps and cracks. Ends that have been in contact with soil may be marked with rot and should be trimmed. Woods that have water-resistant qualities—like cedar, redwood and teak—

have significant value and would be expensive to purchase, so these materials are always worth the time required to carefully disassemble and clean them.

Soil is the most precious resource in any garden and should never be discarded. Even soil of poor quality, such as yellow or blue clay, or soil that is mostly sand, can be easily amended with the missing ingredients to produce fertile loam. You may not want to do this work now, but saving bad soil gives you an opportunity to improve it when needed in the future. Turf grass that has been dug up should also be retained. If the turf is in good condition it can be cleanly lifted in rolls with a rented sod cutter, and you can transfer sections to areas requiring patching, or even move the entire lawn this way and re-lay it elsewhere. If the turf is patchy and comes up in clumps and clods, pile them in some out-of-the-way corner to compost. The combination of green blades and soil clinging to the roots will produce excellent quality soil in two years.

Landscape renovations often involve removal of deciduous woody plants and evergreens from the site, either taking down trees or grubbing out old and overgrown shrubs. These plants may well have served their purpose for many years and now must go with the change, but they still have important value as potential mulch and organic amendments for soil.

If you're doing the removals yourself, you'll either have to cut and tie the branches into neat bunches for garbage pickup or find a way to transport the debris to the dump, and the dump might charge you a drop-off fee. But you can rent a chipper-shredder for about fifty dollars and quickly feed it all through the steel blades, producing high-quality organic material you might spend hundred of dollars to purchase.

Stockpile this valuable material to compost for future use, or spread it as fresh mulch over beds and borders. It's ideal for pathways in vegetable gardens or woodland walks, and can be used along with coarse sand to turn your excavated blue clay into friable soil. If professional contractors or arborists are doing the work, they may bring their own chipper, or they can use your rented machine. Just make sure all the good stuff stays on the site.

Common sense is a valuable guideline and will help you find practical and expedient solutions to most problems. In a busy construction season, hard materials and plants can be in short supply, so be prepared to make substitutions. Natural stone and precast cobblestones can be successfully combined to make up any shortfalls in one or the other material.

If you need to make substitutions for plants, look for something with a similar shape that will grow in the light

FREE FILL AVAILABLE

IF you're removing an old concrete pathway or garage floor you'll need to break up the slabs with a sledgehammer. This process yields that unique product, concrete rubble.

There is no aesthetic value to concrete rubble, but it does make handy fill for an empty space or void. Along with purchased gravel, it can be used as a base to provide elevation for a berm or raised patio, or to preserve a shoreline from water erosion. Some gardeners use chunks of concrete rubble to terrace slopes or build low retaining walls, but this is a last resort.

Rubble is a crude material and should never be prominent or visible in the garden. If you're desperate enough to use it in this way, make sure cascading plants and vines will quickly cover it.

conditions on the site. Many forms of cedar and juniper have similar form and like bright light. In shade, upright Japanese yew and dwarf Alberta spruce make good substitutions for each other.

Be prepared for the unexpected on any job. Professional landscapers frequently unearth old concrete foundations just where trees are planned. Instead of attempting major engineering feats, move the trees slightly to the side of the obstruction. Allowing for some flexibility in your landscape plan is the best problem-solving strategy. And don't forget to photograph the progress of your project so you can relive the satisfaction of a job well done.

hard landscaping

Serious gardeners are sometimes mistrustful of the intent of hard landscaping. They see peony beds displaced by parking pads and lilacs uprooted to make way for a wider path. And perhaps they're right to be guarded, for certainly there is something in humanity that loves to pave and build over the earth. But hard landscaping techniques are important tools for solving garden problems and enhancing the marriage of good soil and beautiful plants. If you want to ensure that plant material is always the heavier end of the garden equation, what's needed is a bit of perspective.

There are several reasons for employing hard materials like stone, brick, concrete, asphalt, wood, steel and iron in the garden. First and most important is problem solving. Problems in the garden are seldom isolated and are likely to compound as time passes. The leaning fence will eventually dip lower and collapse, taking out the delphiniums and crushing your favorite rose. The postal path worn through the lawn will only grow more bald and prominent so long as there is mail delivery. Replacing the fence and making a stepping-stone path are simple solutions that don't infringe on plants and green

space. Using hard materials in this functional way satisfies the gardener's interest in keeping plant material at the top of the priority list.

There comes a time when more and different use is required from garden space. A pressing request for an outdoor dining area or additional parking space may be topics of discussions over several seasons, until something must finally be done to satisfy the urge. These developmental changes require hard surfaces and can eat up quite a bit of soil. But they make the garden more useful, allowing everyone to spend more time there, and maximizing the value of

Walls and other uses of stone add critical structure to a landscape.

Fences and gates can enhance the landscape while marking boundaries.

Steps are part of the welcome you give those who approach your home.

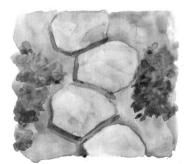

Pathways can take us where we want to go or lead us to a hidden surprise.

opposite: Combining planted beds with hard-surface seating areas takes the edge off a broad expanse of stone and integrates the patio with the garden. A succession of ornamental plants blooming from spring to autumn in patio beds satisfies the gardener's desire that the area appear natural.

GARDENS ARE FOR NATURE, TOO

EVEN the most ardent plant lover will concede that some firm, hard surfaces are necessary. Minor paths and major walkways, retaining walls and fences are some of the useful constructions we absolutely need to make the garden efficient and welcoming. Bear in mind that plant forms should always be the dominant presence and hard surfaces and construction materials are best kept in low profile. When the landscape is overloaded with outdoor furniture, hot tubs and hard surfaces, what you've created is a very pleasant waiting room with a few nice plants.

right: Conservative hard features—bench, fence and rock border—provide structure for green space cleverly laid out to display ornamental plants.

the property. The gardener's conscience might be slightly pricked by this, but the new hard surfaces justifiably enhance the site.

Warning bells should ring when someone suggests laying flagstone over the lawn for a more expansive patio, or plowing a circular driveway right past the front door and through the hybrid hostas. This is where hard landscaping materials meet up with aggressive design purposes and some gardeners will run screaming from the room. There is no point in taking a judgmental position toward gardens where hard surfaces triumph over plant material. Thankfully, gardens are private places we make to suit ourselves and none other. There are good reasons for redesigning patios and driveways—just be sure they fit in with your own perspective of gardening and green space.

The most extraordinary use of hard landscaping has to do with an obsession for the materials. Everyone has seen gardens with excessive use of natural stone, interlock bricks or asphalt exhibiting a fascination with the hard surface. Some garden owners are simply in love with concrete, allowing it to flow like lava from one side of the yard to the other, leaving stingy planting holes where trees struggle and asphyxiate. This vision might put you on red alert and fuel the fear that one brick leads to a flood of brick surface. Just get firm hold of your perspective, take yourself home and kiss the earth.

raised edges and retaining walls

Making a garden has a lot to do with managing soil, keeping it in place and adapting its quantity and distribution to garden use. Some lots are absolutely flat and that is a different problem, because land contour—little elevations and hills—is what brings basic interest to the landscape. But gardens with steep hills or ridges can be a chronic mess as soil is carried down by rain and shifted by wind. Raised edges and retaining walls are simple constructions used to hold soil back, prevent erosion by rainwater and keep plant roots intact. Raised edges can be as low as 3 inches (7.5 cm) and retaining walls can be as high as 3 feet (90 cm). The amount of soil to be kept in place is what determines the need for an edge or a wall.

A little elevation is always a good thing. Where a rise in soil exists, a constructed raised edge (sometimes referred to as a curb) will emphasize the elevation, creating interest and diversity, as well as holding things together. Raising the edge of a bed is a design trick to

Traditional brick-and-mortar walls require professional masonry skills.

Massive natural stones are heavy and difficult to work with, but make an enduring wall.

Straight-cut stones or concrete slabs fit together easily and stay in place.

Plants in the gaps between irregular fieldstones can make a "living" wall.

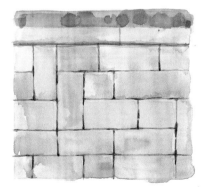
Uniform, precast concrete wall blocks make for quick construction.

Walls made of "scrap" rocks are unstable and will eventually require repair.

make a small place seem larger, but of course it can be used in a large garden to bring definition to an empty space. No matter where it's applied, the raised edge controls soil erosion and prevents lawn grasses from invading the bed. Not much height is required to produce the desired effect and a rise of 3–9 inches (7.5–22.5 cm) will be sufficient to make plants appear larger and more mature.

There is great diversity of materials used for creating a raised edge but some of them are poor choices. House bricks set on end will shatter after just two or three years in contact with wet soil. Railway ties treated with creosote last longer, but begin to rot after eight to ten years and then deteriorate quickly. Pressure-treated lumber lasts about the same time, and both materials will leach long-lasting toxic chemicals into the soil. If you're going to the trouble of installing an edge on the bed, you'll want it to be strong and permanent, and that means using some kind of natural or fabricated stone.

A retaining wall is higher than a raised edge or curb, and it must hold back and contain a greater weight of soil. Because the wall bears the pressure of soil, water and ice pressing forward, its foundation and construction must be stronger in every respect.

Following simple instructions (see page 63), a gardener can build a dry retaining wall (referred to as a gravity wall) less than 18 inches (45 cm) in height that is held together by its own weight.

Walls of greater height are more complicated because of the increased pressure they must contain; they require special construction techniques to build stability and strength through the levels, and the installation of drainage pipes to prevent pockets of water and ice. The low, dry retaining wall is laid with the stones flat on top of each other for additional strength, and slightly "battered" or set back ½ inch (1.2 cm) each level to increase its stability.

If you would like to keep things looking natural, small boulders can be used providing they are generally all of the same size and mineral content. They should be approximately 10–12 inches (25–30 cm) high, allowing for some height to be lost in foundation preparation. Keeping to one mineral family, say all granite or all limestone, will give consistency to the finished bed and avoid a haphazard appearance. Cut stone and precast concrete blocks set on end can also be used. Any kind of machine-cut flagstone with straight sides is a good choice, and it comes in various sizes and thicknesses. Look for rectangular shapes about 1 inch (2.5 cm) thick. Granite cobblestones are adaptable to making a rustic curb, and manufactured cobblestones are also

These natural boulders, used to hold back a steep bank of soil, would have been positioned by heavy machinery. Cascading plants and vines help to soften the massive rocks and blend them into their surroundings.

appropriate edging material and have the advantage of coming in various sizes and colors.

Again, irregular or random-shaped natural stone is fine for a line that requires some turns and curves, or straight-cut stone with a "rock face" (one edge left natural and unfinished) can be used if the wall is to be a straight line. If you're using random flagstone, the pieces will be reasonably flat-surfaced on top and bottom, but the shapes will be irregular and you'll have to fit them together as closely as possible. If you're any good at puzzles you'll enjoy the process as you sort out the shapes. Use the largest stones on the bottom and try to make the stone shapes follow the curves of your line.

Straight-cut stone goes together very quickly, row upon row, with the rock face always outward to offset the severity of the saw cut. If your cut stone is uniform on all sides, you can rock-face it yourself with a mason's mallet and chisel, but this requires special skill and it's best to ask for it to be done at the stone yard.

COPING-STONES are larger and heavier pieces used to cap the top of the wall and are bonded on with an adhesive. Ask at the stone yard for enough coping-stones to cover the top length of your wall, and visit a building center for the appropriate adhesive.

The coping is bonded to rough surfaces like random flagstone with mortar made of Portland cement, mixed one part cement to three parts sand and combined with only enough water to make a stiff paste holding a firm shape. Too much water will weaken the mixture and cause the dried bond to crumble quickly.

A slurry test will tell if you've got the right consistency: turn the bucket upside-down for five seconds; if the cement stays put, the consistency is right.

Smoothly finished stone is bonded with masonry adhesive that has less strength than Portland cement, comes premixed in a squeeze tube and is easier to work with.

It's worth looking at some of the new precast concrete wall systems that have the appearance of natural fieldstone or quarried stone. They're remarkably attractive, easy to work with and combine masonry adhesive with groove and toggle systems to hold them together.

Stones have several uses. The uniform line at the pavement edge separates private and public property, stones along the driveway help to keep a neat edge, and the low retaining wall in the lawn is an ornamental feature that also prevents erosion of the natural slope.

How to Make a Raised Edge

The integrity and durability of every raised edge is based on two factors: a level line to the top edge and the strength of its foundation. Whatever kind of stone material is being used, plan for a third of it to be below ground in the foundation to provide the strength to resist heaving by frost.

1. Constructing the edge begins with stringing a line at the anticipated finished height as a guide for your work. If the edge is curved you will need to move and adjust the line as you turn the corners.

2. Next dig a trench around the bed, deep enough to accommodate 2 inches (5 cm) of coarse sand on the bottom and a third of the stone height. The trench may seem like a lot of work, but it allows you to make the careful adjustments necessary to ensure each stone is level and in line with its neighbor. Sand underneath the stones is essential, helping to drain water and buffering frost action. If you're working with straight-edged stone you'll need a spirit level to check the consistency of the top edges.

   Whenever you use sand or gravel in constructing a foundation, it's necessary to tamp the materials down with a hard and firm tool before setting stone on top. In a limited area like a trench you can smooth the sand with the back of your hand and use a flat brick to tamp it down—never use your foot, which has too much contour.

3. Set stones upright and side-to-side on the foundation and fit them as tightly as possible, working down the whole length of the trench and checking the top edge with the level frequently. You will probably need to make several adjustments and redistribute the sand before everything is perfectly in line and ready for backfilling with soil.

4. Carefully fill the trench with soil and use the brick to tamp it firmly down. Remaining soil can be added to the bed behind the edge, and you may need quite a bit more to fill it in and raise the soil height to 1 inch (2.5 cm) below the edge top.

How to Build a Retaining Wall

Retaining walls require a deeper foundation than curbs or raised edges. This simple construction technique is adequate for retaining walls up to a height of 36 inches (90 cm). Each level of stones is staggered slightly back to increase its strength and ability to disperse the pressure of winter frost. Installing a mowing strip at the bottom edge of the wall makes a clean finish and eliminates the work of edging the lawn. Pockets in the wall can be stuffed with topsoil mixed with damp peat moss and planted with rock-garden plants, such as creeping sedum, thyme and euphorbias, for a natural look. A planting bed atop the wall should contain 12 inches (30 cm) of topsoil for good root development and can be planted with low-growing perennials and ground-cover roses.

1. Dig a trench deep enough to accommodate 6 inches (15 cm) of foundation materials. Line the bare soil at the bottom of the trench and behind the wall with filter cloth (A), a landscaping fabric available at garden centers that allows moisture to drain through but prevents soil from escaping.

2. Lay 6 inches (15 cm) of crushed gravel (B) at the bottom of the trench. The first level of stone (sometimes referred to as a course) should be half-buried in the trench. A perforated drainage pipe (C) can be laid into the gravel behind the first level of stones.

3. Complete each row before laying the next course on top, staggering each level (D) by setting it back by ¼–½ inch (1 cm). Fill in with gravel behind each completed level of stone. The wall with its coping-stones (the top level) in place should gently lean back into the soil. Finish the bottom edge where the wall meets the grass lawn with a mowing strip (E) made of precast patio bricks.

4. Fill gaps between stones (F) with small-sized gravel or stuff with planting mix to make planting pockets. A planting bed (G) can be installed at the top of the wall, 12 inches (30 cm) deep, for perennial plants and small cascading shrubs.

How to Terrace a Slope

Steep slopes in a garden can be difficult to live with. They are hard to maintain when planted with turf grass, and perennial ground-cover plants often make a patchy covering, preferring to grow more at the top of the slope and less at the bottom. Bare areas are often vulnerable to soil erosion and weed invasion. But a slope can be stabilized and made into an attractive feature by terracing.

Terraces are a series of low retaining walls, up to 24 inches (60 cm) in height, cut into the side of a sloping hill. Only one or two terraces may be necessary for a small hill, or any number for a large area of inclining ground. Terraces on a steep hill can be installed consecutively behind each other, or spaced strategically across the hill at varying heights where needed, and can be as short or long as required. The terraces stabilize the slope and distribute the soil pressure, allowing comfortable spaces for permanent plants that can ramble and cascade artistically downward.

1. Excavate the area for terracing (A). Distribute approximately one-half of the soil elsewhere on your property, and amend the remaining half with organic materials (aged manure, peat moss, leaves and pine needles) to be used as planting medium in the finished terraces.

2. Lay 4 inches (10 cm) of crushed gravel (B) into the bottom of the lowest terrace excavation. Fit a sheet of landscape fabric (C) into the bottom, with enough length to run up the front and back walls of the planting space. Place the first level of stone (D) on the gravel, halfway underground. Add the remaining levels of stone, setting each level ½–1 inch (1–2.5 cm) back so that it will lean slightly into the soil behind it. Hold the landscape fabric up against the stones as you fill the planting space with soil. Construct each terrace in the same manner, using the landscape fabric (E) as a barrier between the soil in the lower planting space and the gravel foundation of the upper terrace.

Plants for terraces should be low-growing and of the appropriate scale for small spaces. Tall plants and shrubs will topple over in a terrace, and the expanding roots of large plants will weaken the construction. Dwarf plants with good drought-hardiness will work best in small planting areas. Dwarf groundcover junipers for year-round evergreen display are a good choice. Rock-garden plants and cascading vines are also compatible with terrace planting.

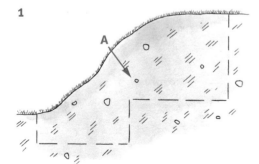

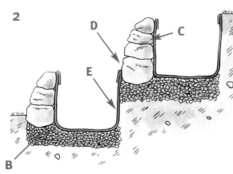

Mowing Ease

A new maintenance task is created where raised edges and retaining walls meet a lawn. The first 3 inches (7.5 cm) of lawn adjacent to the edge are inaccessible to the lawn mower and can quickly become a tatty mess. Grass will need to be cut by hand all along the edge each time the lawn is mowed, and that will become a tiresome procedure. Installing a mowing strip at the edge of the lawn where it meets the raised curb or wall will make a solid bed for the lawn mower's wheel and allow the edge of the grass to be cut efficiently. This labor-saving device can be installed on the edge of any lawn, whether or not there is a raised edge or wall.

The mowing strip is installed all along the edge of the lawn, effectively moving the true edge of grass inward by a few inches/centimeters, and making a solid strip of hard surface at grade level. Any hard paving material like straight-cut flagstone, concrete blocks, cobblestone or hardened brick can be used.

It's important to give the mowing strip a firm foundation so that it won't shift or heave with frost action in the soil. The strip looks and works best if it's a minimum of 6 inches (15 cm) wide, and can be up to 16 inches (40 cm) wide if you're using beautiful stone. Any wider than that and what you've made is a narrow walking path along the lawn.

How to Install a Mowing Strip

1. To keep the strip solid and neat, remove the sod and excavate to the depth of your stone plus an additional 3 inches (7.5 cm) for a bed of compacted and leveled coarse sand.

2. Prepare the bed by laying 3 inches (7.5 cm) of coarse sand. Tamp it down to smooth and compact.

3. Lay the stones on top, butt them tightly together and brush fine jointing sand into any cracks or gaps.

fences and gates

Fencing is a big part of any landscaping budget, so if money is a concern, you might want to consider a hedge. But a fence arrives fully-grown and provides instant privacy, which may be important to you. It's useful to understand just what a fence will and won't do for your garden. It's good for keeping dogs out, but determined people can still find their way in. A fence blocks the view of curiosity seekers, but noise and conversation come through loud and clear. Fences don't provide shelter or food for birds (always welcome in the garden) but they're good support for flowering vines. Fences make good neighbors in the sense that boundary lines are clearly drawn, but differences of opinion can arise over styling and shared cost.

Anything that requires such a quantity of expensive material and construction labor is not going to be simple.

If you're thinking of making the fence yourself, think again. Fences are large and prominent architectural objects and their imperfections are quickly perceived. If your carpentry skills are nothing short of excellent, then making it yourself is a good way to save

A slant-cut pattern is easy to accomplish using a miter box.

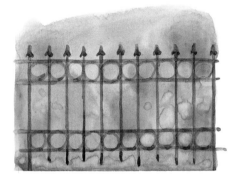

Antique iron fencing can be found at salvage yards.

Lathwood trellis panels are good for clematis and morning glory vines.

Flat, closely jointed panels offer the most complete privacy.

The cost of fencing increases dramatically with the amount of wood to be custom cut.

To maintain balance, symmetrical patterns must be carefully measured and cut.

money. But a poorly made fence is a blot on the landscape, as everyone will tell you. Who can say why the public at large is so insulted by a crooked fence, but it is sure to be a beacon for criticism. A fencing company can do the job for you quickly, but take the time to look at some they've already erected to be sure they've got the skill level you require.

Wood and metal fencing materials have remained consistent for hundreds of years, but the prices have changed dramatically. Pressure-treated wood is the most affordable, and you'll know it by its characteristic green hue. It is impregnated with chemicals that prevent moisture damage, although this protection won't last forever. The preservatives used are highly toxic and include copper, chromium and arsenic, and they will be leached by rain into the soil and remain there permanently. Avoid growing food plants near treated wood and don't touch it with bare hands and feet. Cedar and redwood have natural tolerance to weathering, but be prepared for their hefty price.

Considering the expense of lumber, it's worth looking at metal fencing. Traditional iron fences will stand for a century, although their high cost may be out of reach. The new aluminum fences are an affordable and attractive alternative and, best of all, are maintenance free. Wood can be left raw, but applying a wood preservative every third year extends its durability.

The least desirable and most affordable fencing material is chain link,

This full-moon style allows for roses and vines overhead.

Bamboo is lightweight and remarkably durable.

Contemporary aluminum gates are also lightweight, but look like heavy iron.

Natural stone pillars are strong supports for a cottage garden gate.

This pieced Chippendale design is a classic feature of English gardens.

An American arrowhead gate requires careful and precise cutting.

a modern application of traditional wire fencing. Working successfully with chain link is an aesthetic challenge, but if that's what the budget dictates, at least purchase the material in the color black. It's close to miraculous how well black chain link fades into the background and becomes barely noticeable. You can complete the disappearing act by planting an evergreen hedge in front of the fence, using cedar in a sunny location or yew in shade. If the budget for plants won't cover expensive evergreens, try a hedge of deciduous dwarf lilac or alpine currant.

If the fence is along the front of your property, you'll need an entrance opening, and this raises the issue of a gate. As an architectural feature, gates suggest the nostalgic notion of friendly squeaks and graceful swings. But realistically, most gates are left unlatched and this causes them eventually to hang away from their hinges and fall out of kilter. Essentially, gates are inconvenient because they require a free hand to open and re-latch with every passage through.

Whatever the reason, gates often fall into disrepair and give a derelict impression. If you're going to have a gate, consider one with a spring action and be sure the family are all willing to keep it closed and in good repair. The gate must be wide enough to allow the passage of large objects like furniture and garden equipment. If you decide against the gate, you can enhance the entrance opening with an overhead arbor built into the fence (see box). The arbor entrance works well in either wood or metal, and can be left bare or planted with a flowering vine.

DON'T FENCE ME IN!

HEIGHT is a sensitive issue on both sides of the fence. Most municipalities have guidelines limiting the height of a fence on a lot line and it's important to stay within this limit. A privacy fence of 6 feet (1.8 m) is ideal, but not always allowed. You can possibly consider 54 inches (135 cm) of board fence topped with a 12-inch (30 cm) trellis panel, for a total of 5½ feet (1.6 m).

Of course, it's not always necessary to create such a high wall, and if you want better air and light, a traditional line of pickets or framed trellis fence 48 inches (1.2 m) high makes a graceful division without suggesting a blockade.

It's a courteous gesture to select a style that's presentable on both sides. You're not being a good citizen if the fence looks like the side of a barn to your neighbor. A good style choice is an alternate-board or shadow fence with an identical appearance on each side. It allows good air circulation and enough privacy to satisfy everyone.

A white picket fence is a classic garden image, but far from ideal in reality. Support posts in contact with moist soil will eventually need replacement, and peeling boards will require repainting. Despite the necessary maintenance it's still the perfect support for rambling roses and clematis.

How to Create a Living Fence

If circumstance calls for a casual structure, you might want to consider a living fence of grape vines or climbing roses.

1. Sink 6 x 6-inch (15 x 15 cm) posts (A) into concrete approximately 8 feet (2.4 m) apart.

2. Drill the posts with heavy-duty eyehooks (B) and thread three levels of thick-gauge wire (C) through the entire length—two at top, where the plant will be heavier, one at bottom. If you don't mind the more industrial look, perforated steel T-bars can replace the posts. They are pounded in with a post driver (a heavy metal tube with handles and a closed cap).

3. Plant grapes in light shade, or climbing roses in sun, between the posts and tie the canes horizontally along the wires. Maintenance is one big pruning session a year. Bird fanciers will appreciate the increased avian activity around the grapes, and gardeners will be pleased by the bounty of roses.

steps

Wherever you pass in and out of a garden is an area of high traffic and considerable drama. This is the place where civilization meets the natural world, and it's worth giving some thought to making the transition secure, graceful and inviting. Because most dwellings are elevated above grade, your entrance into the garden is going to involve some number of steps between door and ground, and these are most likely made of stone, concrete pavers or cobbles, or you may have a wood porch and steps. Precast concrete steps are available as a solid block, but they are the least satisfactory, as their size and dimensions are determined at the factory and can't be adjusted. Steps made of wood or large lumber like railway ties are susceptible to moisture damage and have a shorter life.

The flat, horizontal part of the step you stand on is called the tread; the riser is the vertical back of the step that rises upward. The step is a kind of staging, and you want to know it will accommodate your foot and body weight and provide the necessary flex room for launching yourself to the next level.

Wide treads provide easy and secure movement both upwards and down.

Mortared brick steps last longer in climates with mild winters.

Patchwork steps of irregularly shaped stone may need frequent repair.

Steps within a retaining wall must be built to hold back pressure on both sides.

Dry-laid stone steps can withstand ice and snow and repeated freezes and thaws.

Simple stepping stones on a slope work well in a woodland garden.

People prefer not to think of these considerations when using steps, trusting that the required space will be available when they land on it. But this isn't always the case, and poorly fashioned steps can sometimes make nasty surprises.

Presented with a high door frame and limited area below, builders will sometimes compress the steps accordion-fashion, causing the tread to be narrowed and the riser to stretch upward. This configuration creates a kind of rock-climbing experience as you grip each precipice with your toes. Falling as you go up stairs is almost always caused by the riser being too high; your leg automatically lifts to the appropriate level, but the riser trips you up. Going down is also exciting, as there is no place to put your heel and you must hurtle forward on tiptoe with a staccato bounce. And then there are steps with treads too broad and risers too short, forcing you into a lumbering, stretched gait that tries everyone's patience. Will they never get it right? What we want is steps to be so well proportioned and efficient that we hardly notice the passage over them.

A long expanse of front walk that elevates like a ramp as it moves along toward the door can be structured with sections of flat landing areas between shallow steps of only 2–3 inches (5–7.5 cm) in height to accommodate the increasing grade. This will allow comfortable walking with steps strategically spaced out as the level rises. Steps used in this way dispel the sensation of walking uphill, and prevent slipping when the walkway is wet.

If the lawn area has only a subtle raised grade, one step placed where the walkway meets the sidewalk or driveway will visually help to organize the entrance. It really is best to let your foot be your guide and try the walkway without shoes. You will feel immediately where a change in level is uncomfortable, and that is the place to put a step. Manufacturers of precast concrete paving blocks also make attractive step units designed for easy installation. They come in many colors and can be aesthetically combined with pavers and natural stone such as granite, slate, flagstone and limestone.

Steps are the natural partners of garden arbors. If you have an arbor at the entrance to the garden and it is slightly elevated, a stone step is entirely appropriate to bring your foot up to the new level as you pass under. If the arbor is at grade and there is no elevation, you can still use the stone as a design element by setting it under the arbor and lowering it to turf level. Be sure to use enough stone or cobbles to fill the area the arbor covers. One or two simple steps are easily built and require a level and compacted sand base underneath. But steps that rise significantly will require more complex support materials like concrete blocks and gravel, and their installation is best left to professional contractors.

The rule of thumb for perfect steps is a tread of 12 inches (30 cm) and a riser of 6 inches (15 cm). Steps for a deck or at a front door can be slightly wider, with a tread of 14–16 inches (35–40 cm). This horizontal-to-vertical ratio is adaptable to most twenty-first century adults climbing just a few steps or an entire flight of stairs. Where there is not enough room to accommodate properly proportioned steps, they can be split by a landing with the lower steps turned to the side.

How to Build Steps

Steps carry us from one level to another. A simple set of steps provides efficient function and comfortable use, but if they are an inappropriate size for their purpose, wobbly or not level, you'll hate them every time you use them. The construction of two to three steps is easily within the home gardener's grasp, but a longer flight of steps requires more excavation and materials, and the skills of a professional contractor.

Well-made steps provide ease of use and safety; poorly made steps invite accidents and injury. Using the best materials ensures the steps will be safe and durable for many years. If you're installing steps yourself, try to use one solid slab of stone or concrete across the top for each tread, or a maximum of two pieces tightly butted together. Steps that are constructed from materials pieced together in a pattern are difficult to make level and more likely to loosen and perhaps cause someone to trip. A professional contractor, however, has the skills to make pieced and patterned steps stable.

Steps are easy to make, but require thoughtful planning. First, decide how many steps are required, based on the height between the lower level and the upper level that the steps will fit into. Plan to make one step for every 3–4 inches (7.5–10 cm) in height between the bottom and top levels. There may be situations where you require a shallower step of 2–3 inches (5–7.5 cm) in height. Outdoor steps with a rise of more than 4 inches (10 cm) require more complicated materials and construction techniques.

1. Excavate the area, allowing the length to be equal to the combined measurements of your step treads, and providing for a depth that will accommodate the risers plus 2 inches (5 cm) of compacted foundation material. For example, two steps with 14-inch (35 cm) treads and 3-inch (7.5 cm) risers will require an excavation 28 inches (71 cm) long and 8 inches (20 cm) deep.

2. Fill the bottom of the excavation with foundation material made from crushed gravel, limestone screenings or coarse sand, and compact it using a metal tamper or a brick. If the level goes down, add more material and compact again until you have made a solid, compacted base 2 inches (5 cm) deep. Use a carpenter's level to be sure the base is even, and adjust the level of foundation material if necessary.

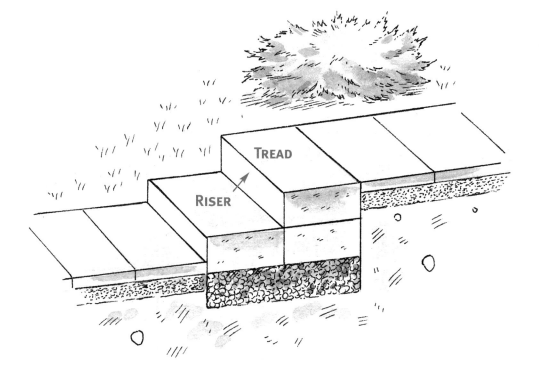

3. Use slabs of stone or concrete that have enough depth to equal the riser height you require. Materials with a thickness of 2–5 inches (5–12 cm) will have sufficient strength to bear the pressure of outdoor use without cracking. (Thinner slabs will require bonding with mortar or a chemical bonding material and should be constructed by a professional contractor.) Set the lowest level of slabs in place to cover the foundation completely. Setting the front slab just slightly lower (⅛ inch/0.5 cm) than the bottom pathway will lock it into place. Then set the subsequent slabs on top of the first level to form the rising steps. The heavy weight of the slabs will hold them in place.

pathways

Humanity can easily be divided between those who focus on the destination and prefer a straight path, and those more interested in the journey, who enjoy a circuitous route. Either way, a nicely made path has great allure, and when you find one you like you'll want to walk up and down it a few times, getting a feel for the texture underfoot. Pathways are as distinctive as the people who walk on them and can be fashioned from crushed corrugated boxes in a vegetable patch or polished granite slabs approaching a front door. Other common materials for building paths include every kind of natural stone, concrete aggregate and cobblestones, brick, asphalt, gravel and wood chips.

All paths have certain things in common. To be successful, they must be suitable to their purpose. Pathways surrounding your home need to be strong enough to withstand the daily traffic of many feet in all weathers and the movement of necessary equipment and heavy objects like furniture and refrigerators.

They also need to be elevated and self-draining so that you won't be walking through puddles and mud. You wouldn't

Uniform concrete blocks are easy and quick to install.

Various sizes of tumbled precast concrete pavers lend an aged appearance.

To get a tight fit, irregularly shaped stones must be cut by hand.

To prevent shattering, use vitrified (hardened) brick in cold climates.

Straight-cut stones are easy for home gardeners to fit together.

Reclaimed brick can be used only where freezing temperatures are not an issue.

want a soft bark-chip path to your front door, but it would be suitable for the stretch of woodland behind the house. Natural flagstone is a luxurious material with a high cost, but precast concrete cobblestones are less expensive and entirely suitable for the job. It's possible to combine and blend the two in a pathway, using the flagstone closest to the door, where it will be most appreciated.

Gardeners relish informal paths meandering through planted beds, but prefer a relaxed material underfoot. If the beds have been widened each year to accommodate more plants, you may end up with grass paths where the lawn used to be. This is a troublesome arrangement as the grass will aggressively invade the beds and plants will be caught by the lawn mower as their fullness sprawls over the path. Gravel is a traditional material for this purpose and the most practical surface for the situation. The gravel drains well, stays permanently in place, prevents weed growth and is just the right amount of support for a casual stroll among the antique roses.

Widely spaced stepping stones allow ground-cover plants the room to fill the gaps.

Edging and inlays using vitrified brick can be set into finely crushed gravel.

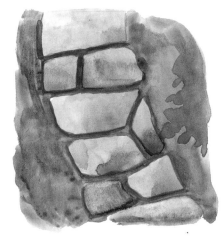

A swayed path is always the most graceful passage between two points.

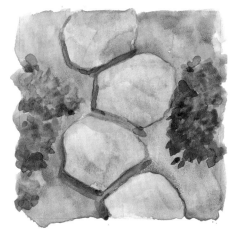

Stepping stones are appropriate for occasional use in informal areas.

Straight paths should be used only for short distances or where options are limited.

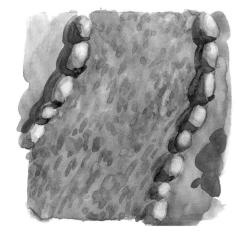

Loose rocks can edge a gravel or bark pathway in woodland areas.

Even the simplest path needs a foundation to be permanent. The heave of winter frost and the invasive movement of plants during the growing season can quickly overwhelm a path that hasn't been strengthened by a permanent base (see below).

Paths of hard materials will require a compacted base of (A) crushed gravel 4–6 inches (10–15 cm) thick, covered with a 2-inch (5 cm) layer of (B) coarse sand that is checked with a spirit level. The paving material is laid on top with joints tightly matched, and jointing sand is swept over the surface to fill in the cracks. A concealed metal edge restraint can be used to hold the edges permanently in place. When you're thinking of construction preparations, it's also important to plan on laying water and electrical sleeves for future use. These are rigid lengths of 4-inch (10 cm) wide PVC piping purchased at a building center, laid horizontally into the foundation and extending 2 inches (5 cm) on each side of the path. In future you may want to run an electrical cable or irrigation line across the path, and the sleeve will be available to thread these through, saving a costly upheaval. The empty sleeve is set into the compacted gravel and sand of the foundation, and the ends are plugged with rags to keep soil out. The sleeve ends are buried shallowly in the soil at the edges of the path until needed. Be sure to mark the spot with a stone set into the soil, or measure carefully and keep a record of the location.

HOW TO INSTALL A PATH FOUNDATION

No amount of deluxe surface stone or bricks can hide an inadequate foundation. A skimpy or poorly made foundation will quickly "unseat" the path, allowing pressure from frost action in surrounding soil to loosen and heave the path materials.

The excavation for the path should be deep enough to accommodate 4–6 inches (10–15 cm) of crushed gravel (A), crushed rock or limestone screenings. Use a hand tamper or brick to compact the soil to a level grade. Set a metal edge restraint in place, if you're using one, and then a layer of crushed foundation materials. Compact the crushed material and check that it is level. Then add a 2-inch (5 cm) layer of coarse sand (B) and compact it to a level grade.

Finally, lay the bricks or stones in place and sweep fine jointing sand across the surface and between the cracks.

opposite: Container plants at corners that allow plants to spill forward, like the chartreuse-flowered lady's mantle (*Alchemilla mollis*) (center), soften and conceal a path's hard edge. But some plants, like the green-and-white goutweed (*Aegopodium podagraria* 'Variegatum') (far left), can pop up in cracks and crevices where they're not welcome and are difficult to remove.

How to Make a Gravel Path

Whatever width you select for your path, if it runs alongside a planting bed it will lose space to sprawling plants beginning in midsummer. A minimum of 36 inches (90 cm) will leave room for your footsteps, and 48 inches (1.2 m) will make the path appear neater and allow you to stroll with a guest. A soldier course of landscaping bricks along the edges of the path makes a crisp line and will keep gravel from drifting. Or if you prefer a less visible treatment, you can use a flexible edging strip of metal or heavy rubber to line the sides.

There is little maintenance required for a gravel path, only occasional redistribution in low spots and a bit of leaf blowing in autumn (the only reasonable use for a leaf blower). After several years, the path may settle and additional gravel can be spread to increase the height and fill any dips or hollows.

Four inches (10 cm) of gravel spread uniformly over the path will make a good walking surface. (To estimate how much gravel to order, use the formula for ordering soil on page 143.) The choice of gravel for the surface has more to do with its particle shape and size than its mineral content. White is the only color that is too bright and out of place in the garden. Look for gravel that is crushed and has small angular pieces less than ¼ inch (0.5 cm) in size. Pea gravel is too large and rounded, and won't compact down to make a firm surface.

It helps the path get off to a good start if it can be compacted in some fashion to settle the gravel and firm the bed. A rented compacting machine will do this very well, or you can use a steel hand tamper—a broad plate with a long pole attached—to smash down the gravel as you move along.

1. Use a field hoe to distribute the soil of the path as evenly as possible and create a smooth bed.

2. Roll the soil to firm it in place. If there is grass on the path area, mow it as low as possible and cover the surface of the path with eight to ten layers of newspaper.

3. Lay down a covering of heavy-duty barrier cloth (A) over the path area to prevent gravel from migrating downward. This is a synthetic, non-woven fabric sold at building supply stores and garden centers. Use homemade staples made from wire coat hangers to tack down the sides of the fabric. Spread the gravel evenly over the path area with a stiff rake, pressing it up to the side edges to conceal all the barrier cloth.

How to Make a Stepping-Stone Pathway

When you need an informal path for occasional use, stepping stones are an attractive and inexpensive solution. They can be installed almost anywhere: down the side of a house not often used to make a garden entry, or across the lawn if the delivery of flyers and mail is wearing a path in the turf. Stepping-stone paths are also useful in a deep flower border as a design element, with the practical benefit of allowing access for plant maintenance.

A stepping-stone pathway through grass or gravel should accommodate comfortable and spontaneous movement. You want to move naturally and quickly without thinking of where to put your foot. Ideally, you should be able to walk the finished path in darkness without missing a step.

1. First, walk the line of the proposed path to determine how many stones you will need. Walk with your normal rhythm and speed to ensure a comfortable distance between stones for your gait and leg length. Drop a small marker with each footstep, and this will tell you how many flagstones to purchase.

For long durability try to purchase stones with a 2-inch (5 cm) thickness. You can use either straight-cut stone for a formal style, or random irregular sizes for a more relaxed setting.

2. Lay the stones out, putting slightly larger stones at the beginning and end of the path to make a substantial entrance and exit, and adjust them until you have a comfortable distance between each step.

If you are setting the stones into existing gravel, remove enough from underneath to allow the stone to be lowered into the space. It should sit approximately ¾ inch (2 cm) above the gravel surface.

If the stones are to be set into grass, use a sharpened blunt-nosed spade to cut an outline around the stone. Set the stone aside, slide the spade under the outlined turf and lift it out.

Use a hand trowel to remove soil to a depth of the stone's thickness plus an additional 2 inches (5 cm) for foundation material.

3. Level the bottom and neaten the sides of the excavation, then put 2 inches (5 cm) of coarse builder's sand in the bottom. Smooth the surface of the sand and fit the stone on top. Use a broad rubber mallet (never a metal hammer) to pound the stone and settle it in place. With a spirit level ensure the stone surface is truly level. If it's not perfect, lift the stone and adjust the sand foundation, replace the stone and check the level again. The stone should sit 1 inch (2.5 cm) above soil level and allow a lawn mower to pass over.

1

2

3

Ten Best Plants for Between Stepping Stones

Stepping stones are useful garden features, making it possible to have a firm surface underfoot in places where you walk occasionally rather than daily. They are cost efficient and easy to install (see page 79) and once in place, will give many years of service.

Stepping stones can be set into a grass lawn or installed in bare soil and surrounded with shredded bark mulch to prevent weed growth. But wherever possible, perennial groundcovers make the most attractive companions to a stepping stone pathway. Select plants that are low growing and suitable to the available light in the location.

If the path will be used year-round, consider planting some evergreens, such as hardy ivy, periwinkle or wintergreen. Their creeping and spreading stems will quickly intertwine to create an ornamental carpet around each stone. For best success, provide regular irrigation, particularly in the first two years. Maintenance should be only a once-a-season trim of any particularly rambunctious growth.

BUGLEWEED *Ajuga reptans* H 6 in (15 cm) W 24–36 in (60–90 cm) −40°F (−40°C) A useful plant with expanding rosettes of leaves rooting from stem nodes, ajuga blooms in late spring on flower spikes up to 8 in (20 cm) tall. Several cultivars and foliage colors are available with blue, pink or white flower spikes and bronze or variegated leaves. Average soil in light shade to part-sun.

EUROPEAN WILD GINGER *Asarum europaeum* H 6 in (15 cm) W to 12 in (30 cm) −20°F (−29°C) Lustrous, kidney-shaped, evergreen leaves on hairy stems. Leaves conceal small, inconspicuous purple-green flowers that bloom in late spring, deepening to brown. Organic woodland soil, shade to part-sun.

SPOTTED DEADNETTLE *Lamium maculatum* H 8 in (20 cm) W 24 in (60 cm) −30°F (−34°C) Another vigorous ground cover that forms expanding clumps to provide a low-growing mat of light to mid-green leaves. Cultivars offer variegated foliage and pink or white flowers. Average soil in part-shade to part-sun.

IRISH MOSS, CORSICAN PEARLWORT *Sagina subulata* H ½ in (1.5 cm) W 8 in (20 cm) −20°F (−29°C) Not a true moss, this has light green, moss-like foliage forming expanding clumps with profuse tiny white flowers in summer. 'Aurea' is a gold cultivar (above). Provide well-drained, moist soil in part-shade to part-sun.

SWEET WOODRUFF *Galium odoratum* H 18 in (45 cm) W indefinite −20°F (−29°C) Delicate, star-shaped, whorled green foliage rapidly forms a dense carpet with pure white, scented flowers in early spring to summer. Tolerates dry shade or part-sun, the leaves will burn in full sun.

WINTERGREEN *Gaultheria procumbens* H 6 in (15 cm) W to 3 ft (1 m) −20°F (−29°C) Glossy evergreen leaves with small pink or white flowers in spring and bright scarlet aromatic berries in autumn. When crushed, the leaves emit the strong fragrance of wintergreen. Part-shade in moist, slightly acid soil.

ENGLISH IVY *Hedera helix* H 3 in (7.5 cm) W indefinite −20°F (−29°C) Vigorous, with cream-veined evergreen leaves rooting from stem nodes. Cultivars, though less hardy, come in colors such as yellow-green or white-veined purple and also with variegated or unusually shaped leaves. Average garden soil in full shade to part-sun.

CREEPING STONECROP *Sedum spurium* (or *S. stoloniferum*) H 6 in (15 cm) W 24 in (60 cm) −40°F (−40°C) Semi-evergreen, trailing plants. Thick, succulent leaves root at joints to form ground-hugging mats. Stonecrop is excellent for rock or terraced gardens. Tolerates dry soil in part-sun to full sun.

MOTHER OF THYME, WILD THYME *Thymus serpyllum* H 4–10 in (10–25 cm) W 18 in (45 cm) −30°F (−34°C) Tiny green leaves on finely hairy stems that creep along to form a dense mat with masses of purple flowers in early summer. Average soil in part-sun to full sun.

PERIWINKLE, CREEPING MYRTLE *Vinca minor* H 4–8 in (10–20 cm) W indefinite −20°F (−29°C) Trailing stems bearing glossy evergreen leaves and light blue spring flowers. Various cultivars offer white-edged leaves, white flowers or purple-red flowers. Periwinkle can be quite invasive. Does well in average soil in full shade to part-sun.

driveways and parking spaces

The idea that we expand to fill our available space is certainly true of driveways. Almost no one wishes for his or her driveway to be reduced in size, and probably they would like it to be larger. Nine feet (2.7 m) is the minimum width for a one-lane driveway, but that accommodates only the car and leaves the driver and passengers walking alongside in the grass or snow. A double width of 18 feet (5.5 m) allows comfortable passage for pedestrians, baby strollers and bicyclists alongside the car, but eats up valuable green space and makes a big visual statement. Oversize and circular driveways invite drivers to abandon cars wherever it suits them, a haphazard approach that appeals to the need for personal privilege and a refusal to walk the extra steps to the garage. Driveways can be a loaded issue.

Comments about the size of a driveway are not always appreciated, and some people are quite defensive of the space. It's required for washing tires, a twice-a-year ritual, or it provides extra parking for guests on holidays, also twice a year, or it's the site of late-night basketball. Gardeners like myself, of course, use the driveway for a personal nursery of plants collected in spring and waiting for permanent sites in the garden, and this precludes tire washing,

A NECESSARY EVIL

PARKING pads are mini-driveways built into front or back lawns, usually as a desperation measure where the competition for street parking is ferocious. Everyone regrets putting the pad in green space where it doesn't belong, but that's often the only choice in a city.

The pad can be constructed of any suitable material, but because of its high visibility it makes sense to use the most attractive surface your purse can afford. Minimum width is 9 feet (2.7 m) across, and the pad should be long enough to accommodate the length of your car plus an additional 3 feet (0.9 m).

If the pad is on your front lawn, a special permit may be necessary and the end of the car must not project over the sidewalk. You can install a 4-foot (1.2 m) high framed-trellis fence along the side closest to the house and, planted with honeysuckle and clematis, this will go a long way to making the situation more acceptable.

Rather than just a narrow strip that meets the driveway at a right angle, this path has an alightment area beside the driveway and is comfortably wide where needed. The small planting bed, with built-in irrigation, softens the hard surface.

guest parking and team sports during the growing season. So size is an issue to be sorted out as everyone competes for square footage on the tarmac.

The matter of "how wide" is quickly resolved on smaller lots where space is at a premium and bylaws prevent driveway incursion into lawn area. Even more restrictive is the circumstance of inner-city shared driveways, a particular challenge to human relations. But much dialogue can ensue in the suburbs, where more space is available and feelings of entitlement run high.

The materials used for driveway surfaces are similar to pathways. Natural stone is an expensive choice, but concrete cobblestones are frequently used and can be tied into the walkway system. With years of use, natural stone and cobblestones can be stained by oil residues from cars' tires and may also sink slightly in areas of greatest weight. The staining can be delayed by slightly altering the parking position by 3–6 feet (90–180 cm) each day, but the best insurance against sinking patterns is a good foundation. Driveways require a 10–12-inch (25–30 cm) base of crushed and compacted gravel to adequately support years of vehicle pressure.

Poured concrete is a poor choice for driveways in cold climates with winter temperatures below freezing. Even with reinforcement grids and pressure seams built in, ice will make its way into fine cracks and begin the process of pitting and crumbling. Crushed and compacted aggregate gravel is a good surface for wheels of all kinds, but may not suit other family uses. Asphalt is by far the best surface for vehicles, and it is ubiquitous in industrial, commercial and residential locations. If you would like to elevate the driveway appearance, asphalt can be banded with natural stone or precast concrete dimensional blocks (the largest size of cobblestone pavers). This design treatment transforms an ordinary asphalt driveway at modest cost and provides a functional surface with good style.

If you are concerned about having too much hard surface, the dilemma of driveway versus green space might be defused by keeping the driveway to a comfortable width of 12 feet (3.6 m) and creating an alightment area or slight flare where you stop the car and open the door. This puts an additional 3–6 feet (90–180 cm) in width by 10 feet (3 m) in length where you need it. Where a double driveway is required, you can help to diminish the hard surface by planting a row of trees along one side, spaced approximately every 8 feet (2.4 m). Trees for this purpose should have a maximum height of 20 feet (6 m) and be pyramidal in form to avoid debris falling on parked cars. When looking at potential tree choices remember that the colder your winter climate, the less likely any tree will reach its maximum height.

HOW WIDE SHOULD A PATH BE?

AN important consideration when making a path is to determine the appropriate width, and this will affect the whole history of its use. A bachelor path accommodates only one person at a time and is any width up to 36 inches (90 cm). While this path in life has its appreciators, it's a nuisance to deal with such a narrow approach to a front door. It can force you to inappropriately invade your companion's private space or break up otherwise loving couples. Two people walking together require the comfort of 4 feet (1.2 m), and a width of 5 feet (1.5 m) makes a deluxe avenue for three abreast. If your path is too narrow for its intended use, people will vote with their feet and step off it, walking wherever they want and abusing the bordering lawn. Providing a reasonable width makes sense in the long run.

patios and decks

The need for patios and decks seems to increase along with our appreciation for outdoor living. The 12-inch (30 cm) hibachi once sufficient for backyard barbecues has been replaced with a 60-inch (1.5 m) stainless steel gas grill. Sling-back canvas chairs and webbed aluminum lounges have been eclipsed by contemporary garden furniture that is substantial in size, comfortable to use—and non-folding. When you consider the cost of aluminum-thread wicker chairs and genuine teak tables, it's apparent the gap is closing between garden and living room furniture. A substantial investment in garden furniture requires a suitable venue for its use, and that will likely be a deck or patio.

The most frequent mistake made in constructing a hard-floor garden surface is misjudging the amount of space needed. We become conservative in estimating the square feet necessary for six chairs and a table, and often make the deck or patio too small. No one can relax when their chair leg is perilously close to the patio edge or they're jammed up against the deck railing. It's useful to set out the furniture if it's already been purchased (or substitutes like garbage cans and cardboard boxes as stand-ins) and get a realistic idea of how much space is required.

Depending on family size, it may be advantageous to have two seating areas in the garden, one larger and attached to the house for family and entertaining purposes, and another smaller and separate for more private use. A second hard surface can be located toward the back of the garden or side of the house and constructed in less formal materials—and at less expense. A small 8 x 12-foot (2.5 x 3.5 m) surface of random-shaped flagstones, set closely together and with coarse sand or fine gravel in the cracks, allows you to have some moments of privacy without totally abandoning the rest of the family. Other materials such as pre-cast cobblestones, aggregate slabs or patterned concrete patio stones are possible materials. Even though the area is small, if you want the surface to be level and firm it should be excavated and given a base of compacted gravel and sand.

If you're going to make a patio or deck, the choice of materials is influenced by the style of construction and, to some extent, the height of your foundation. If your area is elevated, you'll be better off making a wood deck that requires less weighty underpinnings.

Patios are more formal and are usually constructed of stone, either natural or manufactured, or occasionally hardened red brick or outdoor tile. Brick patios laid in traditional designs like herringbone and basket weave are frequently found in homes built before 1950. Bricks make an attractive and affordable outdoor floor. They require a foundation of crushed and compacted gravel,

WHAT SIZE PATIO?

WHATEVER kind of outdoor living space you construct, be sure it's made large enough to be useful. A 10-foot (3 m) square area (100 sq feet [9 sq m]) is comfortable for a small table and four chairs, or two long lounges and two chairs. The best way to estimate how much space is required is to measure it out on the lawn, setting the furniture as you would like to use it and judging how much space is required. You'll quickly know what's possible in the space you've got to work with.

and you need to decide whether to dry lay the bricks on sand or use mortar. In northern climates mortar is shattered by frost and requires repair and patching frequently. Concrete is also a poor choice because of the potential for cracks and breaking up caused by frost damage.

Screened porches are another outdoor room tradition from earlier decades that give much pleasure. They are constructed on a poured concrete base over crushed and compacted gravel and also must have a roof extension from the house. Screen panels are fitted between posts to form the walls, and ceramic tiles are a good choice for flooring. Tiles manufactured for outdoor applications must be set in mortar and should be used only in covered locations like vestibules and porches, where snow and ice won't lie on the surface.

Decks can be constructed at any level from the ground up and can incorporate many stylized design features. Built-in storage areas, seating, planter boxes, privacy screens and overhead pergolas are all extensions of deck design.

The high cost of suitable lumber is an important consideration when building a deck. The most affordable product is pressure-treated wood, but the chemicals used to increase its resistance to moisture are extremely toxic to people and animals and can be absorbed through your skin. Unfortunately, this information is not readily available where lumber is sold, and much pressure treated-wood is used where people will touch it frequently, or where it can leach toxic chemicals into soil used for growing food plants. It can be used safely for the understructure of decks where no one will touch it, but the exposed floor, steps and rails should be untreated wood.

One way to justify the cost of a wood deck is to extend its life in every way possible. Untreated wood is subject to degradation from moisture in all seasons, and you should plan on applying a water-repellent preservative every two years.

Most wood deck floors are constructed with a ⅛–¼-inch (0.25–0.5 cm) space between the boards, but this spacing doesn't allow enough air to circulate and dry the boards quickly. The sides of boards remain wet for a fairly long period, allowing moisture to reach deeper into the wood. The narrow spacing problem is compounded by small pieces of organic duff and debris (leaves, needles, bud casings, seeds) falling from trees and catching in the spaces, where it picks up moisture and begins to decompose and rot the wood. Planning for ½-inch (1 cm) spacing between floorboards will greatly increase airflow, allow organic debris to fall through, and cause rain and melting snow to drain rapidly. An

added benefit is a cost saving in material, as the floor will have larger and better "breathing" spaces and less wood is required in construction. The wider spacing is unnoticeable underfoot and is a concern only to those in stiletto heels.

Naturally rot-resistant woods are available everywhere lumber is sold, and though their cost is high, they will extend the life of a deck many years. Look for cedar, redwood and white oak, all moisture-resistant North American woods. Black locust is also

rot resistant and usually available as 6-foot (1.8 m) posts. Despite the ability of these woods to resist decay, they will last even longer if a water-repellent preservative stain is applied regularly. The preservative stain goes on quickly with a paint roller or brush and is

Small design details can make a big difference in the way you enjoy a deck. The standard step dimensions—a 12-inch (30 cm) tread and 6-inch (15 cm) riser—are absolutely necessary to prevent accidents, and you may want to consider making the tread wider to allow sitting (**left**) and to provide a place to group seasonal flower pots (**right**). If you're building planter boxes along the deck edges, it's worth having metal or vinyl liners to prevent moist soil from coming in contact with wood. Both the wood planter and the liner must have drainage holes, and they should be drilled together so the holes are aligned. An extra spot for plants is provided by incorporating small platforms with steps (**center**).

A railing (**left**, **center** and **right**) is a good safety feature to prevent tumbles, and bylaws make it mandatory above certain heights. Bench-style seats along the edge are a useful option, and their comfort is increased if you provide a 6-inch (15 cm) backing board built into the railing. Crawl space under the deck is a custom-made retreat for local fauna such as raccoons, skunks and groundhogs. A simple trellis baffle, skirted along the open edges and nailed tightly, will reduce interest in this area while maintaining good air circulation under the wood floor.

available at hardware and building supply stores.

A deck constructed of rot-resistant wood and protected every second year with a preservative coating should last twenty years in good condition before selected boards need replacement. If you want a deck to last the ages, wood-blend lumber made of wood and plastic is sometimes available at a high price, but it lasts and looks good without maintenance for many years.

Miracles of transformation are always possible. A former carport can become an expansive patio with the addition of a brick floor and raised planting bed. Similar renovations to unused side yards and once-busy play areas can result in more and better garden space.

garden sheds

Gardeners of a certain age accumulate a lot of necessary baggage and equipment. Shared space in the garage will suffice to accommodate the collection for a while, but then you'll want a shed of your own. Garden sheds are distinct from bicycle, outdoor furniture and garbage bin storage places, or at least they should be. No one but a gardener realizes the value of ancient clay pots and warped compost sifters, and it's best to keep these items in an appropriate place and away from the unenlightened.

If you're fortunate to have space for a garden shed, consider carefully what you plan to put in it. As any shed will cost money either to build or purchase as a kit, be clear on what will be stored inside and how much space is required. If the shed must accommodate a lawn mower and pool skimmer, you'll need quite a bit of space and likely the garden gear will be shortchanged. But if the shed can be dedicated exclusively to garden purposes, a 4 x 8 foot (1.2 x 2.4 m) size can work well and still not dominate the landscape. Such a site should leave room for a small potting bench with space for shelves, hooks and possibly garbage can bins under the bench for sand and soil amendments. Heavy-duty hooks can be mounted on an outside wall for hanging your wheelbarrow, wrapped in plastic, over the winter.

Sheds can be made from wood or purchased as put-together kits of metal, vinyl or hardened rubber materials. Whatever your choice, it will be improved by providing a solid and elevated base for the structure. The base could be poured concrete (requiring a simple wood frame), but it's much easier to purchase inexpensive concrete patio slabs, approximately 2 feet (60 cm) square, and piece them together. The base will keep your equipment dry and extend the life of the shed. Be sure that the shed has a slanted roof to allow rain and snow to drain quickly. The deluxe dream shed has its own power, supplied by a low-voltage outdoor extension from the house, and this will allow you to install a light inside.

left: If the shed is placed face forward, you can mount trellises—they don't have to be as elaborate as these—on either side of the door and grow vines up to camouflage the structure. Vines will go a long way to making the shed more graceful and appropriate in the garden.

opposite: Aesthetics are always an issue with garden sheds, and the question is whether to hide or flaunt it. If your shed resembles a tiny house, you might as well mount window boxes on the front and hang curtains. A hard floor in front makes moving about with wheelbarrow or lawnmower easier, and is a handy holding spot for newly purchased plants.

Ten Best Shed-Covering Vines

Camouflaging a shed or small garage is good work for aggressive vines that also provide some ornamental features in the garden. Their rambunctious style is most appropriate in semi-rough places where you have something to hide, or on a large expanse of bare wall or empty fence. Their super-charged energy is the key to quick coverage, but be prepared to occasionally trim back wayward tendrils before they get away from you.

Most of these will also grow horizontally on a roof or sprawl across the ground to form a thick foliage cover over stumps, rock piles and rough slopes. For use on or near the house, climbing hydrangea, five-leafed akebia and trumpet vine are easy to control and have the most ornamental flowers. Bittersweet and Japanese wisteria have enough strength to squeeze the life out of small trees and woody shrubs, and require firm support on a heavy-duty pergola or post fence. They are best located where they cannot overtake other plants, such as on an arbor or pergola.

FIVELEAF AKEBIA VINE *Akebia quinata* H 30 ft (9 m) −20°F (−29°C) Delicate and charming when grown in shade, this can really take off in a sunny location. The vine climbs by weaving itself through a support and needs a simple trellis to get up a wall, but has great sprawling and creeping abilities once it's up there. On the ground it will roll right over old stumps. A very ornamental vine with an unusually attractive and scented purple flower.

DUTCHMAN'S PIPE *Aristolochia durior* (syn *Aristolochia macrophylla*) H 25–30 ft (7.6–9 m) −30°F (−34°C) Large heart-shaped leaves of deep green lend a tropical effect, and it grows vigorously in sun or shade. This is the vine that shades many old-fashioned country verandas and it needs only a simple trellis to get up and spread its overlapping leaves. The brown pipe-like flowers are an unusual dividend, much appreciated by children.

CLIMBING HYDRANGEA *Hydrangea anomala* subsp. *petiolaris* syn *Hydrangea petiolaris* H 50 ft (15 m) −20°F (−29°C) Slow to start, this requires consistent watering the first few years to encourage roots. Then it quickly scales walls, fences and poles, growing unsupported on a solid, flat surface, but more slowly on an open surface such as a chain-link fence or trellis. The mature, nutty brown, exfoliating bark is a valuable winter ornament as are the spent flowers, gardenia-scented when in bloom.

HALL'S HONEYSUCKLE *Lonicera japonica* 'Halliana' H 30 ft (9 m) −20°F (−29°C) A good vine for covering objects in deep shade, but some curse its vigor in sunlight. The semi-evergreen foliage is a soft dark green and classic blossoms, white fading to pale yellow, scent the early summer air. 'Halliana' has enough vigor to find its way unaided up a shed or fence and then billow forward. In full sun, nothing beats *Lonicera* x *heckrotti* 'Goldflame'.

TRUMPET CREEPER *Campsis radicans* H 30 ft (9 m) −20°F (−29°C) For sunny locations, self-clinging trumpet vine will make a dense cover on walls or over stumps, rock piles and fence posts. The lustrous compound foliage is attractive by itself, but the August-blooming trumpet flowers are large and bold in orange-scarlet, red ('Flamenco' and 'Crimson Trumpet'), yellow ('Flava') or coral ('Mme. Gallen').

BITTERSWEET *Celastrus scandens* H 30 ft (9 m) −50°F (−46°C) Beware the capabilities of this vine, for it has a rampant nature and forms tough, twining tendrils that quickly turn woody. Moving with speed and fortitude, it needs no support to scramble up and over a structure and down the other side. Keep it away from trees, as it can twist and squeeze the life out of them. In sun, it has beautiful orange and red fruit. Plant both sexes for good flower production.

CLEMATIS *Clematis* x *jouiniana* 'Praecox' H 10–13 ft (3–4 m) −20°F (−29°C) Unlike its more delicate cousins, this clematis has a huskier build and rambunctious behavior, and can be led on a few stakes up to the top of a garden shed in sun or partial shade. It produces pale bluish clusters of bell-like flowers in late summer, and will also make a dense ground cover.

BOSTON IVY *Parthenocissus tricuspidata* H 70 ft (21 m) −30°F (−34°C) This ivy's shiny leaves are a familiar site cloaking the walls and roofs of old homes. It climbs with little sticking discs on smooth brick, stucco and wood surfaces, adding the graceful appearance of age even to new structures. It doesn't harm masonry, but the discs are unsightly if the vine is removed. Prefers bright light and will turn blazing scarlet in autumn.

SILVERLACE VINE *Polygonum aubertii* H 40 ft (12 m) −30°F (−34°C) A fast growing and engulfing vine with many tendrils and small light green leaves, silverlace roils over structures and fences for 20 ft (6m) or more. It will need only a tall stake to get up and an occasional object to thread through or wrap around. The joy comes in late summer when the vine is covered with sprays of lacy white flowers.

JAPANESE WISTERIA *Wisteria floribunda* H 28 ft (8.5 m) −20°F (−29°C). The queen of vines needs strong support and shelter when grown in cold regions at the edge of its hardiness zone. It is a twining vine, its long blossoming racemes showing before leaves emerge, and its many tendrils hardening to wood. Hard pruning in late winter encourages flowers—cut lateral tendrils back to a stub with three or four dormant buds.

pools and ponds

Watering holes of every dimension require serious planning. Almost everyone enjoys the presence of water in a garden, although enthusiasts divide sharply between those favoring an ornamental fishpond, and others preferring deep water they can jump in. As the North American climate warms and periods of sustained high heat are more frequent, swimming pools creep closer to the top of some wish lists. When you look down from an airplane, it's always a surprise to see just how many gardeners have satisfied the urge and installed swimming pools in quite limited spaces. Pool companies will dig the big pit just about anywhere you want, but enjoyment of a pool can be spoiled if it's jammed in a tight space or a poor location.

Big objects work well in big spaces and pools need to be located in open areas with a generous buffer of square footage around them. A minimum of 10 feet (3 m) on all sides of the pool will prevent claustrophobic feelings and allow for some simple furniture, water wings and floating mattresses. Shrubs and perennial plants can be damaged by chlorinated water and should be kept beyond the 10-foot (3 m) clearance. A swimming pool should be located away from trees that drop seasonal debris. Filtration systems are meant to catch reasonable amounts of small particles, but can't cope with the full flower and seed drop from overhanging maples.

The smaller your space, the more difficult it will be to site the pool in an appropriate location. If it is placed just a few feet/meters from the property line, you'll compromise the privacy of poolside lounging. Even with a fence in place, you can expect to hear your neighbors' conversation, and they'll hear yours, and they might not appreciate late-night or early-morning splashing. If the pool is placed too close to the house, pool activities and equipment compete for space with passing lawn mowers, the movement of groceries through the back door, and gangs of children and dogs.

If you're determined to put a swimming pool in your small garden, consider scaling down the size of the project. In really hot weather, you can find great relief with a dip in cool water and an extended float. It's not really necessary to swim Olympic laps, and keeping the pool small will preserve growing space. Measure the area of your garden and allow the pool area to cover one-third of the available space. More garden area will keep the pool in perspective, but if the pool takes up half or more of the yard you're making quite a statement about the importance of water. If you eliminate a diving board, there really isn't a need for any swimming pool to have a 10-foot (3 m) depth at one end. You can save money by keeping the depth between 5–6 feet (1.5–1.8 m), deep enough for every swimming activity and safer for pool users.

SAFETY RULES

ABOVE all else, a pool must be adequately fenced to keep out unsupervised children and toddlers. We hear of drownings every summer and no one wants the enjoyment of a pool forever marred by such a tragedy.

Your municipality undoubtedly has regulations regarding pool fencing—in terms of height minimum, surrounding space and adequate locks or other equipment. Besides the importance of adhering to the necessary safety rules, you may want to reconsider a pool altogether if you learn that it requires 6-foot (1.8 m) fencing—of an impermeable, unclimbable type.

Water sounds are the siren songs of the garden, and it seems having an ornamental pond is high on many wish lists. Ponds are fairly elaborate water features, and they can be constructed to fit a broad spectrum of design ideas and preferences.

Ornamental ponds are also smaller and easier to site in a yard. They work best in a semi-shaded location to prevent high water temperature from cooking whatever plants and animals are living in the brew. Too much sun will also encourage the growth of green algae on the surface of the water. It's

Try to place your pond where it won't catch too much falling debris from overhanging trees. If there's just one deluge of leaves for a two-week period, you can cover the pond with a net for that time. But some trees, like maples, are constantly dropping flowers, seeds and leaves, which require frequent removal. Bright sun can raise the water temperature to a critical level, so find a semi-shaded spot to keep fish and plants healthy. And don't be surprised to encounter uninvited wildlife near the water. Raccoons, squirrels and skunks like an evening at the spa and will put you on their circuit.

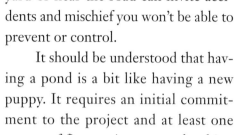

FINDING a place for water in the garden brings us just a little bit closer to paradise. Water features are a naturalizing influence, attracting birds and beneficial insects to form the first line of defense against more destructive garden pests. If you want to encourage the natural predators of caterpillars, aphids and earwigs, you'll need to provide a simple source of water like a bird bath. The bath can be placed in almost any location, but keeping it within window view will provide much satisfaction. No one can resist watching birds enjoy a great splash-up, and they'll bring their fuzzy fledglings, too. A bird bath sits best on a level and solid foundation like a flat piece of flagstone or concrete. In warm weather it will need to be swept out twice a week and filled with fresh water to prevent bacterial growth.

right: Irregular stones and plants combine to hide the liner edge, but it can take a bit of fussing until they fit together. When purchasing aquatic plants, be sure you know which are hardy enough to remain outdoors over winter. Some may be tender and require indoor storage.

difficult to keep pond water clear, particularly if aquatic plants and fish are living in it, although conditions may eventually stabilize and look reasonably healthy. Keeping the water moving with a small cascade will also help to upset the growth of algae. Small ponds are more difficult to stabilize and may remain a bit murky. Put the pond where you can see it often when you're in the garden, and also from windows inside. It's especially nice to include a pond alongside a patio or deck seating area. Although there are seldom bylaw restrictions on ornamental ponds, they should always be where you can supervise them. Putting ponds in a front yard or near the road can invite accidents and mischief you won't be able to prevent or control.

It should be understood that having a pond is a bit like having a new puppy. It requires an initial commitment to the project and at least one season of fine-tuning to get the thing working right. The more life you put

into the water in the form of plants, fish, frogs and snails, the more complex are the potential biological interactions. No one wants to find the creature from the black lagoon lurking near the peonies, but you should be prepared to deal with various kinds of murky scum and a bit of slime until the balance of aquatic life is established. If you're fastidious about keeping your indoor plumbing impeccably clean, you may not be ready for pond ownership.

Basic pond construction isn't difficult and involves either a free-form excavation lined with a sheet of heavy-mil rubber or a pre-molded fiberglass form (see next page). Poured concrete can also be used in regions with a winter temperature no lower than −10°F (12°C). Concrete tends to develop fine line cracks at lower temperatures, and these can lead to chronic leaking problems.

The big issue is concealing the liner rim, and much care goes into the design and structure of stone and plants surrounding the edge. Easiest by far is to select a rectangular or square pond shape with edging of straight-cut stone or bricks. This simple style goes together without frustration and adequately hides the liner edge. The tableau can still include a jungle of plants surrounding the pond to offset the straight lines of the shape. But many gardeners want to make a naturalistic edge of randomly shaped stone, and quite a lot of time can be invested in fitting pieces together and getting them level and stable. Hiding the liner with irregular shapes can be a challenge; if just one bit of high-tech rubber or fiberglass peeks out the idyllic scene can be spoiled.

Masses of shrubs and perennial plants surround a pond and help to soften its simple, contemporary lines. The straight stone edge to the pond is quick and easy to construct.

HOW TO INSTALL A POND

Installing a pond using a fiberglass liner purchased from a garden center is an easy method for home gardeners. Look for a gracefully shaped liner that will easily adapt to your garden space with plenty of room to spare on all sides. The location for the pond should be on flat, level ground and, if possible, with clear sky above. Overhanging trees will drop litter that must be cleaned out of the water every ten days. During the warm months some water will naturally evaporate, and the pond will need to be topped up from time to time. In spring the pond will need a thorough cleaning to remove plant debris, baling out as much of the old water as possible, and filling with fresh water from a hose.

1. Set the liner on the ground and use a sharp shovel to cut an outline of its shape on the ground. Dig out the shape to make an excavation approximately 2 inches (5 cm) deeper and 2 inches (5 cm) wider than the liner on all sides. (Soil that has been dug out should be distributed elsewhere on your property.) Spread a 2-inch (5 cm) layer of coarse sand across the bottom of the hole, leveling it to make a smooth and consistent surface.

2. Set the fiberglass liner into the excavation, fitting and centering it so that there is a 2-inch (5 cm) gap on all sides. The top edge of the liner should be just at ground level and no higher. Remove your shoes and walk carefully in the empty liner to settle it into the excavation. Finally, fill the 2-inch (5 cm) gap all around the sides with coarse sand, to help protect the liner from the action of winter frost.

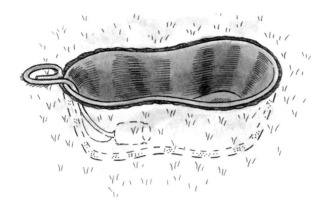

3. Set the pump in a corner at the bottom of the liner, closest to the power source, and conceal it behind one or two rocks. Run the power cord and water tube up the side of the liner and out onto the ground. The power cord can be plugged into an outdoor electrical line after water is in the pond (never run the pump without water in the pond). The electrical connection can come from a heavy-duty power cord that is artfully hidden in nearby foliage or from a permanently installed power source.

4. With the water tube lying on the ground and working in one direction around the pond, place irregularly shaped rocks or flagstones along the pond edge to conceal the rim of the liner. For best concealment, allow the front edge of the stones to protrude slightly out and over the pond by an inch or two (5 cm). Where rocks don't fit together well, dig planting pockets and replace the soil with a premium growing mix for leafy perennials. When you've laid rocks around to the other side of the water tube, construct a small pile of rocks with the water tube threaded up through them to create a small cascade. Lay a flat rock over the tube to hide it without pressing on it. The water can fall directly into the pond for maximum sound effect, or you can place a large flat stone in the pond for the water to fall gently onto.

irrigation

Whatever irrigation system you've got in place, it's likely to be imperfect. Delivering water to adequately meet the needs of all plants is probably the most difficult challenge in any garden. Despite the many watering devices and systems, nothing works so well as rain. If you've struggled for years with hoses, pipes and cans you may be ready to let the lawn return to a natural meadow. But first consider the options.

The most important rule for delivering water where it's needed is to keep the droplets in large sizes and as close to the ground as possible. Watering the lawn should be considered separately from irrigating trees and flowerbeds. In-ground irrigation systems do a good job of this with emitters that pop up only a few inches (several centimeters) and deliver a low fan of water over the turf in each zone. The flexible piping is easily installed without heavy equipment and hooks up to house plumbing. An electronic panel programmed to turn on at pre-set times and days controls the system. You can

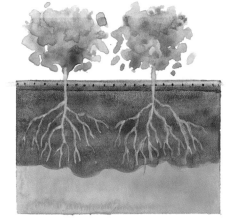

A soaker hose (also called a drip or weeper hose) is the most effective way to deliver adequate water consistently to a plant's roots, which is where it is needed.

While elevated emitters can solve some problems they must be high enough to reach over the tallest plant. This means a good deal of water is lost to evaporation and carried off by the wind.

Pop-up emitters spray water at a 45° angle and are defeated by the plants themselves. Water hits the sides of plants and falls to the ground, making a puddle on one side and dry patches on the other.

A fan oscillator (or sprinkler) delivers water from overhead and uses a broad arc to reach a broad area, but a good deal of the moisture is lost to evaporation and the wind.

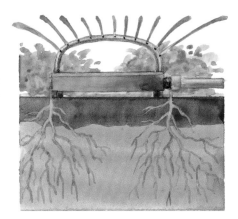

opposite: Plants standing shoulder to shoulder smother weed growth, but are difficult to water effectively. Set down a trickling hose and move it around to deliver moisture at ground level where it will quickly soak into the root zone. The best method, however, is to snake a long weeper hose through the plants and leave it there for the season.

purchase a rain sensor that will shut down the system on rainy days, and also a back-flow regulator to prevent any reversal of outdoor water from flowing back into the indoor water supply.

Gardeners need to be smart about how and when to deliver water, because irrigation companies aren't. The panels for in-ground systems presuppose that all zones of your garden will be watered for a short period each day. That is the worst possible schedule for delivering moisture and will retard growth and keep everything desperate for a deep drink.

Daily sprays of short duration only force grass roots to remain close to the surface, where they remain vulnerable to drought and high soil temperature. The short bursts of water, usually for only ten to twelve minutes, are also insufficient to reach the deeper roots of woody plants and herbaceous perennials. These conditions will keep the garden alive, just barely, but won't encourage growth or high performance. Insisting on a control panel that will allow different cycles each day can solve these problems. Whatever you are irrigating, it should receive water twice a week for an extended period to allow water to percolate down deeply.

Roses are moisture-intensive plants that take a full 2 gallons (9 l) of water from the soil each day during the warm growing months. In full bloom, they take even more to keep petals fresh and hydrated. 'The Fairy' is a pale pink shrub rose that will bloom until November and likes a deep organic mulch, which helps conserve moisture.

opposite: Planting under high trees gives a lush layered look to the garden. But big trees take the lion's share of ground moisture from other ornamental plants, so be prepared to water trees individually with a hose laid at the base. Roses like lots of water, but avoid wetting the foliage to prevent disease.

How Much Water Where?

Trees and specimen plants require special attention and you should never assume water delivered to the lawn would suffice for the needs of these big plants.

Turf grasses are greedy consumers of water and won't allow much to reach the deeper root systems of woody plants. If you think your trees and large shrubs are slow growing, they probably aren't getting enough water. With adequate irrigation, they should grow 1 foot (30 cm) a year, and drip emitters connected to the same automatic system can be installed to meet their needs.

Flowerbeds require taller stake emitters that stand above the height of plants and allow droplets to cascade over and down them. The emitters are available in various heights and remain in the garden year-round.

Although the automatic irrigation systems are affordable, not everyone wants to invest their money in underground piping. Lawns can of course be watered with a hose and some kind of sprinkler device. Select a sprinkler that delivers large-size droplets. The smaller the droplets, the more that's lost to evaporation, and anything that delivers a fine mist is almost useless. Whatever kind of device you're using, avoid watering the lawn at midday, when sun and wind will evaporate most of what you're putting down.

above right: Soaker hoses are an intelligent investment because they use 70% less water than sprinklers, delivering it slowly and at ground level where it's needed. You can put them in place for the season, buried in the soil or hidden under foliage or mulch, and hook them up to the regular garden hose for an overnight soak. The hoses are rolled up and stored in autumn. This method is ideal for flowerbeds, shrubs and trees and is a smaller investment than in-ground automatic systems. If you care about your garden, you won't resent thinking about when to provide water and hooking up the soaker hose system.

lighting

Garden night lighting should do more than drive moths mad. If you want something better than the customary bulb over the back door, there's a wide choice of do-it-yourself lighting kits or you can hire an outdoor lighting contractor. Borrowing from theatrical techniques, outdoor nightscape lighting can create moonlight over the entire garden, flood a patio seating area, or put an intense pin-point spotlight on a piece of statuary. With just a bit of creative light placement, the garden takes on an elevated presence in the evening hours, expanding the time you spend there and maximizing enjoyment of night sounds and fragrances. And whatever lighting you install, it will contribute to winter interest when natural light is quickly fading at day's end.

The first question is whether you prefer prominent lighting fixtures or something a bit more discreet. Many of the lighting kits provide fixtures with a distinctly military flair, containing various forms of missile silos and helmetlike midgets in black and verdigris finishes, all strung out on a line. These fixtures make quite a show of force, if that's your intent. But no one wants to be intimi-

Canister fixtures deliver light straight up under trees or at the corner of the house.

Small ornamental fixtures direct light downward to illuminate a pathway or ornament.

Spotlights are security features and also illuminate dramatic architecture.

Adding a partial deflector to a canister allows light to be directed on an angle.

Intense mini-spotlights send light across steps at an entrance.

Driveway lights should be high enough to clear winter snowdrifts.

dated by his or her lighting system and, ideally, it's the light that should be seen, not the fixture.

Because lighting involves wiring and electrical supply, you might want a contractor to do the job. A transformer will need to be installed on a wall and wires run through buried protective sheaths to various locations. The fixtures themselves will be mounted on fences and trees, concealed in stairways and stones, or perhaps buried in the ground for uplighting. Intense beams can be shot across steps to prevent stumbling, and gates and pathways can be illuminated and the architectural form of trees dramatically lit from the ground up. Although outdoor light fixtures are designed to withstand the elements, they will still require maintenance and should be reasonably accessible. If the source of perpetual moonlight is mounted 20 feet (6 m) up a tree, someone will need to go up there and change the bulb now and then.

Light on steps, doorways and the garage prevents accidents and makes visitors feel more secure and welcome. Key plants and trees can be uplighted with ground fixtures for dramatic night display. Never install light fixtures on a tree trunk; they will provide entry points for disease and insects. Turn off light on plants and trees at midnight to give them a period of darkness.

opposite: Lighting hardware can be discreetly concealed or it can be a prominent element in the garden. An ornamental fixture in the foundation bed near an entrance should be compatible with the period and architecture of the house.

Ten Best Weeping Shrubs and Small Trees

Weeping plants add great style to a garden when planted by an entrance or anchoring one end of a garden bed. They are genetically inclined to grow downward in a variety of postures, some dramatically weeping and others rambling their way downward. They can be particularly dramatic features when highlighted with uplighting (see previous pages).

Height can be kept within human scale (under 6 ft/2 m), and that is a comfortable range for plants you will pass frequently or have close to a doorway.

Some are very slow growing and it's worthwhile purchasing a sizable plant. Others grow vigorously, becoming fatter but not much taller, and occasionally require some thinning out of canes.

LACELEAF JAPANESE MAPLE *Acer palmatum* var. *dissectum* H 5 ft (1.5 m) W 10 ft (3 m) −10°F (−23°C) A valuable plant by a doorway or along a path. Finely cut leaves cascade down in drifts from slender wood. Most stay small for a long time, gaining in foliage and spread. Try 'Garnet', 'Crimson Queen', 'Viridis' and 'Waterfall'. Consistently moist, fertile soil in light shade or part-sun, out of strong winds that can dry their wispy foliage.

YOUNG'S WEEPING BIRCH *Betula pendula* 'Youngii' H 15 ft (5 m) −50°F (−46°C) The white bark of this graceful dwarf birch is a year-round asset, as are its slender and pendulous branches and dome-shaped head. It usually stops at 6–7 ft (1.8–2.1 m) to concentrate on the beautiful sprays of glistening leaves, spring catkins and golden autumn foliage. Consistently moist soil is essential to avoid insect problems; it won't tolerate drought.

JAPANESE GARDEN JUNIPER *Juniperus procumbens* 'Nana' H 2–3 ft (0.6–1 m) −50°F (−46°C) The shiny blue-green juniper needles are familiar, but this plant's form is creeping and procumbent. 'Nana' makes a low weeping feature along a sunny path, and is attractive combined with small boulders and softer plants like dwarf daylily 'Stella d'Oro', the fringed and fern-leaf bleeding hearts (*Dicentra eximia*, *D. formosa*) and miniature roses.

WEEPING NORWAY SPRUCE *Picea abies* 'Pendula' H 8 ft (2.4 m) −40°F (−40°C) This dwarf, weeping form of the massive forest spruce is dramatic in a bed or border. Deep green-needled branches reach out at unpredictable angles as they weep, so allow it room to display itself to advantage. Long purplish cones develop in spring, staying on through the winter. Needs a sunny location and moisture when young, developing drought-hardiness with age.

Cutleaf Weeping Caragana *Caragana arborescens* 'Walker' H 5 ft (1.5 m) −50°F (−46°C) This hybrid has finely cut, light green leaves on long, slender branches that sway in the breeze. Masses of delicate yellow flowers show in June, followed by ornamental pods and yellow autumn color. It needs consistent watering and shelter from strong winds, but does well in normal breezes and a sunny site. For greater drought tolerance try 'Pendula'.

Weeping Katsura *Cercidiphyllum japonicum* 'Pendula' H 6–8 ft (1.8–2.5 m) −30°F (−34°C) With its understated elegance, this is a beautiful complement to plants like *Pinus cembra* or *Picea pungens* 'Glauca Globosa'. New leaves emerge bronzy-purple, fade to light green and then blue-green. Autumn color is deep yellow (alkaline soil) or apricot (acidic soil). Sun or bright shade and consistent moisture; it does not tolerate drought when young.

Corkscrew Hazel *Corylus avellana* 'Contorta' syn 'Harry Lauder's Walking Stick' H 6 ft (1.8 m) −30°F (−34°C) While appearing to need a good drink of water, this fairly drought-hardy shrub grows quickly in medium shade. It is most beautiful in winter when its "corkscrews" are on view, and in spring when catkins elongate in elegant tassels. It grows well in medium shade; direct sun causes twigs to spiral tighter. Cut out suckers each summer.

Weeping Higan Cherry *Prunus* x *subhirtella* 'Pendula Rosea' H 25 ft (8 m) −20°F (−29°C) There is something matrimonial about a weeping cherry in bloom, so many pink and white blossoms on display in early spring. This has a strong architectural form in winter with long canes reaching to the ground. Its single flowers are deep pink in bud, fading to white as blossoms age. For a total spring wedding effect, underplant with early tulips and glory-of-the-snow.

Weeping Purple Osier Willow *Salix purpurea* 'Pendula' H 15 ft (4.5 m) −40°F (−40°C) Plants with blue-green foliage are always valuable in a garden and this one also has a gray underside that flashes when stirred by wind. Very attractive near stiff, dark evergreens and also pretty with roses, it takes on a widespread, weeping form of great vigor. Thin as needed in summer, and give it room to move freely, preferably where wind can reveal its many charms. Full sun.

Sargent's Weeping Hemlock *Tsuga canadensis* 'Pendula' H 12 ft (4 m) W 25 ft (8 m) −30°F (−34°C) A formal and elegant plant for a garden entrance or by a front door, this is a good choice for year-round evergreen display. It's a brittle plant and should be sited where it will not be bumped about and out of strong wind, to protect its delicate cones and wispy twigs. Autumn color is golden yellow. Part-shade to full sun and consistently moist soil.

soft landscaping

Gardens can be divided into floors, walls and ceilings, although we seldom think of green space in that way. Some garden floors are made of hard materials like brick and stone, but most important are the green floors made of turf grass and ground-cover plants. Walls could be fences, but also every kind of hedge and twiggy shrub. And ceilings overhead are either blue sky or the trees you walk under, both the ones you plant and neighboring trees that extend over your space. Every gardener is also an architect and must decide what plant material to use and where to put these elements.

Decisions about soft landscaping begin where hard landscaping leaves off. Once you know where to put hard surfaces like decks, patios and walkways, and large objects like sheds and ponds have been set in place, it's time to consider the basic "bones" of the garden. Soft landscaping refers to permanent plants of size and substance that give the garden form and character in all seasons. Woody trees and shrubs are the biggest bones, but enough herbaceous perennials grouped together to create a substantial mass are also part of the picture. Turf grasses and ground-cover plants are permanent parts of the soft landscaping in your garden, but a cluster of summer annuals changes from year to year in a space reserved for temporary color.

Whatever plants are considered for your soft landscaping, the goal is for everything to grow like Topsy, and that means vigorous, unchecked growth toward mature form. Allowing your plants to do this doesn't require special

Allowing plants to overwhelm hard objects is a graceful submission to the natural world. Vines over a seat or bench provide practical shade on hot days and a rustic winter tableau in snow.

opposite: Staggered layers of woody plants in front of a house create plant context through all seasons. Coniferous trees and shrubs with blue and chartreuse needles provide year-round color. Deciduous trees and shrubs with purple foliage, and variegated perennials and grasses add warm seasonal richness. The combined textures and forms of a diverse planting give the landscape lasting interest.

skill, only thoughtful and conscientious soil preparation. Wherever you intend to plant, do more for the soil than you initially think is necessary. Professional builders of new homes put a skimpy 2 inches (5 cm) of topsoil under new sod, condemning the lawn to a lifetime of struggle. If you supply 4–6 inches (10–15 cm) of triple mix (a combination of loam, peat moss and manure), you'll ensure a strong lawn for many decades.

Every planting area for trees, shrubs and perennials needs enrichment with organic amendments like compost, rotted manure, peat moss, leaves and pine needles, and you can't supply too much of these materials.

Of all the building materials you might purchase through a contractor, soil is the most mysterious and elusive in character. It's often the case that no one knows what it is or where it came from, and it's hard to pin down specifications on soil quality. Triple mix is a premium blend of soil enriched with peat moss and composted manure, but you won't know how much of each constituent makes up the whole. Terms like "topsoil" and "loam" don't guarantee or explain anything about soil contents either.

When you purchase soil, you should expect to see dark material with a fine and consistent texture containing no rocks, large chunks of plant debris or wood chips, or anything else that defies description. You might want to amend the purchased soil with coarse sand and/or composted manure to improve its drainage and fertility, and some soil suppliers will custom-blend their product with your preferred amendments and do the mixing for you.

Initial soil preparation is like packing a school lunch sufficient for twenty years. It's got to have enough substance and nutrition to last until university.

How Good Is Your Soil?

COMPRESS a handful into a ball and then flick it with your finger; if it has good texture, it should shatter easily. Good soil has a sweet and slightly yeasty smell, and it should be used generously where needed: a 6-inch (15 cm) depth under a new sod lawn, and 18 inches (45 cm) in new planting beds. Keep in mind that newly delivered soil is full of air and will sink approximately one-third in the first growing season.

Rich soil with good drainage and consistent moisture results in lush and healthy growth. Dwarf shrubs are best for foundation beds where they won't outgrow their space.

trees

If you love daylilies and are mad for peonies, you've got to put these preoccupations aside for the moment and focus on the task at hand—that is, the big stuff. Every garden has a basic framework of trees and shrubs that are consistent in all seasons. They may lose their leaves, but their size and shape are unchanging. And of course, evergreen plants remain the same in all seasons, though their color may darken slightly in winter.

You can think of these permanent plants as a kind of scaffolding on which to hang the seasonal gardens from spring through summer and late autumn. As early spring bulbs bloom and pass over to summer perennials, the garden "bones" remain a consistent backdrop to the display. In winter the permanent plants are the central focus of the garden, and their winter appearance is an important criteria in selection.

If you're unsure of how to select these important plants, the easiest way to begin is with the largest candidates—trees. You may have smaller understory

Pyramidal trees—perfect for confined spaces—have a vertical form and cast little shade.

Weeping cherry, pear and crabapple trees have a relaxed and informal stature.

Large, flowering shrubs like lilac and viburnum can take the form of small trees.

Multi-trunked serviceberry and birch make dappled shade and allow grass underneath.

Ground-cover plants are more successful than grass under dense maple, oak or ash.

Small shrubs like 'Sarcoxie' euonymus and dwarf lilac are grafted onto small standard trunks.

Beware "Monster" Trees

AN average city or suburban lot can't comfortably contain trees like Norway maples and weeping willows that grow to 60 feet (18 m) and require an acre (about half a hectare) of their own. Big maples and willows look fine for the first five years and then turn into Godzilla trees, consuming everything within their drip line and creeping into the drains. If you take them down in anger, they'll get you back with the revenge of the stumps. No one wins a fight with bullies like these, so it's best not to plant them.

What to Do about Stumps

A stump of any size is a problem. The most expedient course of action is to call in an arborist or tree company with a stump-removing machine to grind it down and out of the earth. You'll be left with bushels of soft chewed-up wood good for mulch over tree roots, and a depression in the ground you can fill with soil and sod over. The "stumper" machine is quite large and will require wide access between houses to remove a stump in your backyard, and the process can be costly.

You can buy products that are applied into drilled holes in the stump to accelerate its decay. These chemicals have an effect, but seldom quickly or completely.

If the stump is very broad and cleanly cut, you might consider it as a base for a bird feeder, art object or planted container. Seeing stumps put to practical use is always a surprise that draws approval. Or you can grow over it with one of the shed-covering vines. But a stump left standing for no purpose is only evidence that violence has taken place in the garden, and no one wants to see it.

trees like lilac and redbud with interesting features, but every garden needs one really terrific tree that is bigger than the others. It should have character and distinction, reasonable size and clear form, but not overwhelming dominance. Thirty feet (9 m) is a comfortable height for a garden tree at maturity if you're standing near it. This height also gives the tree enough presence in the landscape to look good when you're inside the house looking out in winter. If you live in a northern region, there will be fewer growing days in the life of the tree and the cold climate may prevent it from attaining its potential height. In that case, you could select a tree with a slightly higher mature size, knowing it will never reach it.

Trees with dense and unkempt growth are uninteresting and make the garden look messy. Choosing a tree with clear form, such as linden, birch or Serbian spruce, will contribute an immediate element of style to your garden. If the tree must give some filtered shade, you could try one of the lower-growing honey locusts or a magnolia. Trees with greater density are unpleasant to sit near and block airflow through the garden, leading to troubles with disease. The important points are that the tree should have an interesting shape and not outgrow its space.

Placement of a large tree is a crucial issue, for it must be located where it will command the attention it deserves and won't interfere with the house. The textbook recommendation is to put it in a far corner to give perspective to its full form, and that's often a suitable place. You might choose to put it midway on one side of the lot to take advantage of sitting in the shade. If it's too close to the house, you'll lose the full view of the tree from top to bottom and potentially cause problems around windows and doors. Smaller trees can be used near the house, but keep the big beauties at a distance. Often the corner of a house is improved and strengthened with a narrow tree that won't block windows, and many hybrid plants are available for this up-close location.

opposite: Among the trees that don't grow beyond 25 feet (7.6 m), every form of Japanese maple has a long autumn season of vibrant foliage. The fallen leaves are gardener's gold and can be used immediately to mulch planting beds or saved in a pile to produce humus.

Ten Best Trees for House and Garage Corners

Prominent house corners can be architecturally stark. The corner of a wood frame house can appear vacant and somehow "unfinished", while the sharp corners of a brick structure are sometimes severe and rigid. Most houses will benefit from embellishment with large and graceful plants that are in scale with the structure and grow tall rather than wide.

Trees with pyramidal habit are well suited to softening and clothing a sharp corner without interfering with windows and views, and many such trees offer seasonal interest—bark, flowers and ornamental fruit—up close where you can see and enjoy them. When planting your corner tree, remember to set the root ball 6–8 feet (1.8–2.4 m) away from the foundation and beyond the overhanging eaves, where natural rainwater can reach it. Every tree has a slightly flat side that has faced away from the sun during its growth. Place the flat side toward the house wall and the full side facing outward. Remember to provide regular irrigation—particularly the first couple of seasons after planting—and organic mulch over the roots.

ALLEGHENY SERVICEBERRY *Amelanchier laevis* H 18 ft (5.5 m) −30°F (−34°C) Serviceberries are very useful plants for filling space ornamentally without dominating. Any are good for planting by a tall house corner, but in spring this one has the most colorful purple-bronze leaves with nodding 4-in (10 cm) panicles of white flowers. Its branch structure is open and delicate, with gray bark and purple-black berries, the sweetest of their kind. In sun, autumn color is orange-red to brick red.

RIVER BIRCH *Betula nigra* H 40 ft (12 m) −30°F (−34°C) A beautiful and graceful, multi-trunked tree with tan to salmon-pink bark and glossy, dark green leaves that turn golden in autumn. The attractively shaggy bark peels more deeply than any other birch. It is resistant to the bronze birch borer and tolerates heat. It prefers neutral to acidic soil below pH 7.5 and needs consistent moisture to remain healthy. *Betula platyphylla* var. *japonica* 'Whitespire' has smooth, chalk-white bark that doesn't peel.

GOLDEN CHAIN TREE *Laburnum* x *watereri* 'Voissii' H 15 ft (4.6 m) −20°F (−29°C) The sight of this tree in bloom is not quickly forgotten. Its upright, oval form is strung (sometimes smothered) with cascading racemes of golden-yellow wisteria-like flowers in June, followed by olive-green bark and bright green foliage with a bluish tinge. It dislikes excessive heat, growing best in moist soil and a half-day of sun. It is suitable to frame a doorway or at either side of steps.

COLUMNAR SIBERIAN CRABAPPLE *Malus baccata* 'Columnaris' H 24 ft (7.5 m) −50°F (−46°C) Of the more than 700 forms, this crabapple is amazingly straight up and down, with charming pink buds opening to white flowers in spring. Its medium-green leaves are cheerful all summer and hard little red and yellow berries appear in autumn, persisting into winter and causing no litter problem. Provide heavy loam and full sun.

WEEPING NOOTKA FALSE CYPRESS *Chamaecyparis nootkatensis* 'Pendula' H 30 ft (9 m) −20°F (−29°C) You either love or hate this unusual blue-green weeping coniferous tree. It's a valuable ornamental in semi-shade to sun, and as its branches cast no shade it can be angled against a house corner so that it doesn't obstruct views or light. It's particularly attractive in "families" on both corners of a garage or paired, large and small together. Small greenish berries are ornamental in late spring.

'RED OBELISK' BEECH *Fagus sylvatica* 'Red Obelisk' H 30 ft (9 m) −30°F (−34°C) If your house is tan, taupe or gray, the red-bronze leaves of this tree make a stunning corner accent. Its narrow, upright profile is adaptable to several uses, such as to line a driveway or create a screen along a lot line. Autumn color is golden-brown, and as beeches age they begin to hold their foliage through winter. Beeches grow well in part-sun, but their colors show best in sun.

'PRINCETON SENTRY' MAIDENHAIR TREE *Ginkgo biloba* 'Princeton Sentry' H 30 ft (9 m) −30°F (−34°C) Ginkgoes have grown on earth for 150 million years and are commonly found in ancient fossil remains. This slender hybrid has a tapering apex, slightly wider at the bottom with a neatly ascending form. Its dramatic architectural beauty has the typical ginkgo "see-through" appearance, as well as striped bark and golden autumn color.

'KWANZAN' FLOWERING CHERRY *Prunus serrulata* 'Kwanzan' H 18 ft (5.5 m) W 10 ft (3 m) −20°F (−29°C) Little is as flamboyant as a cherry tree in full spring bloom, and 'Kwanzan' has fragrant pink, fully double flowers in pendulous clusters. Its narrow form is useful as a vertical accent on corners or in a line across a bright brick wall. It makes only a few small fruits, which birds take, and its autumn color is reddish-copper.

'CHANTICLEER' ORNAMENTAL PEAR *Pyrus calleryana* H 30 ft (9 m) −20°F (−29°C) Ornamental pear trees are valuable in all seasons for framing doorways or steps, as well as near a house corner. Spring brings white blossoms, followed by rounded glossy leaves turning scarlet in autumn. Their upright pyramidal form makes a formal and precise accent in winter, along with the clinging olive-green mini-pears. All tolerate wet or dry conditions and resist diseases and insects. 'Chanticleer' is the narrowest of the pear trees.

PYRAMIDAL ENGLISH OAK *Quercus robur* 'Fastigiata' H 40 ft (12 m) −20°F (−29°C) This slim hybrid's controlled height and breadth make it suitable for house corners or along fence lines. It grows straight up, bearing classic oak leaves and stylized acorns at maturity. Tall and lanky when young, it benefits from annual pruning early on until it thickens. It needs good air circulation to avoid late-summer mildew, but the seasonal affliction won't affect growth.

Ten Best Distinctive Trees up to 30 Feet (9 m)

Every garden needs one splendid tree with character enough to stand on its own and rise above the crowd. This is meant to be an important plant of substantial size, selected for seasonal features like flowers, ornamental bark and fruit, and for year-round architectural form. Professional landscapers will often refer to trees of distinction as "specimens" or "accent trees."

Although every tree has a potential height at maturity, weather and environmental factors are strong moderators of growth. Woody plants growing close to the northern edge of their hardiness zone seldom achieve potential height. They are healthy and attractive specimens, but the shorter growing season and depth of winter frost keep them smaller than similar plants in warmer regions.

Ruby-red Horse Chestnut *Aesculus carnea* 'Briotii' H 30 ft (9 m) −30°F (−34°C) A classic lawn tree with a full, rounded profile and typical fan-like leaves. Early summer brings a truly remarkable display of 10-in (25 cm) long rosy-red candelabra flowers in great abundance. In winter the branches make a neat and symmetrical profile. A useful tree for creating a limited shade area, without overwhelming coverage.

River Birch *Betula nigra* H 30 ft (9 m) −30°F (−34°C) With beautiful, shaggy, peeling trunks of tan to salmon bark and strong resistance to bronze birch borer, this birch is a short-lived tree with an average lifespan of about 50 years. An optimal site is key to a beautiful and healthy tree. Very sensitive to moisture stress, birches must have consistent irrigation or a naturally moist site in part- to full sun.

Red Jade Crabapple *Malus* 'Red Jade' H 15 ft (4.6 m) −40°F (−40°C) A semi-weeping ornamental with a lavish display of pink and white spring blossoms, lustrous fluted foliage and pendulous clusters of red fruit that persist through winter. Fast-growing, vigorous and disease-resistant. Six-foot (1.8 m) long horizontal branches with trailing twigs make an attractive winter profile. Leave in full form or thin occasionally for a "see-through" style.

Fat Albert Spruce *Picea pungens* 'Fat Albert' H 15 ft (4.6 m) −40°F (−40°C) A true dwarf with dense, upright, pyramidal form and silver-blue needles that are iridescent year-round. Very slow growth makes it worthwhile to buy a larger specimen. Try also 'Bakeri' with deep blue needles and 'Iseli Foxtail' with blue twisted new growth. Plant in full sun and water well for the first two years; thereafter it can tolerate a somewhat dry location.

KOUSA DOGWOOD *Cornus kousa* var. *chinensis* H 20 ft (6 m) −30°F (−34°C) The most winter-hardy and disease-resistant of the flowering dogwoods. Tiny flowers with showy white bracts appear in late spring and persist up to six weeks or longer, turning to pink then lime green. Large, pendulous red berries follow. Magnificent. Many fancy hybrids are available, but the original species var. *chinensis* is still a garden treasure. Part-shade to full sun.

PURPLE FOUNTAIN WEEPING BEECH *Fagus sylvatica* 'Purple Fountain' H 18 ft (5.5 m) −10°F (−23°C) Dramatic impact in a small area, with a slender trunk and glossy deep purple foliage on weeping branches. Its smooth silvery bark bears "ripples" similar to an elephant's skin. Quick-growing, it takes on great character with age. A good choice for small gardens in part-shade to full sun.

LEONARD MESSEL MAGNOLIA *Magnolia* x *loebneri* 'Leonard Messel' H 15 ft (4.6 m) −20°F (−29°C) A wonderful fast-growing four-season tree for a small garden. Its upright and controlled form requires no pruning, and its star-like blossoms are deep pink outside, white inside. Silvery bark and glossy buds are attractive in winter. Requires consistently moist soil in part-shade to full sun. More cold-tolerant (−30°F/−34°C) are 'Susan' and *M.* x *soulangiana*.

SWISS STONE PINE *Pinus cembra* H 30 ft (9 m) −30°F (−34°C) A coniferous tree with a narrow, densely pyramidal form in youth, opening and spreading with age. Long, lustrous deep green needles with bluish white accents show their best color in a sunny location. Slow growing, this tree will remain an admirable and consistent focal point for many years.

SCHUBERT CHOKECHERRY *Prunus virginiana* 'Schubert' H 15 ft (4.5 m) −50°F (46°C) Great value for the price, putting on quite a show with generous white blossoms and bright green leaves. Foliage turns deep purple as summer warms, finishing scarlet-red. Some fruits are produced and relished by birds without dropping to the ground. Dark charcoal bark is attractive in winter. Highly suitable for cool regions and sometimes listed as 'Canada Red'.

CARDINAL ROYAL MOUNTAIN ASH *Sorbus aucuparia* 'Cardinal Royal' H 18 ft (5.5 m) −40°F (−40°C) A favorite lawn tree with clusters of white spring flowers and red autumn berries relished by robins. Symmetrical and oval in youth, it forms a graceful open head in maturity, which allows grass to grow beneath. Fern-like foliage is dark green above, silvery below. Stressed in heat, mountain ash prefers adequate moisture, bright light and cool breezes.

Ten Best Trees to Create Filtered Shade

Japanese Maple *Acer palmatum* H 18 ft (5.5 m) −20°F (−29°C) Upright forms of red and green Japanese maple form loose canopies as they mature. Many species and hybrids exist, and the deepest purple leaf cultivar is 'Bloodgood'. Be sure to purchase an upright tall form and not a laceleaf cascading shrub.

Downy Serviceberry *Amelanchier arborea* H 20 ft (6 m) −30°F (−34°C) Whether sold as a shrub or single trunk, it's all the same plant and the shrub will grow as high as the tree. Its white early spring flowers turn to blue berries favored by birds. The small leaves make a soft, dappled light in summer and turn orange-to-red in autumn. Many hybrid cultivars of this native plant exist, including 'Ballerina', 'Princess Diana' and 'Robin Hill'.

Trees with finely shaped and cut foliage create filtered shade conditions, moderating the light and air temperature below without casting a dense, dark shadow. A healthy lawn can be maintained underneath, particularly if it is made from shade grass seed or shade sod, both of which can be purchased from garden centers.

Any of these trees will cast soft, dappled light over a planting of sun-shy perennial plants, such as hostas and spring-blooming hellebores. A grouping of these trees makes a sheltered glade around a patio seating area.

Trees with smaller foliage make good lawn specimens because their fallen leaves won't damage the grass or require repeated rakings.

Fernleaf Beech *Fagus sylvatica* 'Asplenifolia' H 30 ft (9 m) −30°F (−34°C) This beautiful tree is a bit of an oddity, so unlike its beech cousins, but is very effective as a light-filtering specimen plant. Deeply incised leaves give a distinct ferny effect, and turn nutty brown in autumn. Its youthful structure is quite tight with branching down to the ground, opening with age into a graceful, spreading form.

'Imperial' Honey Locust *Gleditsia triacanthos* var. *inermis* 'Imperial' H 30 ft (9 m) −30°F (−34°C) Favored as a street tree for its no-raking autumn leaf drop, honey locust is a graceful, spreading plant with symmetrically arranged branches in a compact form. Foliage breaks bud late in spring, opening into dainty green leaves. Cultivars, in various heights, include 'Summergold' and 'Sunburst', with golden leaves on new growth turning to chartreuse.

HIMALAYAN BIRCH *Betula jacquemontii* H 25 ft (7.6 m) −20°F (−29°C) Whitest of all the birches, Himalayan birch has shown some resistance to the bronze birch borer when grown in a consistently moist soil. The chalk-white exfoliating bark and glossy green foliage make this tree sparkle in sunlight. The height of birch trees and the fluttering mannerism of their leaves create beautiful dappled shade.

PAGODA DOGWOOD *Cornus alternifolia* H 15 ft (4.6 m) −30°F (−34°C) A graceful native dogwood with deeply veined leaves, open form and horizontal tiered branching, this produces creamy blossom heads in spring followed by blue-black berries. It grows best in moist soil and can be used as an understory tree in partial shade. When grown in sun and adequately watered, autumn foliage turns reddish purple.

RUSSIAN OLIVE *Elaeagnus angustifolia* H 18 ft (5.5 m) −50°F (−46°C) Russian olive is one of the few trees that will make strong growth in dry or sandy soil. It prefers an open, sunny position and is salt-tolerant, making it a good choice near a roadway or salt water. The gray-green foliage is a valuable ornamental asset and will filter the light on a hot corner over perennial beds.

KENTUCKY COFFEE TREE *Gymnocladus dioica* H 40 ft (12 m) −40°F (−40°C) Despite its name, this tree is well adapted to northern regions. Best known for interesting recurving bark and a picturesque winter profile, it is also valued for scented greenish-white flower panicles and ferny foliage. It prefers a moist rich soil, but with age tolerates drought and city conditions. A good choice to filter light over a seating area on a hot lawn or patio.

TATARIAN MAPLE *Acer tataricum* H 20 ft (6 m) W 15 ft (4.6 m) −40°F (−40°C) A slow-growing maple with upright, oval form and small, medium green leaves. Spring flowers are panicles of greenish white color, turning to small red winged fruits in late summer. Tatarian maple's autumn color is a mottled yellow to red, except on the cultivar 'Rubrum', which turns blood red. This maple is highly adaptable to cold, dry climates and worth seeking out.

'IVORY SILK' TREE LILAC *Syringa reticulata* 'Ivory Silk' H 20 ft (6 m) −40°F (−40°C) This is a hybrid cultivar of Japanese tree lilac and the last of all the lilacs to bloom, with large creamy white panicles and privet-like scent. It has a formal shape with a single standard trunk and an oval crown. It is a good choice to moderate light over parked cars or a hot patio. Try also 'Summer Snow', 'Regent' and 'Chantilly Lace'.

shrubs

Shrubs are the most useful materials you have in establishing garden structure. They provide diversity of sizes from under 12 inches (30 cm) to over 12 feet (3.5 m), giving you something to work with in almost any situation. Deciduous flowering shrubs can be combined with coniferous evergreen plants to ensure planting groups have year-round ornamental value. But most important, shrubs allow you to draw lines, erect barriers and create privacy in ornamental ways.

Sage old garden designers will tell you defining its perimeter enhances every space. This simply means staking out your territory to make it look more organized and give it definition. In all matters of real estate, there is some sense to drawing a line around what you own, distinguishing between public and private, yours and the neighbor's. Surveyors do this for a living and mark the boundaries with stakes and bright orange ties. Builders mark the boundaries with fences, and gardeners do it with hedges.

Low, bun-shaped shrubs like nest spruce and euonymus make good accent plants.

Freeform flowering shrubs like quince and forsythia require space for their mature size.

Dwarf flowering shrubs like spirea and daphne are suitable in mixed borders and foundation beds.

The many wide and spreading forms of juniper are efficient, evergreen ground covers.

Dwarf shrubs like Japanese yew and dwarf Alberta spruce are the right size for a foundation bed.

Upright conifers like 'Emerald' and 'Holmstrup' cedars are good specimens at a house corner.

An unadorned fence is a stretch of empty wood or chain link, but a hedge is something alive. Living walls of plants along the perimeter give substance to your garden and make it feel like an environment, rather than an empty space. The garden begins to have context and defines itself. A hedge planted in front of a fence is always an improvement, although the combined cost of fencing and hedging plants makes that wall in your garden more expensive. If there are no serious concerns with keeping anything in or out, it may be sufficient to use the hedge alone and save the cost of the fence.

Hedges can be made in every size and with all kinds of plants, and this versatility allows gardeners to use them for many kinds of problem solving. Low hedges of boxwood are a traditional means of defining planting beds, and this never fails to "elevate" or make the contained plants look better. Walkways set adrift in space are anchored and embellished by a hedge alongside, making walkers feel secure and keeping everyone's footsteps on the path. And privacy, sometimes difficult to acquire in an open space, can be created with hedging screens around a seating area or along a public road.

Shrubs are also important in relaxed garden corners, where their bulk and mass help to fill space and give a sense of depth to planted areas. They are essential to foundation plantings, anchoring the house to the earth, and are the backbone of mixed plantings, partnering with perennials to make displays of flowers and ornamental fruits in a sequence of bloom spanning four seasons. Doorways and entrance beds are ideal locations for distinctive specimen shrubs with controlled growth, particularly weeping plants that become increasingly beautiful without growing upward.

SHAPING A HEDGE

HEDGES of deciduous privet and coniferous yew or cedar are easy to shape if you understand how sunlight falls on the plants. If your hedge is sheared flat on the top and sides, it's important for all areas to receive adequate sunlight.

When you keep the bottom wider than the top, sunlight can fall on the sides from top to bottom and the foliage will be uniformly thick and dense. If the shape is reversed, with the top wider than the bottom, light won't fall on the lower sides and foliage will become sparse. Less formal hedges of Austrian currant or boxwood can be flat-topped, cutting flat across the top and leaving the sides to take a natural form.

The harmonious associations of color, texture and form make a successful shrub border. Upright vertical plants provide diversity, along with anchoring boulders. Flowers are hardly necessary in this lovely grouping.

Ten Best Shrubs for Hedging

Almost any kind of woody plant can be used to make a hedge, although plants with smaller leaves will create a neater and more organized effect. Some hedge plants can be allowed to grow into their natural forms, with their branches entwined. Shearing or "flat-topping" only the top surface of the hedge once or twice a year can create a more controlled style.

Formal hedges are made by shearing both sides and the top of the hedge to create flat planes of foliage (see previous page for how to shape a hedge). Formal hedges require frequent clipping to keep them in shape. All new hedges require consistent watering during the first two years to get them established and growing well.

SMALL-LEAFED BOXWOOD *Buxus microphylla* H 30 in (75 cm) W 5 ft (1.5 m) −20°F (−29°C) Boxwood's tiny broadleaf evergreen leaves are perfect for a hedge that remains green year-round in sun or shade. Many varieties are suitable for hedges as low as 8 in (20 cm) or as high as 2 ft (0.6 m). Flat-topping keeps it neat with little maintenance. For a quick, thick hedge, plant shrubs half as tall as you want the hedge to be and set them out almost touching sides.

AMERICAN HORNBEAM, BLUE BEECH, IRONWOOD *Carpinus caroliniana* H 40 ft (12 m) W 50 ft (15 m) −40°F (−40°C) A vigorous tree suitable for hedges 5 ft (1.5 m) or higher in sun or shade. Foliage is dark green with attractive veining, turning orange and scarlet in autumn when grown in sun. For a hedge, set out with trunks 2–3 ft (0.6–0.9 m) apart. Clip on all sides for a relaxed but controlled appearance, or shear.

ALPINE CURRANT *Ribes alpinum* H 3–5 ft (0.9–1.5 m) −50°F (−46°C) For low or medium hedges, this is densely twiggy with small, bright green lobed leaves. An ornamental variety, it bears no fruit and insignificant flowers, and makes a good sheared hedge alongside a walkway, or can be flat-topped and left with natural sides. Adapts to light shade or full sun, and tolerates any good, reasonably moist soil. Set out with trunks 2–3 ft (0.6–0.9 m) apart.

'BLUE ARCTIC' WILLOW *Salix purpurea nana* H 5 ft (1.5 m) −40°F (−40°C) A dwarf version of the much larger purple osier willow, this has soft blue-green leaves on slender branches that take on a purple tone in winter. It is suitable for low informal hedges where a strong barrier isn't needed. It can be left to take its natural form or sheared. Plants will tolerate heavy wet soil. Set out with trunks 4 ft (1.2 m) apart.

Dwarf Burning Bush, Spindle Tree *Euonymus alatus* 'Compactus' HW 4 ft (1.2 m) –40°F (–40°C) For a low hedge with natural form, this grows best in bright sun and will turn deepest scarlet in autumn. In winter the unusual winged bark is an interesting feature. For a tight hedge, set out with trunks 4 ft (1.2 m) apart, but be sure to get the dwarf variety. Burning bush makes a good hedge alongside a fence or separating a front lawn from the road.

European Beech *Fagus sylvatica* H 5–15 ft (1.5–5 m) –30°F (–34°C) A classic hedging material for tall hedges in green, copper or purple. With maturity, it will hold its leaves through winter. Beech stands close shearing, or can be clipped just to keep within bounds. Established hedges can become high and wide enough to cut out passages and archways. Grows well in light shade or sun. Set out with trunks 2–3 ft (0.6–0.9 m) apart.

Oregon Grapeholly *Mahonia aquifolium* H 5–10 ft (1.5–3 m) –30°F (–34°C) A handsome shrub with lustrous holly-like foliage, bright yellow spring flowers and attractive blue berries. Tolerant of dry soil, it can suffer wind and sun burn in winter. Morning sun is ideal—the north side of a house is suitable; avoid a south or west exposure. It is most beautiful in its natural form or shear or clip on the top. Set out with trunks 3–4 ft (0.9–1.2 m) apart.

Hick's Yew *Taxus x media* 'Hicksii' H 20 ft (6 m) –30°F (–34°C) With its columnar habit, this is ideal for evergreen hedging. Its stems grow straight up and tall, but an ideal hedge height is 3–12 ft (0.9–3.6 m). Yew, very suitable for shearing, is a principal subject for topiary training. Set out with trunks 2 ft (0.6 m) apart. Because of its strongly vertical branches, this hedge can be flat-topped and the sides left natural unless formal shearing is desired.

White Cedar *Thuja occidentalis* H 5–15 ft (1.5–4.5 m) –30°F (–34°C) Young saplings of this plant are sometimes called swamp cedar and commonly sold as cedar hedging. It is excellent for a privacy hedge in a sunny location with consistent moisture, and needs only an annual topping to keep it at the desired height, but is also adaptable to formal shearing. Plants set out 1 ft (0.3 m) apart will form a hedge in three to four years.

Hedge Viburnum *Viburnum opulus* 'Nanum' HW 18–24 in (45–60 cm) –30°F (–34°C) This dwarf viburnum makes an informal low hedge suitable along a path or driveway. It bears no flowers or fruit, and can be lightly clipped or left to take it own mounded form. Hedge viburnum will grow well in light shade to full sun and prefers well-drained soil. In autumn the foliage turns bronze-red. Set out plants with crowns 2 ft (0.6 m) apart.

Garden designers use shrubs to divide space within a garden, making "rooms" for different uses and interests. Instead of looking at your garden as one picture, you can make low shrub walls within a greater space to develop different pictures. The rooms can serve individual purposes, such as private seating and dining, a cutting garden or a pond area.

temporary plantings

Professional landscapers categorize shrubs as either primary or temporary, using inexpensive shrubs as temporary plants to fill space until the largest woody specimens put on some growth. The temporary shrubs are removed as space grows tight, giving more advantage to the primary specimens.

Large plants often have slow beginnings after planting in their new locations. Trees and potentially large shrubs will require two years to make sufficient roots into new soil before they can extend their leaders and side branches, and that can be an impatient time for gardeners. If you would like to see space filled more quickly, satisfaction can be found by augmenting the area with temporary quick-growing plants as fillers.

The temporary plants should be inexpensive to purchase, quick growing and with spreading form to fill the area rapidly. They will remain in place for three to six years, but eventually should be removed when the permanent plants increase their rate of growth and ability to cover more space. Plants with smaller root systems, like low spireas and cinquefoils, dwarf lilacs and weigelas, shrub roses and hydrangeas, can possibly be moved successfully (with a dose of transplant solution in the new hole) to another location. But if they are seriously damaged during removal, their relatively low cost will ensure you've had your best use of them.

Where beds are crowded or if there are gaps waiting for plants, strategically placed containers can focus attention or fill empty spaces. As one pot of blooms fades, another can be whisked into place. But containers require more frequent watering than plants in the ground.

PART-SHADE TO FULL SHADE

FIVE OF THE BEST QUICK-GROWING TEMPORARY PLANTS

While useful to fill in empty spaces among slower-growing plants, these plants need enough room to develop. If too closely spaced, they won't have anywhere to go with their growth and that will defeat the purpose. As the slower permanent plants put on growth, you can begin to move the temporary shrubs to another part of the garden.

ANNABELLE HYDRANGEA *Hydrangea arborescens* HW 4 ft (1.2 m) −50°F (−46°C) Large, globe-shaped, cream-colored flowers in midsummer, lasting until frost.

'HENRY'S GARNET' SWEETSPIRE *Itea virginica* H 4 ft (1.2 m) W 6 ft (1.8 m) −20°F (−29°C) Fragrant, white flowers in spring, a rounded, arching form and deep red autumn color.

PART-SHADE TO FULL SHADE

FIVE OF THE BEST SLOW-GROWING PERMANENT PLANTS

These plants will grow to achieve their full size, but patience is required. When selecting a permanent plant for shade, it's well worth purchasing the largest specimen you can comfortably afford. The larger size gives you a head start on filling the garden space, and saves time waiting for a smaller plant to catch up.

SERVICEBERRY *Amelanchier canadensis* H 20 ft (6 m) W 9 ft (2.7 m) −30°F (−34°C) Small, oval leaves with white spring flowers followed by blue berries and bright autumn color.

AMERICAN HORNBEAM, BLUE BEECH, IRONWOOD *Carpinus caroliniana* H 20−40 ft (6−12 m) W 12 ft (3.6−15 m) −40°F (−40°C) Small leaves and smooth bark, brilliant orange-red in autumn.

AMUR HONEYSUCKLE *Lonicera maackii* H 6 ft (1.8 m) W 8 ft (2.4 m) −50°F (−46°C) Spreading woodland shrub with white to yellow flowers and red berries.

FLOWERING RASPBERRY *Rubus odoratus* HW 6 ft (1.8 m) −30°F (−34°C) Maple-like leaves with fragrant, purple-rose flowers in July. A good filler and screen.

AMERICAN ELDER *Sambucus canadensis* H 12 ft (3.6 m) W 6 ft (1.8 m) −40°F (−40°C) Finely cut green foliage and cream flowers in early summer; purple-black edible fruit.

EASTERN REDBUD *Cercis canadensis* H 12 ft (3.6 m) W 16 ft (4.8 m) −10°F (−23°C) Bare stems are covered with pink flowers in spring, followed by heart-shaped leaves.

GRAY DOGWOOD *Cornus racemosa* H 20 ft (6 m) W 8 ft (2.4 m) −30°F (−34°C) Dense screening shrub for sun or shade, with gray bark, white flowers and berries.

AMERICAN HOP HORNBEAM *Ostrya virginiana* H 30 ft (9 m) W 20 ft (6 m) −30°F (−34°C) Oval tree with small leaves, catkins in spring and yellow autumn color.

PART-SUN TO FULL SUN

FIVE OF THE BEST QUICK-GROWING TEMPORARY PLANTS

These are used to infill space surrounding slower-growing specimens and can be expected to make fast growth. They can also age quickly, however, becoming a bit tatty after a few years. They benefit from pruning every second or third year, cleaning out older stems to induce fresh growth. By the time they must be moved out of the bed, their mature size will be an asset elsewhere in the garden.

DWARF FLOWERING QUINCE *Chaenomeles* x *superba* H 2 ft (0.6 m) W 3 ft (0.9 m) −20°F (−29°C) Low, spreading branches with red, pink or white spring flowers and autumn quince fruits.

WEEPING FORSYTHIA *Forsythia suspensa* H 4 ft (1.2 m) W 6 ft (1.8 m) −10°F (−23°C) Stems gracefully arch outward and down to the ground, with yellow spring flowers.

PART-SUN TO FULL SUN

FIVE OF THE BEST SLOW-GROWING PERMANENT PLANTS

A worthwhile strategy—if you can afford it—is to purchase one of these plants large enough that its size, though not mature, is at least satisfying on the day of arrival. With a larger rootball and huskier trunk than a smaller plant, it will give an immediate sense of its potential bigness.

PAPERBARK MAPLE *Acer griseum* H 18 ft (5.5 m) W 10 ft (3 m) −10°F (−23°C) Exfoliating cinnamon-brown bark peels in strips like birches.

STAR MAGNOLIA *Magnolia stellata* H 18 ft (5.5 m) W 10 ft (3 m) −30°F (−34°C) Lemon-scented white flowers with strap-like petals in early spring and silvery winter buds.

'BLUE PACIFIC' JUNIPER *Juniperus conferta* H 1 ft (0.3 m) W 3 ft (0.9 m) −20°F (−29°C) Low, trailing stems spread outward bearing lacy, coniferous blue-green foliage.

'GOLDFINGER' CINQUEFOIL *Potentilla fruticosa* HW 3 ft (0.9 m) −50°F (−46°C) Large, golden flowers all summer on a relaxed and rounded shrub.

'HANCOCK' CORALBERRY *Symphoricarpos* x *chenaulti* H 3 ft (0.9 m) W 6 ft (1.8 m) −20°F (−29°C) Graceful, fine, blue-green foliage followed by pink flowers in spring and pink berries.

NEST SPRUCE *Picea abies* 'Nidiformis' H 3 ft (0.9 m) W 5 (1.5 m) −40°F (−40°C) Broad, nest-like, low coniferous shrub, good for foundations and bed planting.

SERBIAN SPRUCE *Picea omorika* H 40 ft (12 m) W 10 ft (3 m) −20°F (−29°C) Tall and narrow conifer with classic form. A good specimen or lawn tree on a small lot.

VANDERWOLF PYRAMIDAL PINE *Pinus flexilis* H 15 ft (4.6 m) W 6 ft (1.8 m) −40°F (−40°C) Upright, open branching form with blue-green needles, for specimen use.

foundation plantings

Picture a Monopoly board with little plastic hotels and houses sitting forlornly on their avenues, and you can see how stark any home looks without living plants to connect it to the earth. Dwarf shrubs and small ornamental trees ease the transition between landscape and hard structure, creating a soft, nesting effect along a cold concrete foundation wall. While concealing an unattractive foundation is useful, the plants will also prevent rainwater from pooling near the wall and provide insulation from summer heat and winter cold.

Foundation plants are meant to enhance the structure, not to conceal it, and it's important that they be in scale with the wall they stand against. No one wants to fight their way through a forest just to reach the front door, or find their picture window entirely blocked by a massively spreading shrub. In the "olden days" of garden centers when only a few giant-sized plants were offered, many green monoliths found their way into front borders where they quickly assumed battleship proportions. More recently, consumer interest and increasing gardening skills have encouraged hybridizers to breed many new selections of coniferous and deciduous shrubs. Gardeners now have

their choice of suitably scaled plants for small and large locations. Dwarf plants with a controlled rate of growth will stay within reasonable scale for many years, preferably less than six feet, and most large ornamental plants are available in scaled-down hybrid selections that rarely require pruning.

Coniferous evergreen plants are the backbone of every foundation planting, presenting a consistent green presence through four seasons. Their controlled forms and various shapes provide versatile opportunities to fit a garden around the architecture of a residence. Low, bun-shaped shrubs like globe blue spruce, nest spruce and globe cedar are suitable for filling the spaces under a window. Moderately tall and stately 'Emerald' cedar is suitable for placement on either side of a doorway or front steps. Dwarf mugo pine and 'Mint Julep' juniper can be used between deciduous flowering shrubs. Evergreen trees like Nootka false cypress and 'Fairview' juniper are appropriate at the corners of a house where they can be allowed to grow above the first story.

Although coniferous plants form the main structure of the foundation planting, some softer, flowering shrubs are also a necessity. Flowering shrubs are especially welcome in spring when

everyone is desperate to see some petals and smell wonderful scents. Dwarf selections of lilac, mock orange, viburnum, quince and deutzia are all appropriate partners for an evergreen foundation bed. Add to that some early spring bulbs and a few summer-blooming perennials, and the garden at your front door will be worth a special visit.

This bed has very nice density but would be greatly improved with color. Purple and gold leaves, and more blue needles, are wanted here.

opposite: Consumer interest has encouraged the development of smaller hybrids of coniferous and deciduous shrubs so that today's gardeners have a wide choice of suitably scaled plants for all locations.

Ten Best Dwarf Evergreen Foundation Plants

Permanent evergreen plants around house foundations are essential to connect the house to the landscape and to prevent the structure from looking like it fell off the back of a truck. But it's important to keep the plants in scale to the limited space available. All too often large shrubs end up obscuring windows and crowding doorways. Selecting dwarf plants with clear limits on potential growth is key to a foundation planting that complements the house and is comfortable to live with.

Evergreens' various forms, textures and colors lend themselves well to using several kinds together in close proximity while they provide many years of service with little maintenance. 'Emerald' cedars and dwarf Alberta spruce are useful for framing a doorway or marking a corner, and 'Mint Julep' juniper and 'Green Mountain' boxwood make attractive low hedges. Bristlecone pine and Koster's false cypress are good focal-point plants in a prominent location.

'GREEN MOUNTAIN' BOXWOOD *Buxus microphylla* var. *insularis* H 4 ft (1.2 m) −20°F (−29°C) This unique boxwood is an upright selection with a leader that allows it to grow into a natural conical shape. It is ideal for filling spaces around steps or between plants, and as a high hedge across a wall or inside a wrought iron fence. Clip carefully for formal pyramid shapes. For hedges under 2 ft (0.6 m) use 'Green Velvet' or 'Green Gem'.

KOSTER'S FALSE CYPRESS *Chamaecyparis obtusa* 'Kosteri' H 4 ft (1.2 m) W 3 ft (0.9 m) −30°F (−34°C) Plants in this family are soft blue-green and adaptable to light shade, and prefer consistent moisture. 'Kosteri' grows slowly and its soft foliage has a coral-like formation. Delicate and "see-through," it is good for a prominent spot where it can be seen and admired. Take care in winter that snow does not accumulate on top of it.

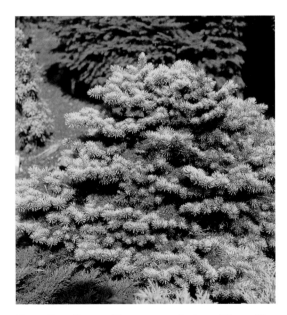

GLOBE BLUE SPRUCE *Picea pungens* f. *glauca* 'Glauca Globosa' H 4 ft (1.2 m) −50°F (−46°C) Amazingly, hybridizers have bred the towering 60-ft (18 m) blue spruce down to this bright powder-blue dwarf shrub with a lovely symmetrically round shape, expanding in girth as it gains height. Its formal, consistent appearance helps organize a bed. Plant two of these blue buns under a large window or one to each side of a step.

BRISTLECONE PINE *Pinus aristata* H 5 ft (1.3 m) −50°F (−46°C) One-of-a-kind plants contribute interest to a foundation planting and this small Rocky Mountain pine has an elegant bonsai-like appearance. Dark needles and stiff branches make an impressive accent in sun combined with 'Gold Mound' spirea or 'Blue Arctic' willow. Its extremely slow growth is reflected in its price. More affordable are *Picea omorika* 'Nana' and *Pinus sylvestris* 'Glauca Nana'.

DWARF JAPANESE YEW *Taxus cuspidata* 'Nana' HW 3 ft (0.9 m) −30°F (−34°C) Yews are excellent for filling space in low light where other evergreen shrubs won't grow. This dwarf has dark green needles and a rounded shape. Smaller 'Aurescens' has yellow-tipped needles that add bright color to shady places. The larger *Taxus* x *media* 'Fairview' (H 6 ft/1.8 m) is good set against a tall, wide brick wall.

'GREY OWL' JUNIPER, *Juniperus scopulorum* H 3 ft (0.9 m) −40°F (−40°C) A low shrub with string-like silver-gray foliage and brilliant blue berries that remain through winter. Small junipers fit easily into foundation plantings and make big color contributions. Other colorful junipers to try are the steel-blue *J. squamata* 'Dwarf Blue Star', deep gold *J. chinensis* 'Paul's Gold' and the turquoise-green *J. horizontalis* 'Turquoise Spreader'.

DWARF ALBERTA SPRUCE *Picea glauca* var. *albertiana* 'Conica' H 3–8 ft (0.9–2.4 m) −30°F (−34°C) Vertical plants organize and formalize an entrance, and this one is excellent for its slow, controlled growth in sun or bright shade. Small, fine green needles are densely packed along its conical shape that it keeps without any clipping. Always best in pairs; plant one slightly more forward than the other, with room for expansion.

DWARF WHITE PINE *Pinus strobus* 'Nana' H 3 ft (0.9 m) W 6 ft (1.8 m) −30°F (−34°C) This is a another small hybrid of a forest giant. Beautiful, soft blue-green needles make it useful as a single specimen or to fill space around a sunny foundation. Other scaled-down forest plants, wider than tall and similarly ornamental, are *Picea abies balsamea* 'Nana', *P. abies* 'Little Gem' and *P. abies* 'Nidiformis'.

NEST SPRUCE *Picea abies* 'Nidiformis' H 36 in (90 cm) −40ßF (−40ßC) Nest spruce is a very consistent plant, maintaining a low, broad, nest-like shape with deep green color all year. It likes at least half a day of sun and is useful for framing either side of steps, or for lining a driveway. It combines well with spring crocus and low flowering groundcovers like periwinkle. *Taxus cuspidata* 'Nana' is useful in low light situations, as are all the yews. Try *T.* x *media* 'Fairview' against a low brick wall.

'EMERALD' CEDAR *Thuja occidentalis* 'Emerald' H 10 ft (3 m) −30°F (−34°C) Pillar-like green shrubs add structure and provide context for smaller plants. This cedar has brilliant winter color, never needs SHAPING AND IS GOOD BRACKETING A DOORWAY OR AGAINST A WALL BETWEEN windows (plant 2 ft/0.6 m beyond the roof overhang). An annual trim of top growth will hold it to a lower height. Shorter are apple-green 'Holmstrup', golden-orange 'Rheingold' and yellow 'Sunkist'.

ground covers and lawns

It's well known that nature embellishes where gardeners fail to plant. Exposed soil must be covered in some way to prevent erosion, and it's just a question of installing plants of choice or allowing weed seeds to grow. Either way, the soil that forms the floor of your garden won't stay bare for long.

COVERING GROUND QUICKLY

EVERYONE has the same frustration with ground-cover plantings, and that is keeping the weeds out in the first two years and getting the plants to fill in quickly. Landscapers address this issue pragmatically by putting in a greater number of plants more closely spaced and then deeply mulching between the plants. These are expensive solutions, but they do work and perhaps it's worth the investment to get good results fast. If you're willing to prepare a season in advance, you can purchase some plants and grow cuttings from them. The following year you might have triple the initial number purchased and you'll be ready for a mass planting.

Turf grass is a universally accepted method of covering soil and if you have need of a sports surface or soft walking area, that's a good place for grass. But lawns are water intensive and require frequent maintenance, and too much of their consistent appearance can be boring. There may be areas of low light where grass won't grow or uneven areas where it's difficult to maintain, so other kinds of ground-cover plants are needed to take creative advantage of floor space.

The category of ground covers includes all plants up to 36 inches (90 cm) in height, although most often gardeners select plants under 12 inches (30 cm) for this purpose. Mat-forming plants and endless ramblers can be used for broad effect, and some are good lawn material. Lawns of English ivy or periwinkle are beautiful surfaces in every season and require almost no maintenance. Some ground covers like sweet woodruff, snow-in-summer and the many forms of thyme will densely carpet exposed soil under trees and hedges as well as providing generous flower displays. Gaps between shrubs leave much floor exposed and these are places to make good use of "running" ground-covers like lamium, pachysandra, peri-

winkle and Siberian carpet cypress. Almost anything with a high leaf count qualifies for floor covering, and long-blooming plants like daylilies, perennial geraniums and alpine strawberries will conceal soil while providing valuable display.

Ground covers provide a textured floor covering that brings worthwhile seasonal interest and can remain effective through the cold months if evergreen plants are used. But there are certain merits to the calm consistency of turf grass and circumstances when a traditional lawn is appropriate. It's important to know just when and where to put a lawn, because once it's down you'll have to maintain it.

A plant's method of growth is often the best key to how it should be used. Grass is a plant that grows outward by stolons, creeping runners with nodes or joints at short intervals where new plants form. It will keep expanding this way until it hits either concrete or air, just about the only things that will stop it. Because grass is an expanding plant it will look unnatural and contrived in a constrained or narrow area. That means putting it where it can be appreciated broadly, with enough space to get a good run.

You might like to have some lawn adjacent to a patio or deck, but don't let it replace the hard surface. Furniture on grass produces disastrous results and will deteriorate the turf by shading areas under chairs and tables. If a grass lawn is to be part of your garden floor plan, don't let it cover more than one third of the square footage. Beyond that, you're shortchanging yourself of more interesting and important plants.

Ten Best Ground-Cover Plants

Consistency and moderate spreading ability are the important characteristics when selecting a ground-cover plant for landscaping purposes. Spaces around woody shrubs and trees and near house foundations, steps and pathways can be dry and often shady, and a consistent ground-cover planting improves these areas considerably.

A good ground-cover plant comes into leaf early in spring, is pest- and disease-free through the growing season and lasts in good form long into autumn. Attractive blossoms are a bonus and so are characteristics that contribute to the winter garden. Ground-cover plants require three to four years to spread and provide good coverage, so be prepared to water and weed them patiently. Once established, however, they'll cover the soil for many years. You can speed up the process by buying extra plants and planting them closer together.

Mat-forming plants like ajuga are useful because they tolerate dry soil in sun or shade and spread outwards with consistent density, growing in harmoniously expanding circles, not in only one direction.

COMMON BUGLEWEED *Ajuga reptans* H 6 in (15 cm) −40°F (−40°C) All ajugas have worthwhile leaves and showy spikes of mid-spring blossoms. Some hybrids have splendid leaf color but less vigor. If you want one that spreads rapidly, try *A. repens* with deep green leaves and blue-purple flowers. But be careful, it can march right through a lawn. 'Bronze Beauty' and 'Braunherz' are slower. The cold-hardiest is *A. genevensis*, which also prefers dry soil, valuable in any plant.

BEARBERRY *Arctostaphylos uva-ursi* HW 12 in (30 cm) −50°F (−56°C) A handsome evergreen plant with woody creeping stems. The small, glossy leaves turn to bronze in winter, and then burst with bell-shaped waxy pink flowers in spring, followed by long-lasting red berries. Use to fill a strip bed, around shrubs or cascading over a wall. Bearberry tolerates acid soil and poor conditions, and does well in sandy or rocky soil enriched with peat moss.

CRANESBILL *Geranium* species and hybrids H 4–24 in (10–60 cm) −30°F (−34°C) Not the frost-tender geranium (*Pelargonium*) for containers, these cold-hardy, pest-free perennials have attractive foliage and a long blooming season. 'Claridge Druce' is the best for a sunny spot, 'Wargrave Pink' does well in part-shade, and in dry shade nothing beats *G. macrorrhizum* 'Ingwersen's Variety'. If leaves become tatty in late summer, cut them back severely for a quick flush of new foliage.

GROUND-COVER JUNIPER *Juniperus horizontalis* hybrids H 1–2 ft (0.3–0.6 m) −40°F (−40°C) This huge family contains many horizontal spreading varieties for dense evergreen cover through all seasons. Many heights are available, but among the lowest are the blue-needled *J. horizontalis* 'Blue Rug' (6 in/15 cm) for a dense, weed-suppressing blanket, and 'Ice Blue' (4 in/10 cm). 'Prince of Wales' is bright green, tinged purple in winter, and 'Turquoise Spreader' has soft, feathery branchelets in turquoise-green.

CANADIAN WILD GINGER *Asarum canadense* H 6 in (15 cm) −30°F (−34°C) Once established, this creates a low wave of broad, heart-shaped leaves for under shrubs and around rocks. Good in a shady woodland. *A. europaeum* has lustrous, round leaves (see page 80).

CANADALE GOLD EUONYMUS *Euonymus fortunei* 'Canadale Gold' HW 36 in (90 cm) −30°F (−34°C) A compact, evergreen, ground-cover shrub with bright golden-yellow margins on glossy green leaves. The upright form is good for foundation plantings and low hedges. There are several similar euonymus with gold markings or entirely gold foliage and all are bright and cheery plants with good winter value. Try also purpleleaf wintercreeper (*E. fortunei* 'Colorata') for its unique purplish coloring.

SWEET WOODRUFF *Galium odoratum* H 18 in (45 cm) −30°F (−34°C) This carpeting ground cover rolls along quickly in shade to part-sun. Its star-shaped green foliage and intense white blossoms make a classic spring display with Virginia bluebells (*Mertensia virginica*) and yellow cowslips (*Primula veris*). Shallow-rooted, it is easy to remove where unwanted and it is one of the few plants that will make a thick stand in the presence of Norway maples.

FALSE LAMIUM *Lamiastrum galeobdolon* H 24 in (60 cm)−50°F (−46°C) Another plant that succeeds in the dry shade of major trees, quickly forming generous mounds of green and silver foliage that quickly spread and root as they go along. Yellow spring flowers and stylish, green-and-silver foliage form a dense ground cover. 'Herman's Pride' has silver-flecked dark green leaves and 'Variegatum' is silver with green markings. Part-sun, consistent moisture.

SIBERIAN CARPET CYPRESS *Microbiota decussata* H 12–36 in (30–90 cm) −40°F (−40°C) This soft-textured evergreen ground-cover plant was found in 1921 growing in the mountains near Vladivostock, Russia. Arching, cedar-like branches quickly form broad sweeping patches of coverage in a border or around trees. It needs well-drained moist soil and will make the most luxuriant foliage in part-shade to full sunlight. Bright green in summer, it turns purple-brown in winter.

DWARF STONECROP *Sedum* species H 2–24 in (5–60 cm) −50°F (−46°C) Succulent leaves form a thick evergreen mat, tumbling over soil and rooting as they roll along. The many varieties, some clump-forming and others spreading, are all heat- and drought-tolerant in bright light, and good to fill a large gap, in a rockery or even to make a small lawn. Spreading kinds include chartreuse *S. acre* 'Aurea', blue-green *S. reflexum* and mulberry-red (in winter) *S. album* 'Murale Cristatum'.

ten steps to a better lawn

1. **Select the right kind of grass** for your garden. Lawns made from seed or sod can include several different kinds of grass plants, and some may perform better than others in your garden. Getting the right kind of seed can make all the difference between a lawn that's chronically thin and another that's thick and lustrous. Most general-purpose seed mixes contain a portion of the three main lawn grasses: Kentucky bluegrass, perennial rye and fescue. The bluegrass has a thick and lush blade with blue-green color and requires a lot of moisture and a sunny site. Perennial ryegrass is a medium-textured green blade with good drought resistance. And fescue grasses are able to establish a greensward in shady locations.

   You can customize your lawn by overseeding with the grass best for your conditions. Grass seeds germinate best in cool, damp seasons, so early spring or mid-autumn are good times to overseed. First mow the lawn and use a rake to rough up areas of bare soil. Then scatter the appropriate grass seed generously over areas where the turf is thin. Cover and mulch the seed with

1 inch (2.5 cm) of peat moss or rotted manure and keep it wet until the seeds germinate and are growing. You can cut the new grass when it reaches a height of 3 inches (7.5 cm).

2. **Keep the mower blades sharp.** Dull blades rip and shred the grass, giving it a ragged appearance and inviting plant problems. The ragged edges are slow to heal and make an easy entry point for the many fungus diseases that can affect lawns. Clean-cutting mower blades are an investment in the health of your lawn; they can be sharpened at a hardware store in spring.

3. **Cut the lawn high.** The roots of grass plants grow in direct proportion to blade length. Short blades will curtail the growth of roots and make the lawn vulnerable to drought conditions. To encourage longer roots that can reach ground water, set the mower high so that the lawn is between 2–3 inches (5–7.5 cm) in height. You'll get used to the longer look and the lawn will stay green longer when drought hits. A taller lawn will shade the soil

better, with the added benefit of retarding the germination of weed and crabgrass seeds.

4. **Leave the clippings in place.** Green grass clippings contain enough nutrients to supply half the fertilizer your lawn needs for the growing season. If they're allowed to fall in place, they'll return 2 pounds (1 kg) of nitrogen to every 1000 square feet (93 sq meters) of lawn, and that's premium plant food. The clippings will also help to mulch the root zone against high temperature, and support biological life in the soil as they're turned into nutrients.

5. **Don't overfeed the lawn.** Applying too much fertilizer causes grass to grow unnaturally fast. The lawn care industry advises five feedings a season, and that's enough to feed a lawn to an early death. Too much nitrogen causes grass plants to work overtime manufacturing green blades that need to be cut with increasing frequency. If you allow the clippings to remain on the lawn, you'll need to fertilize only once or twice each year. The most

important time is mid-autumn, when grass plants will absorb the nutrients and hold them for release the follow spring. If you want to fertilize a second time, wait until June, when growth is under way and strong root systems are established.

If you're interested in free lawn food and less expensive fertilizer, scatter some seeds of white clover (*Trifolium reptans*) over the lawn in early spring. The clover is low growing and has the ability to take nitrogen from air and "fix" it in solid form on its roots, allowing grass plants to share in the meal. Clover will feed itself and everything around it, and you'll quickly appreciate its presence in the lawn.

6. **Water less often, for longer periods.** Frequent watering for short periods causes grass roots to accumulate near the soil surface. When the weather heats up and soil temperature rises, the grass roots can't reach the cooler soil below and begin to deteriorate. Above ground, the lawn starts to look thin and sad. Watering less frequently and for a longer time will allow water to percolate downward. Grass roots follow the water to cooler soil levels and the lawn will be thicker and more resilient in hot weather.

Try to water the lawn twice a week for two hours each time. In very hot weather you can increase the frequency to three times, for a period of two hours each. Different soil structures absorb water at varying rates. Clay soils are slower

Hardy ivy makes an almost maintenance-free lawn in partial shade, taking three years to thicken and cover the soil when plants are spaced 8 inches (20 cm) apart. Rich soil and consistent moisture will keep it lustrous in winter and summer. Weeding is necessary until established, and path edges should be trimmed once a year.

A creeping thyme lawn smells like heaven, but it relies on a dry climate, bright light and sandy soil. Thyme is a hardy plant that will remain green all year in warm regions but defoliates in cold temperatures and may become patchy under snow cover. When in bloom, it's an amazing pink-purple carpet for four weeks.

to wet and need more time for water to enter the soil and percolate down. Sandy soils are quicker to accept water and move it through the root zone. Ideally the water you put down should moisten the top 6 inches (15 cm) of soil. Dig a small hole in a corner of the lawn after watering and check if the soil 6 inches (15 cm) down is at least sponge-damp.

7. **Remove and prevent thatch accumulation.** Lawns that are fed too much nitrogen produce excessive amounts of roots and clippings. In just a few seasons, this accumulates into a mat-like layer of thatch that's too thick to decompose and diminishes the movement of oxygen and water into the soil. The spongy layer provides a breeding ground for insects and fungus diseases that can plague a lawn for years. You'll know you have thatch if the lawn feels soft and spongy, and you can stick your finger in without hitting soil.

Thatch can be removed with a stiff rake or special thatch rake. If the thatch is very thick and resists the rake, you can rent a vertical-cut mower to slice the lawn and allow for efficient raking. It's easier to remove thatch in spring before the grass gets into full growth. Then limit nitrogen fertilizer applications to once or twice a year.

8. **Let the lawn breathe.** The soil under a lawn tends to become compacted and deficient in oxygen. Grass plants need oxygen to grow, and you can help them breathe better by aerating the lawn each year. Core aerating machines are similar to mowers and can be rented from an equipment company or can be supplied by a landscape maintenance service. They cut and remove thousands of small cores from the lawn, allowing oxygen to enter the soil. The cores are left on the ground and will decompose back into the lawn over ten days. You can use a leaf rake to break them up a bit. Spike aerating machines are less effective. The spikes make only a slender hole with compressed sides, adding somewhat to the problem and not admitting enough oxygen.

9. **Develop a weed philosophy.** A healthy lawn will always have some weeds in it and you just need to establish your level of tolerance for these unwanted plants. Perhaps forget about the baby weeds and focus on the big ones that get in your face. Herbicide applications cause serious health and pollution problems no one wants to have. Take the money you would spend on spraying the lawn and use it to pay someone to hand dig

the big weeds in the lawn. You can add your own efforts and that should make the weed problem very manageable.

To dig weeds efficiently so they won't come back, you need to remove as much of the root as possible. To stop dandelions from regrowing, that means taking out 4–5 inches (10–12.5 cm) of the taproot. If you dig weeds in dry soil their tops will snap off, leaving the roots behind. But if you weed in wet soil the roots slip out easily with a nudge from a weeding tool or slim hand trowel. Weeding after rain is always a successful time, or you can saturate the soil with a hose before weeding in dry weather.

10. **Keep the lawn wll dressed.** Top dressing twice a year with organic materials is the best way to condition the soil under the lawn and improve its total performance. In autumn, and again in early spring, mix equal parts of rotted manure and peat moss and sweep the mixture across the lawn evenly with a soft leaf rake. Aim for a 1-inch (5 cm) coverage over all. Finely shredded leaves and short pine needles are also useful in this mix, if you have them handy. You can wet the dressing down or let rain do it, and it will disappear into the lawn within a few days.

opposite: An idyllic setting, but only if the greensward is naturally healthy. Weed-killing chemicals have a bad effect on people, too. It does no harm to allow wild plants to remain in the lawn if it's mowed regularly. Leave the fertilizing until mid-autumn, the most important time to feed a lawn.

beds and borders

Gardeners are natural-born collectors and can't pass through a plant nursery without several unplanned but deeply coveted acquisitions finding their way onto the cart. Restraint is just not their virtue—gardeners are shameless when it comes to impulse buying. Nature obliges this compulsion by producing endless species of ferns and campanulas, but if you're going to enjoy them all you'd better have someplace to put them. And that leads to beds and borders.

The purpose of a planting bed is to provide a showcase for ornamental plants that will complement the landscaped garden. Beds can be situated as focal points that gradually lead you through the garden, and in that respect,

they are directional signals indicating which way to go or when to stop and pause.

Beds and borders can be used to balance a garden, perhaps placed across from large objects like swimming pools or surrounding a gazebo to provide context and tie the structure into the garden. Staggered along the sides of a long and narrow garden, they cause interest to shift from one side to the other, avoiding the bowling lane effect of looking straight to the back.

In a very broad garden, island beds can be set into the lawn area to focus attention inward and keep you from feeling lost in too much space. Making a bed in a very small area is sometimes the best way to bring a diversity of interest

where nothing else will fit. Some townhouse gardens are so tiny that they can be given over to one big bed with a place for two chairs.

In a cold climate it's important to place some beds planned and planted for winter interest where they can be seen from windows, allowing you to anticipate spring while gazing on a display of ornamental bark, berries and dried grasses with tall sedums.

Another important bed is by the front door, where the very earliest daphnes, violets and primulas will perfume the still-frosty air. In this respect beds are vehicles for plants that appeal to the senses, and you can bring them close to where you pass by every day.

Make this static shape interesting with a small weeping tree and a cluster of boulders across a corner.

Corner beds are dynamic, presenting several planting options within a balanced form.

Scalloping adds graceful lines and makes a narrow bed appear wider.

Wherever your beds are located, you want to be sure they provide the best growing environment for plants, and that means paying special attention to soil preparation. The crucial issues of drainage, soil texture and fertility are the underpinnings of all healthy plant life; it's just throwing money down a hole to install new plants without improving the soil.

Older beds will need to be renovated every five years, the plants lifted and sorted out, some divided, others sent to new homes, and the soil improved throughout. Plan on spreading 3 inches (7.5 cm) of coarse sand and another 3 inches (7.5 cm) of rotted manure or leaves, and digging it all in. It's a lot of work, but you do it only twice a decade. This is also an opportunity to change the bed's dimensions and give it a new shape

It's not always necessary to entirely renovate a bed, but certainly each plant can be given a hole with a generous bushel of premium soil. Some gardeners prepare bulk amounts of planting mix made of equal amounts of rotted manure, peat moss and coarse sand, stored in plastic garbage barrels and ready for use in planting holes.

If you're intending to make new beds, first lay them out with a rubber garden hose (vinyl has its own shape and won't cooperate) to find the best shape and line. Spend some time adjusting the hose until you're satisfied, and then use a blunt-nosed spade to etch a notch all around the shape and consider how you want to construct the bed.

You can do it the hard way, digging out the sod and amending the soil with organic materials. Or you can construct a mounded bed by laying ten sheets of black-and-white newspaper over the

grass, piling soil on top and neatening the edges. Plan for a soil mix made of two parts topsoil mixed with one part rotted manure and one part coarse sand. You'll need enough to cover the area with 18 inches (45 cm), and it will sink by almost half in the first season.

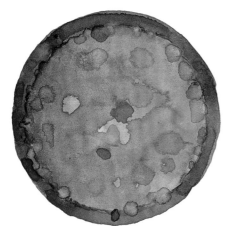

A round bed's formal look becomes relaxed when slightly mounded.

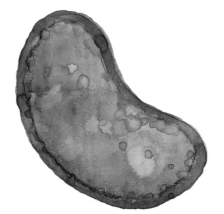

A kidney shape lends itself to Victorian displays of bedding plants and tall ferns at either end.

Crescents are useful for breaking up large areas and defining a lawn.

How to Edge a Bed

Keeping a sharp edge on a planting bed prevents grass from creeping in while enhancing the shape of the planted area.

Use a sharpened blunt-nosed spade to cut the edge. Push the spade in with your foot, 2–3 inches (5–8 cm) deep, and on a 45° angle. Lean back on the spade and pop out a wedge-shaped clod of soil. Continue along the edge until you've made a continuous trench between the lawn and bed.

Expect to have to neaten the edge three times a season. If you won't be changing the bed shape in the near future, you may wish to install a mowing strip (see page 65).

Sharp angles at the corners of hard surfaces are always awkward in the garden. But they can be offset by a curving bed and softened with plants. A stonemason has the skill to cut stone or brick and create a rounded patio edge.

HOW TO RENOVATE AN OLDER GARDEN BED

The best times to renovate an older garden bed are in early autumn or spring when the air is cool and the soil is moist. Plants are semi-dormant when the soil temperature is cold and will suffer far less root trauma in the process. Because the renovation will involve some amount of digging, you'll want to work with soil when it's soft and moist, not in the hard and dry state of warmer seasons.

Select an overcast day, or plan the work for early morning or late afternoon when the sun is low in the sky. If the bed is large and more work than you can handle at one time, plan on dividing it into sections and do one part each autumn and spring.

Overhauling a garden bed begins with an assessment of its contents. This is the time to be ruthless and cunning about what possible potential each plant has for future performance. Anything half-dead or limping along should be discarded, along with plants that chronically suffer from insect or disease infes-

tation. Remember that every space you make by pitching something out represents a wonderful new plant to be purchased.

1. You can dispose of unwanted plants by putting them in containers clearly labeled with both common and botanical names, and setting them out on the sidewalk overnight with a "free to good home" sign. People value any plant with proper identification, and they'll be gone by morning.

2. Now is the time to change the shape of the bed if it needs adjustment. You can use a soft rubber hose to outline a new area if you want to enlarge the bed substantially. Use a blunt-nosed spade to cut out the new lines, lifting sod out and turning the soil underneath.

3. Now carefully lift the remaining plants you intend to keep and store them in pots or plastic bags in a cool shady area. Cut drainage holes in the bag bottoms and give the plants some water. Shrubs in the bed can remain in place, but loosen the soil around their roots with a garden fork.

4. To get the best results from this project you should use a minimum of 3 inches (7.5 cm) of coarse sand and 3 inches (7.5 cm) of organic amendments spread over the bed, but more is better. Organic materials can include compost, rotted manure, peat moss, leaves, pine needles and grass clippings. The coarse

sand will break up heavy clay and bring oxygen into the root zone, and the organic materials will increase soil fertility and help to retain moisture. If your soil is sandy and quick draining, leave out the coarse sand and use as much organic material as you can haul and spread. Dig these materials into the soil and around the roots of shrubs.

5. Set the plants back in, dividing overgrown clumps and changing locations for a modified design to the renovated bed. New plants can be added at this time if you've made a nursery-shopping trip. Water the plants in with a commercial transplant solution, and if you're intending to use organic mulch like shredded leaves or bark, spread it over the soil and around plants.

hills and steep inclines

Gardeners brought low by years of struggling to plant on a slope probably won't fancy a mountain vacation. No one seems to sympathize with the complicated circumstances of a hillside garden until they're afflicted with one. Plants don't stand straight and water doesn't stay in place. Topsoil and mulch drift to the bottom and bare patches of earth crack and erode. It looks like something the glacier left behind.

If your hillside is quite steep, the first consideration is to stabilize the soil and prevent erosion. Root systems of plants aren't enough to prevent the inevitable loss of soil on a steep slope, so some construction measures will be necessary. You might want to speak to a professional contractor about installing rock outcroppings or formal stone terracing, and possibly a drainage tile system at the bottom. This kind of work involves major stone and soil shifting,

and some basic engineering skills.

Not all slopes are steep enough to require restructuring, but they can still be frustrating places to garden. A slope goes up and down; consequently, plants must have characteristics enabling them to follow the terrain. Gravity will cause a vertical shrub like rose of Sharon to slowly lunge forward on a slope with a 45° angle. What's needed is a plant with cascading form, such as weeping forsythia (*Forsythia suspensa*) or

Your hillside can look like a Mediterranean garden using large natural stones for terraced areas (but even concrete rubble will do). Plant lots of creeping and cascading plants—lamb's ears, lavender, ground-cover roses, creeping willow (*Salix repens*), cinquefoil (*Potentilla* hybrids) and cranberry cotoneaster (*Cotoneaster apiculatus*)—and remember to water the slope frequently.

'Hancock' coralberry (*Symphoricarpos* x *chenaulti* 'Hancock'), to effortlessly adapt to the terrain and look good doing it. The anchoring roots of plants like dwarf spireas, 'Gro-Low' sumac and low-spreading junipers under 3 feet (90 cm) in height will easily adapt to a slope. If your design sense says there must be a vertical accent with greater height, it will be necessary to terrace a small area to provide a level foundation for the root ball.

Whether you're landscaping the slope with specimen plants or simply desperate to find something that will grow there, the most essential factor is to plant some carpeting ground covers that will cover the soil and protect it from erosion. The most useful plants are those that ramble along and set down roots from traveling stems, like cutleaf stephanandra (*Stephanandra incisa* 'Crispa'), English ivy, 'Sarcoxie' euonymus, periwinkle and sweet woodruff. Plant them in the shadiest sections and they'll travel toward the lighter areas. Also, strong, vigorous vines with broad leaves such as climbing hydrangea and *Clematis* x *jouiniana* 'Praecox' are well suited to horizontal growth over a slope. Some flowering perennials that combine ground-cover value with slope adaptability are violets, alpine strawberries, cranesbill geraniums, lady's mantle (*Alchemilla mollis*), hostas and daylilies.

Upright plants on steep slopes need firm support to keep from toppling forward. An outcropping of rocks and additional? will hold roots in place. Dry slopes are best planted with vigorous and drought-hardy groundcovers. Try bugleweed (*Ajuga*), snow-in-summer (*Cerastium tomentosum*), creeping speedwell (*Veronica repens*) and evergreen Siberian carpet cypress (*Microbiata decussata*).

berms

It used to be that only golfers and cross-country skiers knew what a berm was. These man-made gentle hills are used to create challenge on the golf course and a little downward glide on the ski trail. But gardeners have realized the value of a well-placed berm and the interest it can bring to a flat and one-dimensional yard. Berms are also useful for creating privacy where fencing is inappropriate or undesirable; planted with small shrubs and perennials, a berm can become a commanding focal point in the landscape.

Berms are another way of making an elevation in the garden, generating interest and dimension similar to a raised edge or bed, but in a more subtle and natural style. The important issues to determine are the right size, shape and scale of berm for the garden if it's to appear natural and spontaneous. Erratic hills steep enough to sled down aren't the work of bionic moles, only the creation of enthusiastic berm builders, and cause people to wonder if you're hiding something there. What you want is a gradual swell of soil with gracefully sloped sides and a flat top.

Contouring a berm to have a natural appearance requires some space, and this is difficult to achieve in a small garden where other techniques (raised edges and curbs) will work better. Berms can be made in any shape, although many are basically round. But a berm can have a kidney shape or can follow the angle of a corner by taking a subtle

A 24-inch (60 cm) berm becomes 3½ feet (1 m) of display area when planted. Choose clump-forming, spreading plants, such as perennial geraniums, pinks and dwarf daylilies, or low-flowering groundcover roses, blue lungwort (*Pulmonaria angustifolia*) and low Chinese astilbe (*Astilbe chinensis*). Avoid tall plants that can lean and topple.

turn, or run in a rectangular form along one side of the garden. In order to be useful and have the appearance of permanence, the berm will need a minimum size of 8 feet (2.4 m) in both length and width if it is to be round. That allows 4 feet (1.2 m) across the top and a gradual 2-foot (60 cm) slope on all sides.

Shape and height are relative to how the berm will be used. If you intend to grow turf grass on the berm, construct it with a gentle swell with gradually sloping sides and slightly rounded top. But remember, the lawn mower must comfortably travel up and down the berm without breaking stride. Steep sides or high elevation will cause maintenance problems. If the berm is to be planted, the top should be fairly flat to give plant roots a secure and firm foundation. To use the berm for privacy, consider planting it with small shrubs, giving you the height of the soil plus the added coverage of 3–4 feet (90–120 cm) of plant material. Any of the *Spiraea bumalda* cultivars, dwarf burning bush or spreading yew would work well.

Height is a tricky issue because small berms seem to just melt away after a few years. Any pile of soil will eventually sink by almost a third of its original height, particularly if it's piled directly on the ground. The best way to stabilize a berm is to give it a base of 8 inches (20 cm) of small gravel covered with landscape fabric or filter cloth, with 24–36 inches (60–90 cm) of soil piled on top of the fabric at the highest point. If you intend to plant small shrubs, you'll need the greater amount of soil. Then use a blunt-nosed spade to make a sharp border or edge all around the berm to keep grass from growing into it.

A subtle berm can replace the front lawn and provide a venue for an interesting collection of specimen coniferous plants. Boulders and groundcovers provide cohesion and help reduce maintenance needs.

LOCATION, LOCATION, LOCATION...

PLACEMENT is critical, because a berm right in the middle of things will take away from the implied naturalism of the elevation. You probably wouldn't be happy to purchase a garden with a berm centered in the middle of the yard, so why build one there? A better site is to one side, possibly near a corner, but not up against any fences. A berm should never appear claustrophobic or jammed in with other features of the garden.

If the berm is being constructed to make some privacy, be sure to put it toward the side on which you are exposed. Placing it toward a corner allows for a tree to grow 10 feet (3 m) behind the berm, and if that's your plan, select a tree like ginkgo, honey locust or birch, which all make gentle dappled shade.

Ten Best Ornamental Grasses

Low ornamental grasses are beautiful lining a stone or brick walkway, and medium to tall sizes are useful fillers in the border, providing interesting form and texture with winter value. Introducing grasses to perennial plantings works best if you use more than one kind, selecting two or three grasses with differing and complementary features and spacing them out through the bed. You'll get the best show from a large clump, so try to buy grasses in 1-gallon (4.5 l) containers. If the grass you want is only available in small pots, buy three and group them together.

LITTLE BLUE STEM *Andropogon scoparium* syn *Schizachyrium scoparius* H 36 in (90 cm) −40°F (−40°C) A classic prairie grass with blue-green to silvery blue blades standing straightly vertical. After a late-summer cloud of delicate, wispy flowers, the foliage turns red in autumn. For a lovely privacy barrier by a summer seating area try the larger version, big blue stem *A. gerardii* (5 ft/1.5 m).

QUAKING GRASS *Briza media* H 2 ft (1.6 m) −20°F (−29°C) Often mistaken for a flowering herbaceous plant, this soft grass forms lantern-like seed heads that sway and rattle in the wind. Always welcome toward the front of a border, in a rock garden or along a path where its subtle sound can be caught. Seed heads and the long stems can be dried for floral arrangements. Evenly moist soil, full sun to part-shade.

BLUE OAT GRASS *Helichtotrichon* syn *Avena sempervirens* H 2 ft (0.6 m) −20°F (−29°C) Spiny, vase-shaped clumps of thin, blue-gray foliage look good massed in a group in a sunny spot at the bottom of steps or along a boulevard. Soft, arching, bluish-brown sprays form above the clump in early summer. Full sun, organic soil with peat moss and sand.

JAPANESE BLOOD GRASS *Imperata cylindrica* H 2 ft (0.6 m) −10°F (−23°C) A spectacular, truly dark red when backlit by sunlight. Plant in clusters to show off to best effect, in sun to part-shade and moist but well-drained soil. Intense color all season, but no flower. Also with intense color is black-bladed *Ophiopogon jubatum* (6 in/15 cm), good as a ground-cover grass, and sometimes called 'Arabicus' or 'Nigrescens'.

FEATHER REED GRASS *Calamagrostis arundinacea* H 5 ft (1.5 m) −20°F (−29°C) Ideal for accent or background planting, its strong vertical line and rigid stems act as architectural accents in a blowsy midsummer perennial border or combined with woody shrubs. Yellow flower spikes appear in June, lasting into winter. *C. a.* 'Oredam' has gold flowers and green-and-white striped foliage. Sun to part-shade.

SILVER JAPANESE SEDGE *Carex morrowii* 'Variegata' H 12 in (30 cm) −20°F (−29°C) A mounding grass, with stiff, flat, thickly textured blades of green and white stripes. Similarly colored is *C. m.* 'Aureo-Variegata', and a shorter black sedge is *C. nigra*, with dark blue-green tufts and a black flower spike in spring. Both part-shade; *C. morrowii* is drought-tolerant, but *C. nigra* needs moist soil.

WHITE PAMPAS GRASS *Cortaderia selloana* H 7–10 ft (2.1–3 m) 0°F (−18°C) The tallest and most dramatic of the pampas grasses. Needs to be near an object of substance for balance, such as a house corner or a driveway entry post. There's a pink variety also, if you've the nerve to try it. *C. s. pumila* is a more conservative choice at 4 ft (1.2 m), with beautiful white August blossoms. Full sun.

CORKSCREW RUSH *Juncus effusus* 'Spiralis' H 2 ft (0.6 m) −30°F (−34°C) Spiraled stems similar to the fine, twisted twiggery of corkscrew hazel. The species plant is used to weave Japanese tatami floor coverings. Plant in moist soil near water, by a pond or streamside, in full sun to part-shade.

ZEBRA GRASS *Miscanthus sinensis* 'Zebrinus' H 5 ft (1.5 m) −20°F (−29°C) Tall vertical blades, green with horizontal gold stripes or blotches and pale yellow plumes. Use a big clump at the end of a border or in the center of an island bed. Also beautiful are green-and-white *M. s.* 'Variegatus' and reddish purple *M. s.* var. *purpurascens* (12 in/30 cm). Full sun to part-shade; no fertilizer.

SWITCH GRASS *Panicum virgatum* H 4 ft (1.2 m) −20°F (−29°C) Flat leaves are green in summer, yellow and red in autumn, fading to beige in winter. 'Heavy Metal' is a hybrid with stiff, erect growth and metallic blue color; 'Strictum' is a softer blue. Bright location with moist soil.

installing landscape plants

5

Looking at plants in a nursery is like visiting cats and dogs at the pound—you're not seeing them in the best circumstance or at their full potential. But hopefully you know what you want and can recognize a good specimen when you see it. Most plants for nursery sales to home gardeners are container grown so that they can be efficiently watered and moved with the least disturbance in the root zone or damage to their woody structure.

By the time you purchase a plant at the nursery in spring, it's likely the root system has filled most of the container. When the plant is settled into a hole of its own in your garden, the first growing season will be used to make root growth, with only a little twig and leaf extension. Plants first grow below-ground roots and then above-ground shoots, so that the system is in place to deliver moisture and nutrients to new top growth when it appears. It's in the second growing season that you'll begin to see significant top growth and branch extension, and the initial tightness of the

Newly purchased plants meet up with a full border—clearly something must go. Start by dividing large clumps in half and removing plants that haven't performed well. Then, while no one is looking, remove 8 inches (20 cm) of lawn from the border edge and give your new babies a home.

opposite: The spring garden can put on an amazing display of massed tulips, weeping apple blossoms and carpets of grape hyacinths. With careful planning and knowledge of the growing conditions, and by using plants that thrive in your region, you can have plants blooming from earliest spring to autumn.

PLANTS may have been growing in their pots for several years before reaching the nursery, a practice that encourages a densely compact root system. Large plants that are balled and burlapped also arrive with dense root systems as the result of periodic root pruning in the field to keep the root ball compact. Top growth tends to remain "tight", reflecting the constraints on the root system, with branches not much extended and minimal twiggy growth. But if the woody scaffold is nicely proportioned and balanced, the twigs are gently flexible and foliage appears robust and healthy, it is a good buy for your garden.

woody structure will begin to expand and open up. If you purchase the plant in autumn when the ground has begun to cool, there may not be any new root growth until the following spring. Sometimes very good plants are ugly ducklings for the first few seasons, but eventually extend their branches and become swans. What you need is patience and an appreciation of the process to help you keep the faith.

A plant is established after five years of growth in your garden, and that means the root system is well developed and top growth has begun to assume its mature form. But there's still lots of growing ahead, and you can expect the plant to put on quite a bit more size, especially if it's a tree. If you've been conscientious about providing water and good organic nutrients, the plant should look full of vigor and have many buds in spring. Not all plants are easily established and grow this well. If you're tempted to dig up wild shrubs and seedling trees and transport them to your garden (with permission, of course), their pattern of development will be slower.

Because they have been growing without constraint, their branches and root systems are more extended and likely to suffer trauma when lifted. It may take a few growing seasons and a bit of tender loving care to get them over the shock of it all.

Some gardeners prefer to purchase very young plants, on the premise that smaller plants make a better transition to the open garden. Certainly they're easier to install by yourself and won't require trailer transport, cranes and chains, iron wrecking bars, tree buggies, wire baskets, stakes and root feeders. Nurseries can supply very large sizes of woody shrubs and trees that arrive in good condition, ready to make a fresh start in a new hole. Everything about their planting is more complicated because of their size and weight, and you'll need some strong-arm help when the truck pulls up. If you want the instant garden effect of large-scale plants, just be prepared for the drama of installation. You're going to need help with this baby.

shopping

A spring afternoon in a plant nursery can unsettle the most ardent shopper, presuming you even get into the parking lot. On the way in, you're distracted by something wonderful in full bloom in someone's cart, and no one knows the name. You've come to purchase forsythia and there are six varieties to choose from. The only employee with plant information hasn't been seen for a long time. You want to stock up on columbines, but everything is organized by botanical names and you never took Latin. The checkout line takes twenty minutes to clear and all you bought is gloves. What's wrong with this picture?

Purchasing plants requires a strategy. Some plant families are very large and you must know both the common name and the Latin botanical name to get exactly what you're after. A bit of research in good books, either your own or at the library, will give you these important identifications. If your plant isn't locally available, you can check a plant source guide to find out what nurseries carry it and if they service mail orders.

If you're hunting for plants in a rural area, you may find a nursery or tree farm that allows you to walk the rows and make a selection. If plants are growing in the ground, the staff will dig, ball and burlap them for you if the season is still cold and buds aren't yet swelling. Woody shrubs and trees can safely be field dug only when dormant, in earliest spring or late autumn. Dormant plants haven't started into active growth and are less susceptible to transplant shock. Your chances of successful transition are improved and soon the plant will burst into leaf and bloom in your garden.

Nurseries in big population centers carry plants that sell quickly and are very familiar. If you're looking for unusual plants you may find them in the mail order catalogues of distant nurseries. This is a good way to acquire extraordinary plants, but you should know what to expect. Most mail orders are shipped in very early spring when the plants are still dormant, or if they're particularly good travelers like violets and scented geraniums, they might be just coming into leaf. Perennials received this way must be planted immediately into the garden or in pots kept in a cool indoor space if the ground is still frozen. Woody plants and roses are shipped bare root and look most unpromising on arrival. They've been taken from cold storage at about 35°F (1–2°C) and need to be planted promptly. You can hold them for two or three days in a cold garage with temperatures of 35–40°F (2–4°C), but then they need to go into soil. If the garden isn't ready, you can pot them up temporarily in containers with purchased soil and put them out in the daytime and back into the garage for the nights, along with potted perennials waiting for garden space.

GET AN EARLY START

DON'T wait for a nice warm day to visit the garden center, because everyone else will have the same idea. Nurseries begin bringing in plants at the end of winter and they welcome early business. To be alone and unhurried in the nursery aisles is a rare form of pleasure, and you can bring along your best gardening book for on-the-spot information.

selecting plants

Always bring a pair of thin cotton garden gloves when you visit a nursery, and wear them. So much plant material gathered in one place is an opportunity for many kinds of pests to proliferate, and nurseries will guard against plant damage by spraying. Some wholesale suppliers spray all plants with pesticide before they're delivered, and nurseries will spray if there's a local problem before plants are sold. But you won't know about it while you're walking the aisles, so wear the gloves. If you haven't got gloves, keep your hands away from your face and wash them when you get home.

Hygiene is an important factor in nurseries and indicates the level of care that's taken to prevent problems with good cultural practices. The outsides of perennial pots should be relatively clean, not sitting in a muddy tray, and there shouldn't be any weeds sharing the inside. If there is enough staff to water plants regularly, you shouldn't see pots that are completely dry. If the plants dry out and wilt repeatedly, their growth will be checked and they become targets for insects and disease. Plant foliage should be a consistent green color with-

When buying a shrub or tree, look for a balanced placement of main branches and limbs. A little bit of twig injury isn't unusual and can be trimmed off. If the plant is still dormant, check if the buds are slightly glossy and possibly swelling, and that will tell you the wood is alive. Don't scratch the bark to see if it's green inside because the plant isn't yours yet. Have a look at the main trunk where it meets the soil and make sure there are no open cracks or fissures with decayed interior. Also avoid girdling roots circling the trunk at soil level, a condition that will shorten the life of the plant.

STORIES TO TELL

WOODY plants can tell you a lot about themselves. The bark shows the pruning history of the plant and you can find the places where wood has been removed as it grew. If old seed heads still cling to twigs or can be found around the trunk in the pot, you know the plant is mature enough to bloom. That can be valuable information if you're looking at lilac or wisteria, which won't flower if too young.

The woody scaffold shows the front and back of the plant. The back is the darkest side and will be flat, while branches at the front have had more light and are fuller. This shows you how to face the plant outward when you set it into a hole.

Clean pruning scars that heal quickly are no problem, but watch for ragged injuries in the wood, particularly if you're purchasing a tree. The ragged edges of accidental damage are slow to heal and allow disease organisms to enter, infecting the interior wood. Some nurseries wrap a protective sheath of corrugated paper around tree trunks to prevent damage.

out yellow patches or spots and the leaves should have good turgidity, a firm resilience indicating the root system is moving water efficiently up the stems. You can check turgidity by gently depressing a leaf and watching it spring back into position. If it doesn't spring back, something's wrong in the pot.

If you see insects on plants, at least you know they haven't been sprayed recently and are safe to touch. Mostly you'll see sucking insects like spittlebugs and aphids that are easily removed with a spray of water at home. (Another efficient method of removing a few insects is by hand-picking. A pair of "bug dedicated" rubber gloves will embolden even the most squeamish.) But if the undersides of leaves show a collection of tiny white flies, that's a problem to be avoided. Whiteflies are difficult to suppress and can breed very rapidly. Needless to say, any plants with mushy or spotted leaves are diseased and shouldn't even be offered for sale.

Perennial plants increase their size in mid-spring by expanding from the crown and putting up more stems, but they need to be out of the pot and in the ground to do this. If you can get them planted early in the season, the plants will put on good growth their first year in your garden. Perennials sold in 4-inch (10 cm) pots are unlikely to put up more than a token blossom the first year but will enlarge their crowns and flower well in the second growing season. If you want a perennial to bloom the first year, you can purchase larger plants in gallon containers. The number of growing points sprouting from the crown is an indication of the number of flowers that plant will produce. Plants with multiple growing points are good bargains and can usually be divided at the end of the first season if you want to make several small plants from one big specimen.

Plant sizes and pricing are fairly consistent between nurseries, and it's unwise to look for a bargain. Reduced prices in spring or summer indicate something amiss in the nursery. But you can find predictable reductions in autumn, usually during the month of October, when garden centers try to sell off as much stock as possible to reduce their winter storage costs. If you're shopping then, the selection is more limited and plants have spent a long, hot season in containers, but you might find some good buys. You should be able to tell from the condition of the foliage if the root system is still in good working order. Large trees and shrubs are the big-ticket items in any season, and if their root balls are big enough to require a wire basket wrapping, you'll know that's where the money is. A large root ball and thick trunk are indicators of maturity and the length of time the tree has been held before sale. Tree value is measured by the width of the trunk and not by height. Trees produce a new layer of bark each year of their lives and this is an accurate measurement of age and maturity. Vertical growth is sporadic and will slow down or accelerate at different stages of development, as well as being directly affected by cultural practices. If trees are grown in soils deficient inoxygen, moisture and fertility they will slow their vertical growth. If you want your trees to grow quickly, be good to them in every way.

using mail order to purchase plants

Many wonderful plants can be acquired through local garden centers. But once you've got the gardening bug, you'll probably want to look further afield for new plants you've read about or seen in your travels. And that will open the door to mail order nursery catalogues, a rich source of plants and information. Thousands of interesting catalogues are available to gardeners, and many are focused on an area of interest. Some are from specialist growers of plants like hostas, magnolias or antique roses, and others feature plants for a specific region or climate category, such as dry prairie or moist shade plants. Whatever your interest or growing conditions, you're certain to find a nursery grower with plants to meet your needs. Begin by looking for advertised catalogues in the back pages of your favorite gardening magazines. You'll also find lots of catalogues on the Internet, particularly through Cyndi's Catalog of Garden Catalogs (www.qnet.com/~johnsonj/), which lists 2000 mail order nurseries and is updated frequently. The site is organized by the types of plants (perennials, shrubs, trees, water plants,

etc.) and also provides links to plant societies.

Try to select a nursery that's within your climate zone. Plants grown in climate conditions similar to the summer high and winter low temperatures in your own garden will be the most reliable. If you have questions about a plant's adaptability to your location, don't hesitate to contact the nurseries with your questions. They want their plants to succeed in your garden, and they rely on satisfied customers for repeat business and recommendations to their customers' gardening friends.

Be sure to place your order well in advance of delivery date schedules, which are outlined in the catalogues. Nurseries prepare months in advance for their shipping season, and many plants can sell out before shipping begins. Mail order nurseries do a great job of delivering healthy plants in good condition. To do that, they will ship only at specific times (usually late autumn and earliest spring) when plants are dormant and less vulnerable to shock. Nurseries will often schedule their shipments to coincide with spring planting season in each region.

Most plants arrive in a dormant state with bare roots and special packing materials to maintain humidity in the box. If you notice swelling buds on woody plants, they are semi-dormant and will soon be in an active state of growth. Open the box to prevent the accumulation of excessive moisture and possible fungus growth, and put it in a cool, frost-free place.

Your plants should be settled into permanent garden homes as soon as possible. They can wait in their packing material for a day or two, but then need to be planted. If late frosts delay planting outdoors, herbaceous perennials can be put into pots with soilless mix and set in a sunny window. Or if day temperatures are above freezing, the potted perennials can be set out in sun for the day and taken in a cold garage at night until finally planted into the garden. Bare-root woody plants should be kept as cool as possible without freezing. If woody plants begin to break buds and sprout, they can be held for another 48 hours with their roots in a bucket of water, but then must be planted in the ground. In all cases, these temporary conditions should be limited to as short time as possible.

zone guidelines

The zone system is based on the principle that all plants have a minimum temperature that they can survive. To ensure a plant is winter hardy in your garden, you must know the minimum coldest winter temperature in your region. Then you can confidently select plants with hardiness ratings that at least correspond to your minimum coldest temperature, and preferably have a lower rating. As an example, if your garden's temperature falls to –20°F (–29°C) every winter, you are in Zone 5. When selecting plants, be sure that they are hardy to Zone 5 or lower. If you attempt to put plants hardy only to Zone 6 (–10°F/–23°C) into the garden, there is a good chance you will lose them to frost damage.

There are several zone guidelines used in North America, and it can be confusing to know which one to follow. What is most important is to know the minimum low winter temperature in your garden, and then check that against the hardiness rating of plants before you purchase them. Landscape plants of all kinds have labels that list the degree of cold they can tolerate. Don't purchase plants that aren't evaluated for cold-hardiness.

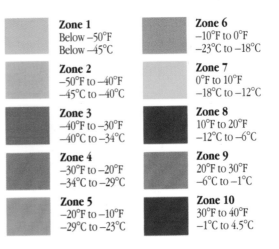

USDA AVERAGE MINIMUM WINTER TEMPERATURES

Zone 1
Below –50°F
Below –45°C

Zone 2
–50°F to –40°F
–45°C to –40°C

Zone 3
–40°F to –30°F
–40°C to –34°C

Zone 4
–30°F to –20°F
–34°C to –29°C

Zone 5
–20°F to –10°F
–29°C to –23°C

Zone 6
–10°F to 0°F
–23°C to –18°C

Zone 7
0°F to 10°F
–18°C to –12°C

Zone 8
10°F to 20°F
–12°C to –6°C

Zone 9
20°F to 30°F
–6°C to –1°C

Zone 10
30°F to 40°F
–1°C to 4.5°C

traveling with plants

A shopping spree at the garden center can lead to moments of panic in the parking lot. How can three cartloads of plants possibly fit into a compact car? It's not an easy puzzle to solve, but you can try. It's better to shop alone because people take up a lot of room in the car. Also, if you have bought tall plants it helps if the back seat can fold flat. Some nurseries supply plastic to protect car upholstery, but you should always have a small plastic tarp, large garbage bags, old bedsheets or blankets, a roll of jute twine and scissors in the trunk for these occasions.

Garden centers offer delivery with their truck but usually charge a substantial fee for the service. If staff is available, they'll even help load a few heavy containers into the trunk, but you should consider if you'll need help getting them out at home. And staff won't be able to cope with elaborate packing jobs when you've purchased a small forest. If you're going to attempt the transport yourself, begin with the largest and heaviest plants. Tie the jute twine around the branches of shrubs, lightly compressing their shape to prevent twig damage. Every place in the car is useful for packing plants except the driver's seat, so open the trunk and all the doors. Put shrubs in head first, with the heavy container ends closest to the trunk and door openings to make removal easier.

Try to line containers up so they'll support each other and prevent rolling. Bags of manure can be laid between or on top of heavy containers for bracing. Tall plants may have to be put into the trunk diagonally or straight across the back seat. It's all right if twiggy plant bodies overlap each other so long as their heavy bottoms are stationary. If the top twigs of a tall plant are reasonably pliable, it won't hurt if they're gently bent for the duration of the trip. Use gallon-size pots of perennial plants to fill in the gaps between larger containers to prevent rolling.

If plants must protrude slightly from windows or from the trunk, it's crucial that the exposed parts be wrapped or covered. High-speed wind will desiccate buds and shrivel leaves and evergreens quickly. Bring along old pillowcases and tie them over exposed parts. The back-seat footwells are good places for tall perennials with tender stems. If a passenger is riding in front he or she can manage a small shrub between the legs and hold a tray of annuals or small perennials. Tighten the caps of liquid fertilizers and put them, along with books and hand tools, under the front seats and you're ready to buckle up and hit the road. Don't mind the stares and take it easy on turns.

temporary storage

Getting the best selection means shopping early, so you may end up purchasing plants before the garden site is ready for installation. The plants can stay in their containers for a few weeks if you're conscientious about keeping them healthy. Staff in the garden center gave them daily attention, so you can pick up where they left off. It's important to keep plants in a shady location with protection from wind. Even in cool weather, direct sunlight can seriously stress plants and check growth. Black plastic containers can heat up quickly, cooking plant roots and disrupting delivery of water to stems and leaves. If there's any danger of frost at night, plants should be taken into an unheated garage, or if that's not possible, a blanket can be carefully arranged over them until morning. Large plants that are balled and burlapped will need to be heeled in with their root balls temporarily protected (see box).

The gardener's job is to make sure soil is moist and pots feel heavy each day. Perennials grown in peat-based soil mixes will dry out quickly and may be hard to re-wet. Watering them with hot tap water will reactivate the absorbing action. Large or small containers that are very dry can be stood in a bucket of hot water for an hour and will rapidly take up the warm drink.

Ground-cover plants are the least tolerant of temporary storage while waiting for a hole of their own. They want to make horizontal growth outward and their root systems begin to expand early in spring. They deteriorate more rapidly as roots press against the sides of containers and are frustrated in their growth process. If you must hold ground covers for more than two weeks, it might be a good idea to transplant them into larger pots or find a temporary place in the ground where they can wait.

HEELING IN

IF you need to hold the plant for a while before getting it in the ground, it will need to be heeled in somewhere. Dig a shallow depression in a shady spot and set the root ball in it, then cover the exposed portion with a purchased bag of shredded bark and keep it wet. If you've no area where this is possible, you can put the root ball and the shredded bark in a large plastic garbage bag and prop it up in a shady corner. Poke drainage holes in the bottom of the bag and keep the root ball damp but not dripping.

right: Plants won't grow significantly while still in containers, with the exception of twining vines. Clematis, honeysuckle and wisteria can shoot up overnight, making several inches (or centimeters) of growth each day. The tender stems will wave around in the breeze and eventually begin twining and climbing on themselves and each other, creating a mess that's impossible to unravel. You have two choices in this situation. Either snip off the current growth and be prepared to wait for new tendrils to generate after the vine goes into the ground, or arrange an impromptu trellis to keep them separate and undamaged. The easiest vine support is made by slipping two slender canes into the sides of each pot and weaving a length of pliable chicken wire between them. Once the plant is in the ground, install a permanent trellis.

Ten Best Perennials for April and May

It is the clumps of fresh green perennials that bring a landscape back to life in early to mid-spring. Soft herbaceous plants partnered with woody shrubs, at the foot of a hedge or within a foundation planting ideally should have a long period of bloom, strong stems that don't require staking and resistance to insects and diseases.

If possible, be generous with the numbers of spring perennials in your garden. Drifts and sheets of color are what revive the gardener's spirit after a long winter. Many spring perennials have low foliage that can continue to be attractive all summer, once blooms have faded. If the leaves of cranesbill geranium become tatty in mid-summer, they can be cut back to stimulate a new flush of foliage that will last until frost. The foliage of columbines and pinks also continues to be ornamental until the snow flies.

COLUMBINE *Aquilegia* many species H 10–36 in (25–90 cm) –40°F (–40°C) A delicate, woodland gem with spurred flowers on stiff stems and blue-green foliage in late spring to early summer. Available with single or double flowers, some bi-colored. Provide moist, organic soil in sun to part-shade.

BASKET-OF-GOLD *Aurinia saxatilis* H 12 in (30 cm) W 24 in (60 cm) –30°F (–34°C) This mounded plant, also known as yellow alyssum, is excellent for rock gardens, in a terraced garden or atop a stone wall where it can drop over the edge. Thrives in sandy soil in sun to part-shade.

CARDINAL FLOWER *Lobelia syphilitica* H 36 in (90 cm) –30°F (–34°C) Tall spikes of flowers, similar to snapdragons, in jewel tones of deep red, blue and purple. Provide moist soil in sun to part-shade.

VIRGINIA BLUEBELLS *Mertensia pulmonarioides* syn. *M. virginica* H 16 in (40 cm) –40°F (–40°C) Nodding clusters of sky-blue bells are charming planted with daffodils and species tulips, or naturalized in a woodland setting. Will spread slowly in moist, humus-rich soil. Part-sun to light shade.

CRANESBILL GERANIUM *many species* H 6–48 in (15–120 cm) −40°F (−40°C) Not the traditional patio plant, the many species are effective ground covers in circumstances from dry shade to full sun. Clumps of attractive foliage with flowers in white and many shades of pink, violet, blue and purple.

PINKS *Dianthus* many species H 6–18 in (15–45 cm) −40°F (−40°C) Tufts of grass-like, blue-green foliage with single or double flowers on erect stems. Scented flowers have notched or laced petals in colors including shades of pink, scarlet, white and purple, often with darker eyes. Well drained, sandy soil in sun.

LEOPARD'S BANE *Doronicum cordatum* H 12 in (30 cm) −30°F (−34°C) This plant produces early daisy-like blossoms of intense yellow tinged with orange on tall stems above heart-shaped, dark green leaves. Leopard's bane does well in part-shade to light shade, but avoid deep shade.

MOSS PHLOX *Phlox subulata* H 6 in (15 cm) −30°F (−34°C) Creeping mat-forming plants with star-shaped, single flowers in brilliant shades of pink, cerise, blue or white, many with contrasting eye. Good groundcover in a rock garden or will cascade over the edge of a retaining wall. Sun to part-shade.

GIANT SOLOMON'S SEAL *Polygonatum commutatum* H 48 in (120 cm) −30°F (−34°C) Tall, arching stems with attractive tiered leaves, strung with pendant white pockets. Beautiful in spring and a useful architectural plant all summer. Provide moist organic soil in part-shade.

PRIMROSE *Primula vulgaris* H 8 in (20 cm) −20°F (−29°C) Simple open-faced primroses and cowslips (*Primula veris*) are lovely with perennial hellebores (*Hellebore niger* and *Hellebore orientalis*), and small early bulbs like blue scilla (*Scilla*) and blue-and-white glory-of-the-snow (*Chionodoxa*). Provide light shade to part-sun.

Ten Best Perennials for June and July

More than half of all perennial plants bloom in June and July. This is a colorful time in the garden, and resilient long-blooming perennials are important assets.

The blooming period for perennials can be lengthened by an average of two weeks if spent flowers are removed just as they finish blooming. If browning flower heads are left on the plants, they soon begin producing seed and shut down flower production. Prompt deadheading frustrates their efforts to manufacture seed, resulting in more flushes of flower buds. Plants can be divided in late summer when flowering is over.

All perennials benefit from regular watering, but can withstand slightly dry locations. Tickseed, meadow rue and blanket flower tolerate hot and dry locations if irrigation is available. For moist, half-shade garden corners, dame's rocket and foxglove look after themselves nicely.

Yarrow *Achillea* many species H 18–48 in (45–120 cm) –40°F (–40°C) These tall, sun-loving plants have flat clusters of tiny flowers in pink, yellow, rust, red and white. Deadhead spent flowers regularly for a long season of bloom. They are excellent for cut flowers and the seed heads are ornamental in winter. Yarrow tolerates heavy soil and full sun.

Shasta Daisy *Chrysanthemum* x *superbum* H 12–24 in (30–60 cm) –20°F (–29°C) The classic white daisy with a yellow center disk. Many species and hybrids are available, and the most familiar is 'Alaska' with single 2-in (5 cm) daisies on 2-ft (0.6 m) stems. 'Aglaya' has frilly double flowers and 'Little Miss Muffet' has semi-double blossoms on shorter stems (14 in /35 cm). 'Majestic' has the largest flowers (6 in/15 cm).

Blanket Flower *Gaillardia* x *grandiflora* H 24–36 in (60–90 cm) –40°F (–40°C) Cheerful, deep orange-and-yellow or maroon-russet daisy-like flowers on a very vigorous plant that tolerates just about everything: drought, heat, cold, wind and poor soil. The rich colors of blanket flowers are useful to add a distinctive dark note to a perennial border, against which to accent other flowers in whites, blues, purples or pale yellow. Full sun.

Daylilies *Hemerocallis* x *hybrida* H 10–40 in (25–100 cm) –40°F (–40°C) An enormous range of daylilies is available in scarlet, apricot, yellow, peach and violet shades, many with scented or patterned petals and crimped "pie-crust" edges. 'Hyperion' is a pale yellow, perfumed blossom that should be in every collection. Flowers are broad or narrow, some rebloom and the leaves make dense sword-shaped clumps. Full sun to part-shade.

TICKSEED *Coreopsis* many species H 12–24 in (30–60 cm) –20°F (–29°C) Tickseed is the easiest flower to grow and also long-blooming. Its daisy-like flowers sit atop vigorous, wiry stems and are consistently bright yellow, except for the pink 'Rosea'. It will tolerate dry soil. Thread-leaf varieties (*C. verticillata*) have divided foliage and superior flowers—'Golden Showers' is brightest gold, 'Moonbeam' is palest yellow.

FRINGED BLEEDING HEART *Dicentra eximia* H 12–18 in (30–45 cm) –40°F (–40°C) A well-loved perennial with elegant pendants of heart-shaped pink blossoms dangling from long, arching stems above finely dissected blue-gray foliage. The fringed plant blooms from June to August, longer than its larger, spring-blooming cousin. Needs well-drained, moist humus-rich soil in part-sun to light shade.

FOXGLOVE *Digitalis* many species H 24–60 in (60–150 cm) –30°F (–34°C) Flaming, speckle-throated flowers in shades of pink, muted purple and white cluster along tall distinctive spikes above basal rosettes of simple, deep green foliage. Provide shelter from wind and moist humus-rich soil. Modestly self-seeding plants develop flowering side spikes and may be biennial or perennial, depending on garden conditions. Sun to part-shade.

DAME'S ROCKET *Hesperis matronalis* H 36 in (90 cm) –40°F (–40°C) This is one of my favorite perennials, an old-fashioned plant similar to summer phlox, with clusters of white or mauve night-scented flowers over a long blooming period. Plants may be short-lived but will self-seed. It is good for woodland and casual gardens in full sun to part-shade.

ORIENTAL POPPY *Papaver orientale* H 24–48 in (60–120 cm) –40°F (–40°C) Poppies are simply spectacular flowers with crinkled, papery petals on enormous 4-in (10-cm) flowers heads marked by rich black centers. They are available in several watercolor shades and the classic red, and they need cold winters to do best. Spent blooms should be quickly deadheaded to produce more flowers and postpone going to seed. Full sun.

MEADOW RUE *Thalictrum* many species H 24–60 in (60–150 cm) –20°F (–29°C) Another of my favorite old-fashioned perennials, meadow rue has elegant sprays of delicate flowers in cream, mauve and purple, nodding from tall slender stems amid finely divided blue-green foliage. Provide some shade or dappled light in hot regions. Full sun to part-shade.

TEN BEST PERENNIALS FOR AUGUST AND SEPTEMBER

The last weeks of summer and into early autumn are good opportunities to enjoy landscape perennials. As cooler temperatures and moisture return, the partnership between woody plants and herbaceous perennials is renewed, extending the flowering season as long as possible.

Obedient plant and black-eyed Susans will still be bright in the first weeks of September, and Michaelmas daisy and showy stonecrop are strong right up to the first hard frost.

When the leaves of perennials begin to turn brown, they are no longer producing energy for the plant and can be cut back to the ground, leaving just a 2-inch (5 cm) stubble. Oversize clumps can be divided now, or left for attention in early spring. Clumps of the latest blooming plants can be allowed to stand through winter to make attractive features in the snow.

MICHAELMAS DAISY *Aster novi-belgi* H 12–36 in (30–90 cm) –30°F (–34°C) Michaelmas produces daisy-like flowers in pink, violet, blue or purple sitting on strong branching stems. The mounding dwarf varieties are especially good for rock gardens. This daisy prefers cool moist conditions in full sun.

TURTLEHEAD *Chelone obliqua* H 24–36 in (60–90 cm) –40°F (–40°C) These clumping plants are useful in damp gardens. Their showy, deep pink, hooded blossoms appear in late summer. It is a native plant from the southeast United States and requires rich, moist soil in full sun to light shade.

SUMMER PHLOX *Phlox paniculata* mildew-resistant hybrids H 24–48 in (60–120 cm) –40°F (–40°C) Small fragrant flowers in clear colors of pink, red, lavender, cerise and white for sunny beds. Mulch and keep moist. Full sun.

OBEDIENT PLANT *Physostegia virginiana* H 36 in (90 cm) –40°F (–40°C) Also named "false dragonhead" for its resemblance to snapdragons, these are lovely in a border of tall mixed perennials. Taller plants may need staking. Full sun to light shade.

KAMCHATKA BUGBANE *Cimicifuga simplex* H 36–60 in (90–150 cm) –40°F (–40°C) A lovely plant with tiny, late-summer and fall-blooming white flowers on tall, graceful spikes for planting at the edge of a woodland garden or at the back of bed, in moist soil. Provide full sun to light shade.

PURPLE CONEFLOWER *Echinacea purpurea* H 24–48 in (60–120 cm) –40°F (–40°C) A bright plant with tall stems bearing pink-purple, daisy-like blooms with dark centers all summer long. Leave the last flush of flowers, as the seed heads are ornamental in winter and well appreciated by birds. Full sun to part-shade conditions.

ROSE-MALLOW *Hibiscus moscheutos* H 36–48 in (90–120 cm) –10°F (–23°C) The "cold-climate hibiscus" has huge flowers (12 in/30 cm) on a shrub, blooming all summer to frost. Cut back hard in late fall. Feed it regularly and provide shelter from wind. For full sun to part-shade.

BLACK-EYED SUSAN *Rudbeckia* many species H 24–60 in (60–150 cm) –30°F (–34°C) Another well-loved, daisy-like flower to light up a garden. Sunshine yellow blooms with dark centers are excellent for cutting. Provide moist, loamy soil in part-shade to full sun.

SHOWY STONECROP *Sedum spectabile* H 18–24 in (45–60 cm) –30°F (–34°C) Succulent, branching stems with gray-green leaves and long lasting late-summer blooms loved by butterflies. A good rock garden plant, stonecrop is drought-resistant and does well in full sun to part-shade.

TOAD LILY *Tricyrtis hirta* H 12–36 in (30–90 cm) –20°F (–29°C) Much more elegant than the name reveals, these are waxy, orchid-like flowers that perch atop slender branched stems from late summer into fall. They require moist, humus-rich and warm soil in partial to light shade.

Ten Best Summer Annuals

Take a look at the annuals section of a garden center, and you'll probably be very confused. There is such a large selection of plants, from old-fashioned favorites your grandmother grew to the latest hybrids, that you'll have a hard time making a selection.

The important issue with summer annuals is getting them into the right amount of light. Annuals are genetically programmed to excel in flower production, and almost any annual plant will produce an avalanche of flowers, providing it has found its place in the sun (or shade).

Sufficient water is an important factor with annual plants, which put out great numbers of flowers over a long season of 20 weeks. Petal tissues require more water than leaf tissues to remain turgid and in good condition.

Along with their requirement for regular and generous amounts of water, annuals also appreciate feeding with commercially prepared water-soluble fertilizer solutions to support their high energy requirements. Feeding with a 10-15-10 fertilizer every three weeks will keep them bursting with bloom all season.

BEGONIA *Begonia* (large tuberous and small fibrous) H 8–24 in (20–60 cm) The larger begonias grow from tubers and the smaller bedding begonias have fibrous roots. These bright flowers will bloom all summer and into autumn in consistently moist (but not wet) soil. Be sure to provide water in hot spells. Brings vivid color to part-sun and light shade conditions.

SPIDER FLOWER *Cleome hasslerana* H 60 in (150 cm) These distinctive plants have airy ball-shaped flowers in purple, rose, pink or white atop long arching 48-in (120 cm) stems. They are useful at the back of a border or between tall shrubs. Spider flowers will tolerate dry soil and they self-seed easily. For full sun to part-shade.

FLOWERING TOBACCO *Nicotiana alata* and *N. sylvestris* H 10–48 in (25–120 cm) Flared, long-necked flowers come in shades of red, pink, lime green and white on plants from 10–48 in (25–120 cm) tall. The species plant *N. affinis* (syn *N. alata grandiflorus*) is deeply and luxuriously scented at night. Provide consistent moisture in part-sun to light shade.

COLEUS *Solenostemon scutellarioides* syn *Coleus blumei* Flower spikes H 10–24 in (25–60 cm) A wide variety of colorful and intriguingly patterned foliage in many shades of red, purple, pink, yellow and black, with varieties being developed regularly. Pinch early in the summer to encourage branching. If you wish ornamental display beyond the valuable foliage, allow the flower spikes to develop. Part-sun to light shade.

BUSY LIZZIE, PATIENCE PLANT *Impatiens wallerana* H 12–24 in (30–60 cm) Mounding plants with brilliantly colored single or double flowers that bloom from late spring until the first frost. Impatiens plants require humus-rich soil and consistent moisture. They should not be allowed to dry out in hot weather. Valuable for part-sun to light shade.

TREE MALLOW, ANNUAL MALLOW *Lavatera trimestris* H 36–48 in (90–120 cm) Large, rose-pink, cerise or white blooms are perched atop substantial mounding plants from midsummer until frost. Do not leave to set seed—deadhead regularly to keep plants productive. Requires full sun.

SWEET ALLYSUM *Lobularia maritima* H 8 in (20 cm) Masses of tiny, honey-scented flowers clustered on stems that form mats of bloom from late spring to frost. Alyssum is useful and colorful in a rock garden, as an edging plant in a border and in planters. It prefers full sun to light shade. Cut back hard if plants become leggy.

NASTURTIUM *Tropaeolum majus* H 12–24 in (30–60 cm) These mounding plants have unique rounded foliage and intensely bright flowers in near-neon shades of orange, red, pink and yellow, some with contrasting blotch marks. Nasturtium's leaves have a peppery taste and are used in salads and sandwiches. Suitable for cutting; they require full to part-sun.

SCARLET SAGE *Salvia splendens* H 12–36 in (30–90 cm) Sturdy upright plants with central and side flower spikes in shades of purple, red and white, with other colors increasingly available. Deadhead spent blooms frequently and promptly so plants keep producing flower spikes. This is a true heat-loving plant that requires full sun. However, the cultivars in pastel colors, such as 'Sizzler Series', require some shelter from full sun.

ZINNIA *Zinnia angustifolia*, *Z. elegans* and *Z. haageana* H 12–60 in (30–150 cm) A variety of single, double and cactus-flowered plants with many branching side stems and blossoms in every color except blue. As with all annuals, remove the spent flowers to keep buds coming. Zinnias are heat-loving plants that are ideal for locations in bright sun.

garden tools

Good tools take the strain off muscles and accomplish the job quickly and efficiently. What's important is that the tool be the right size for the job, and that it be kept in good condition. Attempting to cut a 2-inch (5 cm) woody branch with hand secateurs (pruners) will likely hurt your hand, break the pruning blade and cause unnecessary damage to the plant. Using a large lopper or pruning saw will remove the branch in moments, with no stress to the gardener.

Expensive stainless steel shovels look nice hanging from a peg in the garage, but they can't be sharpened and that seriously limits their long-term usability. The best buys in digging tools are moderately priced and available at hardware stores and garden centers. Shovels and spades should be fabricated from metals that can be sharpened with a flint stone. Cutting tools like pruners with replaceable blades, loppers and pruning saws are worth spending serious money for. With thoughtful care your tools will perform for many years, although if you use them incorrectly, and that includes using them for a job other than the one they were designed to do, you will certainly (and quickly) ruin them. If you attempt to cut a large branch with small pruning shears rather than a large lopper, the blades will be unable to accommodate the girth of the branch and they may even become stuck or wedged in. Our first reaction is to press sideways in an attempt to loosen the shears, but blades and saws are designed for straight-line, forward and backward motions only— sideways movements will surely ruin them. The rule is always to use the right tool for the job at hand.

CARING FOR YOUR TOOLS

DON'T leave tools outside overnight where they may be soaked by rain or dew. Use a wire brush to remove clinging soil and store them in a dry place. Clean them thoroughly at the end of the gardening season, rubbing small spots of rust with sand, and brush the blades lightly with mineral oil to protect the metal surface.

left: A long-handled rake gives you better reach and control of the soil. Use a long-handled shovel to dig a deep hole; it will carry the weight for your back and prevent fatigue.

THE TEN MOST NECESSARY TOOLS

Extraordinary strength isn't required for garden chores, if you've got the right tool. Tools do the work for us, providing we select the right tool for the right job. Digging a shallow hole for a large perennial clump is quick and easy using a sharp blunt-nosed spade. But the same work is more difficult with a larger shovel, which would be difficult to maneuver in a small space. Excavating a larger and deeper hole for a heavy shrub requires a long-handled shovel to carry the weight of soil and shift stress away from your back. Digging the same hole with a small spade would put the burden of lift and weight onto your own muscles. Using tools in scale with the work to be accomplished also applies to small hand tools. Always select pruners, trowels and saws that fit your hand comfortably. The best tool for the job is the one that fits your hand, not the largest one available.

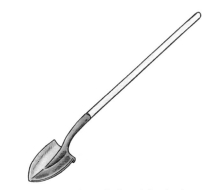

1. Long-handled shovel for digging heavy soil.

2. Blunt-nosed spade for edging beds, planting shrubs and dividing large perennials.

3. Garden forks for mixing, aerating and turning soil.

4. Stiff rake for spreading soil and organic materials and grading beds and lawns.

5. Soft rake for gathering leaves.

6. Wide-blade trowels for planting small perennials and annuals.

7. Narrow-blade trowel for planting bulbs and removing weeds.

8. Folding pruning saw for removing heavy rose canes and thick shrub branches.

9. Bypass pruners (also called secateurs) for trimming shrubs and roses.

10. Wheelbarrow for moving soil, rocks and plants, and mixing organic amendments.

How to Plant Perennials

More than Just a Hole in the Ground with Some Dirt

Making a good hole is the best form of life insurance for your plants. A plant hole is structured to encourage rapid and strong root development that is crucial to winter hardiness. Plants with well-developed root systems are able to manufacture generous amounts of carbohydrate energy used to build the fibers that protect them from deep frost. When root development is slow and limited, plants may suffer extensive twig dieback in winter. If you've made a good hole for your plant, you can be reasonably certain it will be healthy and intact through the winter months.

The ideal planting soil is a mixture of what's taken from the hole combined with organic amendments and coarse sand. If your soil is already sandy, you'll only need to add generous amounts of organic ingredients. Remove the soil from the hole and put half of it in a bucket and spread the remaining half over another part of the planting area. In the bucket, mix in similar amounts of organic material and coarse sand to equal the original volume. You can also mix in ½ cup (125 ml) of bone meal to encourage root growth. The organic amendments will supply nutrients to the plants, and the coarse sand will break up clay and bring oxygen into the hole.

1. The day a plant goes into the ground is the most important for its future growth. How you dig the hole and what you put into it could make or break this plant. If you've purchased plants suitable to your hardiness zone and available light conditions, and if you have amended the soil as needed, you're ready to start constructing a hole.

Small pots of perennial plants are sold in divisions made by dividing larger clumps into many smaller pieces. Plants sold in 4- or 6-inch (10 or 15 cm) pots will grow into big clumps within three seasons. You'll get quicker performance and more flowers by digging the hole twice as deep and three times as wide as the plant's root ball. A perennial in a 4-inch (10 cm) pot should have a hole dug 8 inches (20 cm) deep and 12 inches (30 cm) wide. Larger pots of purchased perennials can be planted in holes using the same ratio of twice the depth and three times the width.

2. Trim off any broken stems and decaying leaves. Remove the plant from its pot by turning it upside down and gently pressing on the bottom and sides until it slides out. Don't pull on leaves or the central stem if the plant resists movement; if necessary, you can soak the entire pot in warm water to loosen the root ball. Gently tease the roots apart.

3. Put enough of the amended soil mix in the hole to bring the new plant up to ground level, set the plant in the hole and fill in around it with the soil mix. Gently firm the plant down, but don't compact and press oxygen out of the soil surrounding the root ball.

4. Cover the root area with a mulch and provide a generous drink of water to settle the plant. Wet the soil throughout the hole. A transplant fertilizer can be mixed into the drink to promote quick root growth. If the plant has wilted visibly, provide temporary shade for a day or two by putting a box or garden chair nearby to block direct sunlight.

How to Plant a Shrub

Shrubs can be weighty and are best moved in a wheelbarrow or garden cart. If you've pushed, kicked and dragged it across the lawn, there's no point bothering to plant what's left of the poor thing. Grasping the shrub around the trunk to lift and carry it can sometimes result in a torn root system. So if you can't move a heavy shrub in something with wheels, consider laying it on a tarp or old blanket so that two people can carry it sling-fashion between them. Getting to the hole safely is half the job.

Before planting a shrub, trim off any broken twigs and determine which side is the front of the shrub. The front will have a fuller growth of branches fanning outward, and the back will be flatter. If the plant has had strong light from all directions during its growth, you may have difficulty determining the true front, but one side may have better branch structure.

1. The hole for a shrub is similar to the hole for a perennial plant: it should be dug twice as deep as the root ball and three times as wide. Half the soil is retained and amended with organic materials and coarse sand to bring the volume back to the original amount, and the remaining portion of soil from the hole is spread elsewhere in the garden. Two cups (500 ml) of bone meal can be added to promote root growth. Shrubs planted in holes without added soil amendments will certainly live, but growth is usually slow and frustrating because of the diminished amounts of oxygen and nutrients in the hole.

2. Lay the shrub on its side and firmly hold the trunk where it meets the top of the root ball while gently pulling the container away. If nothing budges, press gently on all sides of the container to loosen the root ball and try again. If the plant has been in the container for too long a time, it may not be easily removed. The best thing is to use a heavy pair of garden clippers to cut the container off. If the container is made of degradable fiberboard, it must still be completely removed. Healthy soil doesn't contain enough moisture to effectively decompose such thick fiber, and if portions of the container inhibit root growth underground, the plant will quickly decline.

3. Fill the hole with enough soil mix to bring the shrub up to ground level, set the root ball in the hole and fill in with remaining soil. Using your hands, not your feet, firm the plant in and then give it a deep drink of water. This is a crucial step in guaranteeing healthy growth for the plant. If the soil is compacted too firmly (as would happen if you used your feet), fine pore spaces in the soil will collapse and drive out oxygen. The plant will be deprived of oxygen in the root zone and growth will never assume normal vigor. It's always better to have a looser fit in the hole, rather than compacting the soil too firmly around the root ball.

You can add transplant fertilizer to the water for a quick growth start even if you've already mixed bone meal into the soil. Woody shrubs don't require frequent or excessive fertilizer feeding. If grass surrounds the shrub, lawn fertilizer applied to the turf once or twice a year will be sufficient for the grass and the shrub. Or a thick mulch of homemade garden compost or aged manure applied over the roots in spring will provide all the nourishment required to keep shrubs healthy and vigorous. In autumn, allow a generous layer of leaves to remain under and around the shrub. Leaves are the most natural form of plant food, and will also encourage earthworms to fertilize the soil with their castings.

How to Plant a Tree

How to Stake a Tree

INCORRECT staking deforms, mutilates and kills more trees than insects, disease and lightning do. Although tree trunks seem to be thick and unwieldy, they will struggle desperately to get away from a too-close stake. Tying a tree directly to a stake causes cells on the dark side of the trunk to lengthen as the tree bends into a bow shape to escape the shadow of the stake. Once this curvature develops, there is no setting it straight again, and structural problems follow as growth proceeds on the unbalanced structure. If the stake remains in place, bark will eventually grow over the bindings, drawing them into the interior of the wood, where vital circulatory avenues will be severed. Problems compound as wood dies and rotting diseases set in.

Trees over 8 feet (2.4 m) high need two stakes, placed on opposite sides of the trunk. The pointed end of the stake should be driven into the soil outside of the root ball. Heavy wire is tightened around the stake and an 8-inch (20 cm) length of rubber hose is slipped onto the wire and gently looped around the tree trunk. The hose section protects the bark from damage and the wire is fastened back at the stake. Repeat the process with the stake on the opposite side. The purpose of the stakes isn't to hold the tree up, but rather to prevent wind from rocking the root ball and tearing new roots. The pressure on the wires should be gently firm, but not tight. Check every month to be sure the pressure continues to be correct, and remove the stakes after one to two years.

Woody plants that grow higher than 15 feet (4.5m) are considered to be trees, no matter if they have a single standard trunk or are multi-trunked and shrub-formed. The height of these plants requires a broad root structure to keep them stable in the soil; despite popular mythology, trees seldom have deep taproots. Instead, they develop saucer-shaped root balls as they mature. Very large trees will have most of their roots distributed in the top 36 inches (90 cm) of soil, where moisture and nutrients are available. If you've ever seen large trees "lifted" out of the soil by violent windstorms, you may have been surprised to see this saucer formation of the roots.

1. Soil preparation for tree planting is a bit different. The hole should be just deep enough to equal the height of the root ball, and about twice as wide. Use a stiff tape measure to get the depth and width dimensions of the root ball. Trees require good drainage under their roots, so cover the bottom of the hole with 2 inches (5 cm) of coarse sand and use a garden fork to dig it in. Tamp the soil down with the back of a shovel, but don't tread on it with your feet. The addition of sand will raise the bottom of the hole slightly and help to drain water that might accumulate in the hole. Put half the excavated soil in a wheelbarrow or on a tarp and amend it with organic materials and more coarse sand, and spread the other half of the original soil elsewhere in the garden.

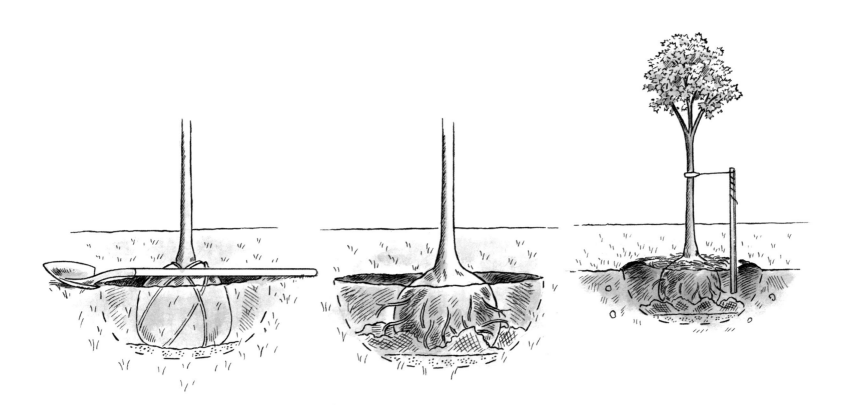

2. If the tree is in a container, lay it on its side, grasp the trunk where it meets the soil and pull the container off. Press lightly on the container to help release it, or cut it off if necessary and lift the tree into the hole. If the tree is large enough to have burlap wrap and also a wire basket, these coverings stay on and go into the hole. Unlike other woody plants, trees need to sit high in the saddle. The tree should be elevated approximately 1–2 inches (2.5–5 cm) above the grade of the soil; the sand dug into the bottom of the hole will help raise it up.

3. Once the tree is centered in the hole, bend the wire basket back and away from the top of the root ball, and untie the burlap. Pull the burlap away from the top of the root ball and use scissors to cut off as much as possible without exerting pressure or pulling. The bent-back basket and remaining burlap will be buried. The basket continues to hold the root ball securely and protect it from shattering before roots have taken hold in the new soil. The burlap that remains in the hole will decompose. Make sure the tree you purchase is wrapped in genuine burlap; synthetic burlap has a shiny green appearance and won't degrade underground. If left in the hole, synthetic burlap may prevent roots from extending.

4. Fill in the rest of the hole with amended soil, covering the sides and top edges of the root ball, but leave the top section of the root ball closest to the trunk exposed. Firm the soil with the back of a shovel and use your hands to form the extra soil into a saucer-shaped rim all around the hole to collect rain and irrigation water. Water the hole deeply, adding a transplant fertilizer if you wish. Trees planted in this manner will require staking for their first year (see box, opposite) until stabilizing roots have grown into the soil. Adding a 2-inch (5 cm) mulch of shredded bark over the root ball will conserve moisture and prevent sun and wind from dehydrating the root ball.

planting for difficult situations

Every gardener wants the best growing conditions possible, but all too often circumstances fall short of ideal. Although poor soil can be amended to improve texture and fertility, environmental factors are hard to control. Intense light and heat, wind exposure in summer and winter, deep shade and soil that is chronically dry or permanently saturated are some of the most difficult conditions for plants.

Too Bright, Hot and Dry

Southwestern gardens are some of the most successful at adapting to bright, hot and dry conditions. Plants that evolve in

Stone is a material found naturally in hot, dry sites. Use it as mulch and for architectural interest.

that climate have developed their own methods of conserving moisture and preserving leaf tissues. But similar weather extremes can occur in other climates and stress plants to the point of extinction. Gardens with full exposure to sunlight and dry soil are the most challenging for plants, and in summer months heroic rescue measures are frequently required. Ultraviolet rays can exhaust plant tissues and send leaves into full wilt by midday, when the sun is directly overhead. Water pressure in plant tissues keeps leaves and stems turgid, a term describing the normal erect posture of plant parts. But even with adequate moisture in the soil, internal hydraulic systems can't pump water fast enough into the slumping upper portions of the plant. Although stems and leaves may return to their normal rigid posture when the sun passes away, repeated wilts diminish plant performance.

The first defense against extreme heat and sun exposure is an organic soil. Amending the soil with organic materials like compost, aged manure, peat moss and shredded leaves will ensure water is held in the root zone and available when plants need it. It's important to prevent soil moisture from evaporating. Shredded bark mulch 2–3 inches (5–7.5 cm) thick covering exposed soil around plants will preserve the water

underground. Soil exposed to intense sunlight can heat up enough to cook plant roots, and thick mulch also helps to lower temperature in the root zone.

Selecting plants with drought-hardy characteristics is a smart approach to planting in hot places. Foliage covered with fine hairs that shade the leaf surface, such as perennial cornflower (*Centaurea montana*), are usually prepared to make a good show in a hot site. Plants with deep taproots, like musk mallow (*Malva moschata*), can rely on water stored deeper underground, away from the sunlight. Gray-leafed plants, like Russian sage (*Perovskia atriplicifolia*), evolved in arid regions and want a bright, hot and dry site. Grouping plant clumps in clusters allows them to provide a little shade to the others, and also forms a slight microclimate of cooler air inside the cluster. Consider making some shade with the addition of a shrub or small tree on the southwest side of the planting. Even a large rock will provide some relief from sun if plants are gathered on the east and north sides.

Of course, a regular irrigation program will make a great difference to the well-being of plants in hot and dry conditions. Even cast-iron plants with drought-hardy characteristics will give much better performance with regular watering. They may be able to survive on rainwater alone, but if you want them to have an attractive appearance, supplemental watering is key. A brief watering that wets just the top 1–2 inches (3–6 cm) of soil is inadequate and will mostly be lost to evaporation. Provide water in early morning or early evening when the sun is down. It's important to water long and slowly, allowing moisture to seep deeply into the root zone. A weeper hose is the best way to ensure water goes where it's needed. Put it down for the season, turning it on for several hours in the evening or early part of the day.

TOO MUCH WIND

Although we think of wind as a relief on a hot day, it's dangerously stressful to plants in a permanently windy location. Wind passing across plant foliage causes as much moisture evaporation as hot sun, and can permanently desiccate plant tissues in the course of an afternoon. While wind may be unstoppable, it's possible to affect the pattern of air currents with simple windbreaks.

Windbreaks work by breaking up a current of air, not by stopping it. When wind hits a trellis panel or a woody shrub, the mass of air is shattered into several smaller and weaker currents. Pergolas, trellis panels and deck railings all provide some wind screening to plants. Windbreaks don't need to be

Use structures and woody shrubs to filter wind and protect flowering plants.

large, and actually function better when smaller in stature. Flowering shrubs with woody stems provide good windbreaks for herbaceous perennial plants. Tough landscape roses, low junipers and mugo pines are excellent wind moderators and stand up well to the constant battering. Tall and slender trees like pyramidal oaks (*Quercus robur* 'Fastigiata', Zone 5) will also break the force of wind without taking up much valuable gardening space. Serbian spruce (*Picea omorika*, Zone 5) is a tall and slender coniferous tree that makes a good all-season windbreak on an exposed corner.

TOO MUCH SHADE

In a shady garden you'll need to make the most of what light you have. If large trees cause the shade, call in an arborist to have them high-pruned, removing the lowest limbs and having the crowns thinned and opened. You may be surprised at how much light is increased by adjusting the trees. But don't do it yourself. Any tree-climbing above 10 feet (3 m) is work for a professional with the best equipment and safety precautions. If shade is caused by a neighboring structure, that's a more permanent problem. Painting fences and trellises a light color of gray or taupe (but not white, which is too bright) will help to reflect available light onto plants. It's also possible to use outdoor mirrors (framed with trellis and climbing vines to disguise the edges) mounted on fences or walls to significantly increase reflected light.

You can have a lovely garden in shade—the right plants and healthy soil are a good start.

Plants in a shady site are already struggling with low light, and poor soil conditions will create a double deprivation. Amending the soil generously with organic materials like compost, aged manure, peat moss and leaves will ensure that moisture is available in the root zone. If the massive roots of mature trees take all available water, creating dry shade conditions, it may be useful to make mounded or raised beds to elevate shrubs and perennial plants.

A shady garden imposes limits on what can be grown, eliminating the big bloomers like roses, peonies and lilacs. In the biological processes of plants, low light means low energy, and shady conditions result in fewer flowers and fruits. Plants make energy by combining ultraviolet light and basic nutrients they take from the soil. Fortunately, some plants can adapt to the diminished light and provide generous blossoms and ornamental foliage. Select shade-tolerant plants and buy slightly more than you think are necessary. Plants in shade tend to grow more tall and slender as they reach for light, and you will need more to fill the space. Try to include plants with variegated green-and-white foliage that will reflect light and brighten the scene.

TOO WET

Of all the difficult planting conditions, excessive water in the soil is by far the worst. When water is trapped in soil it locks air and oxygen out of the root zone, stunting growth and eventually asphyxiating plants. Normally water

Soil drainage is the important issue in this wet garden, where weeping plants emphasize the lush setting.

drains out of soil through a system of pores and spaces and is replaced with air. Whether in bright or shady light, the difficulties of water-saturated soil will be similar, and so will the solutions.

If the soil is dense clay it's possible to improve the soil texture and, by digging in coarse builder's sand and even ¼-inch (1cm) gravel, to break up the clay and allow water to drain through. Digging in organic materials will also help establish spaces in the soil for the exchange of moisture and air. Select plants that tolerate wet soil, such as red chokeberry (*Aronia arbutifolia*, Zone 5), summersweet (*Clethra alnifolia*, Zone 4), silverleaf dogwood (*Cornus alba*, Zone 2) and American elder (*Sambucus canadensis*, Zone 3).

But if the soil is deeply saturated it will be necessary to install a system of drainage tiles and perhaps a drainage pit. If you prefer to avoid solutions involving construction and digging, it's possible to establish plantings using raised mounds and beds. The idea of making a wet garden with bog plants is unlikely to be successful. Bog plants require a slow but reliable exchange of moving water and oxygen through the soil, and most wet sites don't have those special conditions.

opposite: A red border in autumn always catches attention. Here, several shades of red work together to intensify the effect. Woody shrubs, tall sedum and ornamental grasses are good choices for a dry area. Provide water regularly to extend the red display until hard frost.

Ten Best Drought-Resistant Shrubs

Shrubs are endlessly useful and particularly so in dry soils where it's hard to fill space. Just remember that "drought-resistant" does not mean that they don't need water.

New plants require weekly deep watering in the first two growing seasons to establish roots. After that, drought-resistant shrubs will become increasingly self-reliant and find their way to groundwater.

You can simplify the watering process by using a soaker hose on the ground to provide water consistently. Flowering shrubs that don't receive enough water will drop their flower buds for next year.

Fiveleaf Aralia *Acanthopanax sieboldianus* H 6–8 ft (1.8–2.4 m) −30°F (−34°C) Glossy, deeply cut leaves with prickles along the stems and canes make this a good privacy hedge or barrier plant. A useful plant, fiveleaf aralia will grow in shade and dry soil and withstands urban pollution and windy locations.

Siberian Pea-shrub *Caragana arborescens* H 12 ft (3.6 m) −50°F (−46°C) Pea-shrubs can take a lot of drought and survive well on the dry western prairies, and that they thrive in windy locations makes them a good screen or windbreak. Caragana's yellow sweet pea-like flowers appear in June, becoming ornamental pods in August. Pea-shrubs are also available as attractive weeping standards with finely cut leaves.

Vernal Witch Hazel *Hamamelis vernalis* H 8 ft (2.4 m) −30°F (−34°C) This witch hazel has interesting rounded green leaves that turn golden in autumn and thread-like, scented yellow-to-red flowers in earliest spring. Virginian witch hazel (*Hamamelis virginiana*) reaches 12–15 ft (3.6–4.5 m) and blooms in autumn. The several fancy hybrids, such as 'Arnold's Promise' and 'Diane', are not as drought-hardy.

'Tabletop' Juniper *Juniperus scopulorum* H 5 ft (1.5 m) W 6 ft (1.8 m) −30°F (−34°C) Junipers are drought-hardy plants and 'Tabletop' is a good one for filling sunny corners or standing next to a gate. It has a versatile flat-top form with silvery-blue foliage. Two smaller and equally useful junipers are blue-green *Juniperus sabina* 'Blue Danube' and dark green, vase-shaped Hick's juniper (*J. sabina* 'Hicksii').

SMOKE BUSH *Cotinus coggygria* H 16 ft (4.8 m) −20°F (−29°C) A small tree at full height, this can be kept to about 8 ft (2.4 m) if pruned annually. The matte blue-green leaves have a distinctive round shape and the inflorescence is an airy blush-pink cluster. The more dramatic 'Nordine' has purple-red leaves, ruby-red flowers and yellow-orange autumn color. 'Royal Purple' has dark maroon leaves and pinkish-purple blossoms.

PEKING COTONEASTER *Cotoneaster acutifolius* H 8 ft (2.4 m) −50°F (−46°C) For a sunny roadside hedge, you simply can't beat Peking cotoneaster. Its canes are long, slender and spreading and have small dark green leaves that turn flaming orange-red in autumn. The mass of branches and small black berries are attractive features for birds, but the hedge can also be sheared or trimmed into a formal shape.

WINGED BURNING BUSH, **SPINDLE TREE** *Euonymus alatus* H 10 ft (3 m) −40°F (−40°C) Sometimes referred to as "two-car-garage burning bush", this large shrub can quickly reach its potential height and width. It has intriguing winged ridges along its mature wood and, when grown in full sun, the foliage turns deepest scarlet in autumn. Smaller 'Compactus' is just right for smaller gardens, and either size is a good hedge or accent plant.

'ARNOLD RED' HONEYSUCKLE *Lonicera tatarica* H 6 ft (1.8 m) −40°F (−40°C) Honeysuckles will grow in sun or light shade and tolerate dry soil. This one blooms more profusely than other honeysuckles, with dark red flowers in spring followed by bright red berries in summer. Its open, arching branches create a good scaffold for clematis to wander through. A good plant to cover an unattractive wire fence.

'DART'S GOLD' NINEBARK *Physocarpus opulifolius* HW 4 ft (1.2 m) −50°F (−46°C) Ninebarks offer a good selection in foliage color and excellent drought resistance in a sunny location. This one is a dwarf plant suitable for the garden, with rounded yellow foliage and white flowers followed by red berries. 'Diablo' is taller, with upright form and dark purple leaves. Both are good for a foundation bed or small informal hedge.

MUGO PINE *Pinus mugo* var. *pumillo* H 36 in (90 cm) −50°F (−46°C) Mugo pine provides strong coniferous form and deep green color year-round. Its low mound shape is useful in group plantings on dry corners or individually in a bed or border, but get the dwarf variety that will stay low. The tall form of mugo pine wants to be a small tree. If you buy the tall one by mistake, let it reach the height you want, then each summer cut back the new growth tips, or "candles", to keep it down.

Ten Best Ornamental Shrubs for Shade

It's not always easy gardening in shady places, but there are some ornamental shrubs that are tolerant of low light and will fill up dark corners if they are given optimum growing conditions. These hardy shrubs are capable of making leaves and blossoms without direct sunlight if they are watered consistently and are growing in fertile soil. Spreading organic mulch, such as shredded bark or leaves, over and around their roots will help to conserve moisture.

Plant growth is always slower in shade, and shaded woody shrubs are inclined to be more vertical as they reach for light. A grouping of three to five shrubs will fill a space more rapidly. In shade conditions, shrubs will put out more leaves in the upper third of the plant, leaving the lower portions more bare. Underplanting with low ground-cover plants, like sweet woodruff and pachysandra, will help to fill in space at ground level.

FIVELEAF ARALIA *Acanthopanax sieboldianus* HW 8 ft (2.4 m) −30°F (−34°C) This has attractive, medium-green leaves but no appreciable flower, and it will grow and spread out its arching branches in full shade. It is a fast-growing plant for dark corners or to fill space alongside a garage. With thorny twigs, it is a good screen or "security" plant. It grows in a variety of soil conditions and is quite resistant to city pollution. The variegated form is quite handsome.

BOTTLEBRUSH BUCKEYE *Aesculus parviflora* H 10 ft (3 m) W 10 ft (3 m) −40°F (−40°C) This shrub, a member of the chestnut family, can become big in sun. In light shade its size is more moderate. It has an open, architectural form with splendid cream-colored blossoms showing in June, though they do not appear reliably in shade. This is a good understory woodland plant or for a shrub border. It suckers in moist soil—an asset if you want to fill space. Lovely paired with sweet woodruff.

WINTER HONEYSUCKLE *Lonicera fragrantissima* H 6 ft (1.8 m) W 10 ft (3 m) −20°F (−29°C) Most honeysuckles grow well and blossom in full shade, as does this highly scented gem. Small, lemon-scented flowers show in great numbers for several weeks on a large, spreading shrub with dull blue-green foliage. It tolerates sand, clay and alkaline soils. Massed on the dark side of a fence or wall, it will perfume the entire garden in March and April.

SWEET MOCK ORANGE *Philadelphus coronarius* H 10 ft (3 m) W 8 ft (2.4 m) −30°F (−34°C) This large, old-fashioned shrub with fountain form and cascading branches grows in light shade. White-petaled flowers and golden stamens produce clouds of citrus scent for two weeks in June. Smaller, golden-leafed 'Aureus' fades to medium green in summer. Very useful in dark spaces among large trees, and adaptable to dry and alkaline soils. None of the other hybrid cultivars do as well in low light.

OAKLEAF HYDRANGEA *Hydrangea quercifolia* H 6 ft (1.8 m) W 8 ft (2.4 m) −20°F (−29°C) Very ornamental with lobed leaves, exfoliating brown bark and large panicles of white flowers that fade to pale green. In full sun, the leaves turn rich burgundy in autumn. Hydrangeas look best in groups set out with trunks 4 ft (1.2 m) apart. Moist, fertile woodland soil. Lovely on a slight slope in light shade, with violets and early crocus.

HYBRID HOLLY, BLUE HOLLY *Ilex* x *meserveae* H 15 ft (4.5 m) W 10 ft (3 m) −20°F (−29°C) Classic holly is a broadleaf evergreen shrub that thrives in light shade and moist soil, with ornamental features year-round. Bright red berries lasting for several months complement the lustrous blue-green foliage; place the plant where it can be seen in winter. Both male and female plants are needed to produce berries. One male plant can pollinate six female plants up to 25 ft (7.5 m) away.

DOUBLE JAPANESE KERRIA *Kerria japonica* 'Pleniflora' H 6 ft (1.8 m) W 8 ft (2.4 m) −20°F (29°C) Hardy kerria grows in light shade and tolerates dry soil, and with ample moisture it will sucker readily. The thin apple-green canes have a distinctive posture, arching gracefully forward, and are laden in June with fully double golden flowers. Kerria is useful to fill a corner or cover a vacant space on the dark side of a shrub or coniferous tree.

LILY-OF-THE-VALLEY BUSH *Pieris japonica* H 4–8 ft (1.2–2.4 m) −20°F (−29°C) A beautiful broadleaf evergreen shrub well deserving of prominent placement. Glossy dark green leaves remain smooth and uncurled in the coldest winter temperature. In spring, long cascades of fragrant, urn-shaped white flowers are followed by new foliage in light green, bronze or rich claret. Requires light shade and moist soil rich with organic materials such as compost, peat moss and rotted manure.

BLACK JETBEAD *Rhodotypos scandens* H 3–6 ft (0.9–1.8 m) −30°F (−34°C) This softly mounding shrub has distinctively veined foliage and many four-petaled white flowers in spring, followed by shiny black berries that persist through winter. Its informal style is best in a large plant grouping or shrub border, but it's attractive, so keep it visible. Tolerates poor soil and city conditions; once established, it takes a lot of environmental abuse. Full shade.

WAYFARING TREE *Viburnum lantana* H 15 ft (4.5 m) W 10 ft (3 m) −30°F (−34°C) A stylish shrub for a lightly shaded garden. Ornamental berries follow creamy blossoms. Its distinctive, veined, leathery leaves can be semi-evergreen in milder regions. Smaller, less cold-hardy (−10°F/−23°C) *V. plicatum* var. *tomentosum* 'Summer Snowflake' produces pure white flowers in light shade; *V.* x *carlcephalum* (−10°F/−23°C) and *V. carlessi* (−30°F/−34°C) produce deeply scented blossoms in part-sun.

planting for seasonal interest

Every season has its interesting images that are composed of plants, natural elements of the earth such as stone, wood and water, and perhaps architectural features like arbors, pergolas, sundials, statuary and all manner of ornaments. Of course, beauty is in the eye of the beholder, and there's no shortage of material to work with as one season rolls into the next. But organizing events to unfold sequentially, with one group of plants finishing their display as another comes into bloom, can be a challenge.

The easiest approach is to divide the year into the four basic seasons—spring, summer, autumn, winter—and make a list for each season of plants already in the garden and when they bloom or display ornamental features. Right away you should be able to see when you have lots of display, and perhaps one or two seasons that are without interest. Most gardens are loaded with blossoming plants in spring and early summer, when more than half of flowering perennials, shrubs and trees bloom. Planning for the later seasons may require some reading and visits to local garden centers to learn about plants with colorful foliage in autumn, and fruits and ornamental bark in winter.

Dividing the year into more and shorter time periods—early and late spring, early and late summer, early and late autumn, and winter—can make a more complex plan. Planning for these seven time periods will require more careful record keeping, using a diary or calendar to record when flowering plants bloom. A good method is to keep a weekly record of what's blooming in the garden or offering ornamental display. You'll soon see the blank spaces where more seasonal display is required and can begin researching a shopping list. With careful observation of the garden and good note taking, you should be able to develop a successful sequence of seasonal display in one or two gardening years.

A plan for seasonal interest can be made for an entire garden or just one section. Areas that you see most frequently, like a bed near the front door, are good places to start planning for four seasons of ornamental display. Consider including a tree with beautiful winter bark, such as the paperbark maple (*Acer griseum*, Zone 6), which has shiny cinnamon-brown bark and brilliant red autumn foliage; a small spring-flowering shrub like slender deutzia, with frilly white blossoms; and then a selection of spring bulbs and early perennials like violets, primulas and bleeding hearts. Early summer might include columbines, peonies and roses, followed by shasta daisies, campanulas and purple coneflowers. A hydrangea could bridge early to late summer, accompanied by tall phlox, rudbeckias (black-eyed Susans) and helianthus (perennial sunflowers). Rose of Sharon is another bridging shrub for late summer to early autumn. Flowering display continues in autumn with Japanese anemones, tall sedums and Michaelmas daisies. If you allow the purple coneflowers and sedums to stand into winter, you'll have the benefit of their forms in snow.

opposite: Though deep in snow, a garden is more than a memory when delicate crab apples create such a fetching winter picture. Hydrangea blossoms left on twigs create beautiful floral ornaments, and the bench is a seat for all seasons.

TEN BEST EARLY-FLOWERING SPRING SHRUBS

Flowering shrubs of every kind are useful and pleasurable woody plants, but the most gratifying are those that bloom very early, at the end of winter when gardeners begin to think there is no hope of spring. Early-blooming shrubs have flowers (some highly scented) that are unaffected by frosty nights or late snowfalls. In fact, they stay on the branches longer when temperatures remain cool to cold—a sudden flash of early warmth quickly terminates their blossoms.

Should these early-flowering plants require pruning, be sure to wait until their flowers have finished, or you will be removing their best ornamental features.

KOREAN ABELIALEAF, WHITE FORSYTHIA *Abeliophyllum distichum* H 3–5 ft (1–1.5 m) –30°F (–34°C) This isn't true forsythia, although the sparkling pink-tinged white flowers look like one. *Abeliophyllum* blooms much earlier than yellow forsythia and its small size allows it to be set into sunny spring borders with primulas and hellebores. Keep its branches thinned out or they'll become a muddled tangle.

CORNELIAN CHERRY DOGWOOD *Cornus mas* HW 15 ft (4.5 m) –30°F (–34°C) Earliest to bloom in spring is the ethereal yellow haze of cornelian cherry, with blossoms springing out of the hardwood branches and followed by edible red fruits in August. Although more subtle, the elegance of *Cornus mas* will make you forget about the brashness of forsythia. The green foliage is stylized with veining, turning orange-red in autumn.

WINTER HONEYSUCKLE *Lonicera fragrantissima* H 6 ft (1.8 m) W 10 ft (3 m) –20°F (–29°C) A powerful fragrance drifts in clouds from this shrub's small creamy flowers in late winter or earliest spring. Its large size restricts it to shrub borders, fence lines or vacant corners, but its tolerance of shade or sun, heavy clay or sandy soils, and high pH alkalinity makes it entirely worthwhile. You can put it anywhere and know there will be a glorious end to winter.

MANCHU or **NANKING CHERRY** *Prunus tomentosa* H 6–10 ft (1.8–3 m) W 15 ft (4.5 m) –50°F (–46°C) For a sunny location, Manchu cherry will provide the most delicate pale pink to white cherry blossoms with subtle scent. This can be a big shrub, so give it room or make a hedge of it for inspiring early display. Edible red berries follow flowers in summer, and it's worth pruning to expose the attractive exfoliating bark.

FRAGRANT WINTERHAZEL *Corylopsis glabrescens* HW 15 ft (4.5 m) −20°F (−29°C) This delicate and wide-spreading low shrub is well suited to a woodland garden. It produces fragrant, pale yellow flowers that dangle from the bare branches in an elegant display in early spring. The leaves are quite distinctive, broadly oval and deeply veined, turning yellow in autumn. An equally beautiful cousin is spike winterhazel, *Corylopsis spicata*.

FEBRUARY DAPHNE *Daphne mezereum* H 4 ft (1.2 m) W 3 ft (1 m) −30°F (−34°C) Outstanding for fragrance in any season, place this by a doorway where the pink-purple flowers can be appreciated in early spring. It may not bloom in February, but this will bloom early. In Ireland, flowers appear in January; in Ontario they're out in March. The blue-green foliage is attractive all season and ornamental (poisonous) red berries appear in early autumn.

'WESTERSTEDE' WITCH HAZEL *Hamamelis* x *intermedia* HW 12 ft (3.6 m) − 20°F (−29°C) One of the earliest of the witch-hazels, and that's something, because most leap into bloom while snow still lingers. 'Westerstede' unfurls its primrose-yellow petals in late February if planted in sun, later in partial shade, and with a delicious scent. It needs room, but will grow in almost any condition, light or shade, wet or dry soil, high or low pH. Everyone can fit it in someplace.

'PJM' RHODODENDRON *Rhododendron* hybrid HW 4 ft (1.2 m) −30°F (−34°C) This lepidote (small-leafed) rhododendron is famously early and bright. Bright mauve-pink to lavender flowers that seem lit from within will shake up the early spring garden. Autumn foliage is a beautiful mahogany with touches of scarlet, and the shrub doesn't require any winter wrapping if planted away from strong wind.

GOAT WILLOW *Salix caprea* 'Kilmarnock' H 15 ft (4.6 m) −30°F (−34°C) The classic form of pussy willow in a shrub form with a broad oval shape and good height. It does best in bright light and moist soil, and can be kept low by removing some older and taller canes from the base each year. The catkins begin to open in late winter and continue to develop over four to six weeks. A grafted weeping form, *S. caprea* 'Pendula', can be used in small spaces.

FRAGRANT VIBURNUM *Viburnum farreri* H 10 ft (3 m) W 8 ft (2.4 m) −20°F (−29°C) The earliest viburnum, this large shrub is loose and unkempt, but has lovely pink panicle flowers and deeply veined foliage. It needs room to spread but its very early scented blooms justify the space. Thin from the base each year to prevent it from consuming passersby. 'Nanum' is compact and neatly mounding, just 3 ft (0.9 m) high, and perfect for a small garden. Part-shade to full sun.

TEN BEST SPRING-FLOWERING BULBS, CORMS AND TUBERS

In the earliest spring days, it's still a long way to go before the first leaves sprout from the bare branches of lonely woody shrubs and trees. Spring-flowering bulbs and woodland plants can be naturalized to provide a reliable show of fresh foliage and blossoms as early as late winter. Not all bulbs, corms and tubers are reliably perennial, though some will appear indefinitely through the years and will increase their numbers over time.

These plants all naturalize easily and can be left to roam through beds and borders and even into the lawn. They naturalize more rapidly if planted in generous clusters, the bulbs almost touching each other. In moist soil, new colonies of self-sown seedlings should appear within four or five years, then spread more rapidly. Always leave foliage to ripen to at least half-brown before removing, to ensure enough energy is stored in the bulb for reproduction. Let stems with seed heads remain until dry and their contents have spilled into the garden. If small bulbs, such as scilla and species crocus, are planted in the lawn, resist mowing until their foliage has fully ripened. Letting the grass grow tall and shaggy in spring promotes deep root growth and drought-hardiness.

CROCUS *Crocus* species and hybrids H 1½–10 in (4–25 cm) The earliest small crocus, sometimes referred to as snow crocus, will bloom for many years in the garden. This colorful group contains species and simple hybrids of wild bulbs. Look for two-toned *C. tomasinianus* 'Barr's Purple', yellow, white-and-purple *C. sieberi* 'Tricolor', and *C. chrysanthus* 'Gypsy Girl' (yellow and maroon), 'Prince Claus' (royal purple) and 'Lady Killer' in white and purple.

CYCLAMEN *Cyclamen* species H 2–12 in (5–30 cm) There are three hardy varieties that are adaptable to outdoor planting, their beautiful patterned foliage and charming scented blossoms braving the cold weather in autumn and early spring. Easy and prolific *C. hederifolium* blooms August–December, *C. coum* shows early and into June, and *C. purpurascens* flowers all summer. Good drainage, woodland soil, light shade to part-sun, with lots of leaf litter. Self-seeding, they can live for a century.

VIRGINIA BLUEBELLS *Mertensia virginica* H 18 in (45 cm) Bluebells' lobed blue-green foliage rises early in spring, followed by clusters of bright blue bells. They will live for many years in shade or sun and need moist soil to spread. Fellow bloomers are the species daffodils (*Narcissus*), although to naturalize they prefer meadow-like conditions in sun, with soil that is moist in spring, drier in summer. Also charming are *N. bulbocodium* and *N. jonquilla*.

GRAPE HYACINTH *Muscari* species and hybrids H 4–8 in (10–20 cm) Cold-hardy and easy growing, deep blue *Muscari* are lovely with yellow *Narcissus* and trout lilies. The grape-like blue clusters of *M. neglectum* and *M. azureum* will in time form drifts through a garden bed or shrub border. Cultivars include white *M. botryoides album*, two-toned blue *M. tubergianum* 'Oxford and Cambridge' and the strangely fluffy *M. armeniacum* 'Fantasy Creation'. Part-shade to full sun.

TROUT LILY *Erythronium* species and hybrids H 3–14 in (8–35 cm) Along woodland walks and in dappled shade on the dark side of a large shrub, the distinctive mottled foliage of trout lilies will eventually form colonies of graceful bells blooming each spring. Try yellow *E. americanum* or the larger, bright yellow *E.* 'Pagoda' (which does not spread). Another early bloomer is star of Bethlehem (*Ornithogalum umbellatum*), with white upturned flowers.

SNAKESHEAD FRITILLARY *Fritillaria meleagris* H 12 in (30 cm) The one spring plant no gardener should be without. Truly curious and beautiful checkered purple-and-white hanging bells pair perfectly with slim blue-green leaves. As meadowland plants, if left undisturbed these will set seed and drift about the garden. Buy bulbs early and plant them right away to prevent them from drying out. Part-shade to full sun.

SNOWDROP *Galanthus* species and hybrids H 3–9 in (7–23 cm) Snowdrops are up in late winter or earliest spring, and will appear when the ground is still frozen. Their nodding, opaque white flowers are especially brilliant clustered as a skirt around the dark branches of evergreens such as yew and boxwood. Reliable *G. nivalis* prefers moist soil in light shade to part-sun, spreading slowly. Showier, giant *G. elwesii* and double *G.* 'Flore Pleno' do not spread.

GLORY-OF-THE-SNOW *Chionodoxa* species H 3–8 in (7–20 cm) This blue-and-white spring beauty will lift spirits in the last days of winter. Plant it under trees, where it looks particularly lovely with dark blue scilla (*Scilla*) and blue-striped white Siberian squills (*Puschkinia*). Hybrids of these early bloomers are generally not as virile nor do they spread as well as the species plants.

WAKE-ROBIN *Trillium* species H 5–24 in (12–60 cm) W 4–12 in (10–30 cm) Every garden should have these woodland beauties, loved for their three-petaled flowers and unfailing constancy. Most familiar is the classic white trillium, *T. grandiflorum*. Other species include red trilliums, *T. sessile* (toad trillium), *T. erectum* (stinking Benjamin) and the yellow *T. luteum* with attractively mottled foliage. All bloom in damp shady corners, slowly increasing in number. Avoid digging within 4 ft (1.2 m) of a clump.

TULIP *Tulipa* species and hybrids H 6–30 in (15–75 cm) These smaller, early-blooming species tulips will return over many years if their foliage is allowed to ripen, although they won't spread like the minor bulbs. The intense yellow-and-white *T. tarda* opens and closes with the sun and *T. saxatilis* 'Lilac Wonder' is lilac-pink with yellow and white. Try also *T. pulchella* 'Violacea', *T. sylvestris* and *T. acuminata*. The larger Darwin hybrids will return for a decade.

Ten Best Plants for Autumn Display

It's easy to admire bright autumn color during the crisp days of winter's approach, but the time to plan for vivid foliage display is in spring, as days lengthen and warm. That is the time to strategically plant shrubs and trees that will give bursts of color at the end of the season. Select at least four plants with colorful autumn foliage from this list and plant them in your garden where their impact will be visible.

Keep in mind that sunlight is a factor in the production of autumn leaf color. Some plants, like burning bush, must be placed in full sun to produce their crimson leaves. But Japanese maples of all kinds will give good color with only half-day sun, as will many of the perennial cranesbill geraniums. Moisture is the second important factor; plants that have suffered from drought during midsummer won't be able to give their brightest effects in autumn. That's just another good reason for a reliable and sufficient irrigation program for every garden.

JAPANESE MAPLE *Acer palmatum* H 15–25 ft (4.5–7.6 m) −20°F (−29°C) Dozens of species and hybrids are available, all producing vividly colored autumn foliage with other joys through the year. Lesser known is purpleblow or Shantung maple (*Acer truncatum*), with miniature maple leaves that are reddish purple in spring, changing to glossy dark green then glistening yellow-orange in autumn. Half-day sun and consistently moist, organic soil.

RED CHOKEBERRY *Aronia arbutifolia* HW 6–8 ft (1.8–2.4 m) −30°F (−34°C) A good shrub for the sunny back of the border or a corner in a large garden. *Aronia* has lustrous, deep green leaves that turn deepest scarlet in autumn. There is also a heavy set of bright red fruits. Look for the cultivar 'Brilliantissima', which is brightest of all.

BURNING BUSH, SPINDLE TREE *Euonymus alatus* HW 15–20 ft (4.6–6 m) −30°F (−34°C) Burning scarlet foliage in autumn is this shrub's attraction. Smaller *Euonymus alatus* 'Compactus' (5–8 ft/1.5–2.5 m) is similar and a good hedging plant needing no pruning or shaping if planted 5 ft (1.5 m) apart. *E. europaeus* (H 12–30 ft/ 3.6–9 m) has deep pink and orange fruit from September to November. All need full sun to color up.

GINKGO *Ginkgo biloba* H 50ft (18 m) −40°F (−40°C) This ancient tree (also known as maidenhair tree) has unique foliage. Despite its height, it takes up relatively little room and doesn't cast shade for many decades. Drought-tolerant and pollution-resistant, they take on a beautiful golden hue in autumn, lighting up a garden. The females, which produce malodorous fruit, are not sold commercially.

BLUEBEARD, BLUE SPIREA *Caryopteris* x *cladonensis* H 4 ft (1.2 m) −20°F (−29°C) A small shrub with narrow, gray-green foliage and feathery blue flowers in late summer through early autumn. Darkest blue are 'Dark Knight' and 'Kew Blue'; 'Azure' is brighter and 'Blue Mist' is powder blue. Flowers best in sun with ordinary soil. Blue flowers appear on new wood of the current season. Wait until mid-spring to remove dead wood.

AMERICAN BITTERSWEET VINE *Celastrus scandens* H 30 ft (9 m) −40° (−40°C) You need two—male 'Hercules' and female 'Diane'—to get the fabulous scarlet and orange fruits that load the vines, which are used for holiday decorations. Beware, this rambunctious vine has enough energy to devour old stumps and strangle the life out of a tree, but in a "rough" area it's just right. Full sun and poor soil.

REDBARK DOGWOOD *Cornus alba* 'Sibirica' HW 10 ft (3 m) −50°F (−46°C) Green leaves and brilliant coral-red canes; 'Sibirica Variegata' has white-bordered leaves. Either mixed with yellow *Cornus sericea* 'Flaviramea' is dazzling. Most beautiful is *Cornus sanguinea* 'Winter Beauty', with glowing yellow to orange twigs tinged red. Give them all an annual cutting of half their canes at ground level to stimulate new wood and bright color. Full sun.

OAKLEAF HYDRANGEA *Hydrangea quercifolia* H 4–6 ft (1.2–1.8 m) −20°F (−29°C) Like all hydrangeas, this grows well and flowers in partial sun. But in brighter light the oak-like leaves take on vibrant autumn shades of red, orange-brown and purple. For spectacular autumn flowers try *Hydrangea paniculata* 'Grandiflora' (syn P.G. or Pee Gee). Its conical summer blossoms turn pink-bronze and dry well.

HIGHBUSH BLUEBERRY *Vaccinium corymbosum* H 6–12 ft (1.8–3.6 m) −40°F (−40°C) Upright, multi-stemmed shrub with urn-shaped, pink-tinged white flowers followed by tart blue-black berries. Autumn leaves are bright yellow, orange and red. Easy to grow in moist, organic soil with a low pH (4.5–5.5). Plant in a raised bed of shredded bark, peat moss, aged manure or compost with coarse sand for drainage. Pellet or powdered sulfur could also be added.

DOUBLEFILE VIBURNUM *Viburnum plicatum* var. *tomentosum* HW 8–10 ft (2.4–3 m) −20°F (−29°C) Named for the double rows of white blossoms smothering its branches in early summer. The leaves of this shrub turn to glowing burgundy-mahogany in autumn. Has an intriguing winter outline of tiered horizontal growth. Cultivars include 'Mariessii', 'Lanarth', 'Shasta' and dwarf 'Newport', which is suitable for a hedge.

Ten Best Shrubs for Winter Interest

Gardeners who are easily seduced by flowers may need a bit of consciousness-raising to recognize the ornamental features of plants in winter. In the absence of blossoms and foliage, woody shrubs are free to show their true character. After the fireworks of autumn color, the winter stems of burning bush are unexpectedly spangled with small, intensely red fruits. Double kerria carries a heavy burden of golden blooms in summer and then surprisingly reveals vivid apple-green stems in winter. Plants with ornamental winter features often have intriguing twig formation, like the corkscrew hazel, or dazzling red berries, like the highbush cranberry.

Placement is the important issue if ornamental winter features are to be best appreciated. Keeping plants with interesting architecture or colorful bark and fruits near doors and windows is the best way to enjoy them each day. It doesn't take many and often just one is enough, but by placing winter interest plants close at hand, your garden becomes a truly year-round pleasure.

REDBARK DOGWOOD *Cornus alba* 'Sibirica' HW 10 ft (3 m) −50°F (−46°C) Green leaves in summer drop to reveal coral-red bark against winter snow. 'Flaviramea' is a bright yellow-stemmed variety, also with plain green leaves. 'Gouchaultii' has green, yellow and rose foliage carried on red stems. For best bark color, grow the shrubs in bright sun, removing some older canes every year to encourage new wood.

CORKSCREW HAZEL *Corylus avellana* 'Contorta' HW 15 ft (4.5 m) −30°F (−34°C) Intriguing in winter, with spiraled and corkscrewed twigs and silver-burnished wood. The catkin-like inflorescences lengthen through winter, opening into elegant tassels in spring. Grows in light shade to full sun, with the corkscrews being tighter in a sunny location. Cut out any smooth or straight stems emerging from below the base.

'YUKON BELLE' FIRETHORN *Pyracantha angustifolia* HW 10 ft (3 m) −30°F (−34°C) A broadleaf evergreen shrub with an upright and spreading posture and generous clusters of bright orange-red berries in winter. It should always be grown against something—a house corner, by an entranceway door or against a garden fence—so it will be sheltered from winter wind. Cousin *P. coccinea* 'Chadwick' has arching branches.

CUTLEAF STAGHORN SUMAC *Rhus typhina* 'Dissecta' H 6 ft (1.8 m) W 10 ft (3 m) −40°F (−40°C) Graceful plants with lacy foliage that turns flamboyantly yellow-orange in autumn. The prominent fruit cones are crimson-red and a treat for gardeners and birds while they last. Sumac is aggressive and will colonize rapidly, so plant it where fill is needed in a hard-to-plant area.

AUTUMN FIRE COTONEASTER *Cotoneaster salicifolius* 'Herbst-feuer' HW 15 ft (4.5 m) −30°F (−34°C) This low and spreading broadleaf evergreen has strong architectural branching that looks best displayed near rocks or cascading into a pond. Its small pink flowers turn to red berries and hold into winter. 'Coral Beauty' is another, similar variety with white flowers turning to orange-red fruit.

WINTERBERRY, DECIDUOUS HOLLY *Ilex verticillata* HW 15 ft (4.5 m) −30°F (−34°C) The species plant doesn't require a male pollinator and will carry bunches of bright red fruits after its leaves drop. Hybrids, with larger berry clusters, need one male plant for up to six females, and should be bought in matched sets: 'Jim Dandy' (M) with 'Afterglow' or 'Red Sprite' (F), and 'Southern Gentleman' (M) with 'Winter Red' (F).

DOUBLE KERRIA *Kerria japonica* 'Pleniflora' HW 6 ft (1.8 m) −20°F (−29°C) Slender apple-green stems remain bright through winter. Large arching clumps carrying golden rosette flowers in early summer are useful to fill a corner or hide a stump. 'Picta' has white-edged, gray-green leaves. Lovely with *Hesperis matronalis* and *Aquilegia*, which bloom at the same time. Part-shade to full sun.

SPECIES ROSE *Rosa* species HW 4–15 ft (1.2–4.5 m) −20°F (−29°C) Roses make seed-carrying hips when spent blossoms are left on the shrub. Species roses have the largest and brightest display of hips. For a small and sunny corner, the low-growing alpine rose (*R. pendulina*) has orange-red pendant hips. For the back of a border, try the larger, arching *R. holodonta* or *R. highdownensis*.

CORKSCREW WILLOW *Salix* x 'Erythroflexuosa' HW 15 ft (4.5 m) −20°F (−29°C) Smallest of the contorted willows, 'Erythroflexuosa' makes a large shrub or small tree. Its spirally twisted and widely spreading branches have golden-yellow to orange bark. The gold to green foliage is also ornamentally twisted.

HIGHBUSH CRANBERRY *Viburnum trilobum* H 15 ft (4.5 m) W 12 ft (3.6 m) −40°F (−40°C) This is the most colorful of all the viburnums, with generous white flowers in spring, scarlet foliage in autumn and heavy, jewel-like fruits that last deep into winter. The clusters of deep scarlet berries become almost translucent in late winter. Equally attractive is the dwarf *V. trilobum* 'Compactum'.

looking after the landscape

6

After so much thoughtful preparation, the landscape plan is finally in place and you can rest. But not quite. Gardens never stand still. They continue to grow, evolve and change, even through the winter months. The cycles of the natural world are always at work on soil, plants and hard materials. Stone and wood materials weather and develop the patina of age. Plants are preparing for change from the day they go into your garden. After five years of growth, their woody structures will have expanded, reaching for light and taking on mature form. Some plants may not have met expectations, while others might excel and scatter their seedlings. Storms change gardens, insects and disease come and go, and environmental conditions like heat and drought cause prolonged stress. Many changes are acceptable, some you'll want to correct, but mostly gardeners are concerned for the continuing health and performance of plants and soil.

FERTILIZING PLANTS

It's well to remember that plants prospered over the earth for millions of years before there was anyone to fertilize them. Clearly they're capable of reaching mature growth powered by plant foods made in their own foliage. But what gardener can resist doing just a little extra for the plants so carefully selected? If it's yours, you'll want to feed it.

Nutrients for plants are available in natural organic forms or as manufactured preparations. Organic fertilizers like compost, manure, blood meal and bone meal contain slow-release nutrients plus the complete range of trace elements important for healthy growth. Most manufactured preparations are fast-release and contain the three main plant nutrients without the trace elements. The organic fertilizers are a better deal for plants, providing a full, nutritious meal. Manufactured fertilizers are also nutritionally valuable, but offer a less complete menu.

EASY AS 1-2-3

THE main plant nutrients are nitrogen for deep green color and strong leaf growth, phosphorus for aggressive root development and bud set, and potassium for healthy tissues. Every fertilizer bag or box has three numbers on it representing the amounts of the basic nutrients contained, and they are always listed in the order of nitrogen, phosphorus and potassium. If the numbers are 10-15-6, that means the fertilizer is 10% (by weight) nitrogen, 15% phosphorus and 6% potassium.

Basic fertilizers for ornamental garden plants should have all their numbers below twenty. Anything higher is too much and runs the risk of damaging the plant.

opposite: A beautiful garden requires maintenance to stay that way. Self-sufficient ornamental grasses need to be cut back every year and perennials will need to be divided. Plants always benefit from the increase in soil fertility that comes from organic soil amendments and insulating mulches.

APPLY fertilizers in the spring after indications of new growth are evident. Evergreens will show light green tips of new growth and deciduous trees, shrubs and roses will have swollen buds cracking open to reveal the tips of new leaves.

Manure, blood meal and bone meal are slow-release fertilizers with low numbers that can be lightly dug into the top 6 inches (15 cm) of soil surrounding plant roots. The bone meal and blood meal boxes will recommend how much to use.

You can be generous with well-rotted manure and homemade garden compost. Both are ideal plant fertilizers and can be dug in or simply used as mulch over the roots.

Manufactured fertilizers in granular form can be lightly scratched into the top 3 inches (7.5 cm) of soil, following the instructions on the bag for amounts to use. These are the forms of fertilizer with which gardeners are most likely to burn plants. Always water plants deeply after applying and never use in greater quantity or more frequently than the manufacturer recommends.

Liquid fertilizers applied with a hose-end sprayer are convenient to use, but more is lost to evaporation than is delivered to the plant.

Applying fertilizer to a plant before it's ready to grow can have the opposite effect and cause a check or temporary halt to potential growth. First watch for new buds or leaves, indications that the plant is in a growth cycle, before providing supplemental feeding. Plants manufacture most of the nutrition they require, so go easy on the extra meals you provide. They don't really need it, but will perform better with just a little extra food. Too much fertilizer can burn tender roots and cause toxic accumulations of sodium in the soil.

Applying fertilizers late in the growing season can force new growth that won't have time to harden before frost. This predisposes the plant to serious winter dieback and can cause a general weakening of winter hardiness. If you live in a cold region with deep winter frost, don't apply any manufactured fertilizers after the middle of July. Organic fertilizers with low numbers, such as manure and compost, can be used at any time. If plants don't need the energy for immediate growth, they'll store it in their roots and crowns for future use.

Shredded bark is a superior garden mulch. It keeps soil temperatures cool during summer heat and conserves moisture in the root zones of plants.

soil condition and fertility

Healthy soil is constantly alive with microbes producing the basic nutrient building blocks plants need to grow. Organic materials and texture are the keys to maintaining good soil condition, and they must be renewed and amended every year. You don't need to know anything about science to keep your garden soil productive. Providing common organic materials like leaves, pine needles, rotted manure and compost will renew fertility and ensure that oxygen and moisture are plentiful in the root zone.

The easiest and least expensive method of improving soil texture and natural fertility is to allow leaves to remain on the ground in autumn. Leaves are the ideal soil conditioner, containing appropriate amounts of fiber and basic plant nutrients that microbes can process into humus. Worms will consume large amounts of leaves and deposit their nutrient-rich castings where plants have easy access. The more worms you find in your soil, the higher its fertility.

Shredding your leaves is the best way to make them stay where you put them; also, the smaller pieces are more accessible to composting soil microbes and worms. Many power mowers have leaf-shredding capability, and simple leaf-shredding machines (no sticks or branches) are reasonably priced and produce a fine mulch that can be put 2–3 inches (5–7.5 cm) deep on exposed soil in flowerbeds and over the roots of woody shrubs and trees. Or you can collect many bags of neighborhood leaves and rent a shredder for all-day mulch production. Wind won't disturb shredded leaves and they'll quickly settle down to half the height. But if time doesn't allow for the shredding operation, most leaves can be put down whole on the ground and will be con-

Blue-flowered hydrangeas rely on low soil pH. If the pH is above 6.0, the blossoms will be pink.

DOES SOIL pH MATTER?

THE fertility of garden soil is influenced by its pH rating, a measurement of the acid or alkaline character of the soil. The rating scale runs from 1 to 14, from extremely acid in the low numbers to extremely alkaline in the higher numbers. Essential plant nutrients present in the soil are easily available to plants when the pH rating is slightly acid or neutral, between 6.5 and 7.0. At lower acidic or higher alkaline ratings, nutrients can be "tied up" or tightly bound within molecules of soil and inaccessible to plants.

It's useful to know the average pH rating for your region, and you can easily have your garden soil tested by a soil testing service or government agency. You can dig lime into an acid soil or sulfur into an alkaline soil to temporarily adjust pH, but the results will last only for a few weeks. The most effective thing to do is add generous amounts of organic material to the soil each year, digging it into planting holes and laying it on beds and borders as a mulch. Organic materials like leaves, shredded bark and pine needles buffer and adjust the soil pH, and make the soil climate more conducive to plant growth.

NITROGEN makes deep green color, and enhances strong blade and stem growth.

PHOSPHORUS stimulates the growth of roots and stems, and encourages flower buds.

POTASSIUM promotes plant health and strength, and influences drought and disease resistance.

sumed by worms and microbes in less than twelve months. Only very broad leaves like those of Norway maple must be shredded to prevent packing down on the soil and sealing out oxygen. Oak leaves are high in resin, which slows their decomposition, but they are still good for mulch and won't pack into an impermeable layer.

Homemade garden compost and rotted manure are more finished forms of plant food and you can spread them on the soil surface or incorporate them in planting holes. Compost, manure and leaves are the most natural and important contributors to soil fertility, providing the full spectrum of macro and micronutrients needed for plant growth. These organic materials are also the base components of humus, the invaluable end product of the composting process. Given the choice of building healthy soil structure and nutrients with organic materials or using packaged manufactured fertilizers, you'd do well to put the box back on the shelf.

Deluxe compost-making bins are a gardener's dream, but you can easily compost in simple piles stashed in obscure corners. Low compost piles up to 2½ feet (0.8 m) high will stay in place without sliding. Taller piles can be kept in place with twiggy shrub branches laid around the edges.

pests and diseases

Insects and fungus diseases are natural parts of the garden's ecology, though it's hard to remember that when confronted with chewed petals and mildew-coated leaves. But consider that only ten percent of insects are capable of damaging plants, and ninety percent are more interested in preserving and protecting plant material. It helps if the gardener can develop a bit of tolerance and accept some animal interference. Plants that are less than perfect still provide a great deal of pleasure.

Fungus pathogens are naturally resident in your garden and it's impossible to completely eradicate them. But good hygiene (picking up rotting plant parts), and increasing air circulation by not planting too densely, will go a long way to preventing diseases. The first line of defense against insects is a large bird population. Their hungry nestlings require constant feeding with protein-rich insects, just at the time bugs are proliferating. Beneficial insects like lacewings and ladybugs will be drawn by plantings of fennel, yarrow, chamomile and clover and then will eat the bad guys.

Regular inspection of plants will draw you into a more pleasurable experience with your garden, and alert you to pest problems before they get out of hand. If a pest problem becomes overwhelming, it might be better to remove the plant for the season rather than resort to heavy-duty chemicals. If you must spray, use only a botanical poison like pyrethrum, available in several organic pesticide products. It is an effective pesticide, and must be used responsibly. Wear rubber gloves when spraying, cover your arms, legs and feet, and avoid breathing in any spray mist.

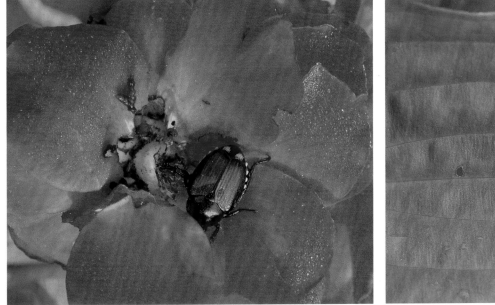

Japanese Beetles Hand pick, or spray with pyrethrum and alcohol mixture (see Aphids). A purchased pheromone (sex attractant) trap can be purchased and set into garden beds away from vulnerable plants.

Slugs Mix equal parts water and ammonia to spray on slugs or sprinkle with table salt. Spread a generous band of powdered sulfur on the soil around vulnerable plants (slugs won't cross it).

Whiteflies   Use pyrethrum mixture (see Aphids) and spray twice, 7 days apart. Drench flies thoroughly, especially on undersides of leaves.

Scales   Spray with a 3 percent solution of light horticultural oil (also called superior oil) directly on the scales to suffocate them. Or spray with a pyrethrum and alcohol solution (see Aphids).

Aphids   Spray with a pyrethrum insecticide, adding 1 tbsp (15 mL) of isopropyl alcohol to 2 cups (500 mL) of prepared pyrethrum product. Spray directly on aphids; they must get wet to be affected.

Earwigs   Make a trap by stapling shut one end of a cardboard tube and laying it flat on the ground under plant leaves. Earwigs will hide in the tube during daylight and can be shaken out into soapy water.

horticultural sprays

INSECT SPRAYS

Homemade pesticides are most effective when used as repellent sprays before large infestations develop. Large populations of destructive bugs can be prevented when repellents are applied regularly to plants that destructive pests are known to infest. It's important to treat only the plants that are frequently damaged by insects, because repellents will kill or discourage beneficial insects, too. And remember, perfection has no place in the garden. It's important to work at acquiring a little tolerance for damage.

Whether you are using commercial or homemade preparations, label all bottles and containers clearly with waterproof marker.

PEPPER AND GARLIC SPRAY

This spray contains enough hot volatile oils to burn the chewing and sucking mouth parts of insects, but it is very hot and will also burn human skin, so be careful not to splash yourself. Wearing rubber kitchen gloves and a pair of shop safety glasses is a reasonable precaution.

1/2 cup (125 mL) fresh hot peppers
2 large cloves fresh garlic
2 cups (500 mL) water
1 tbsp (15 mL) vegetable oil

Liquefy ingredients in a blender or food processor and strain the mixture through a kitchen sieve lined with a handkerchief. Transfer to a spray bottle and label. Spray the upper and lower leaf surfaces of plants that show insect damage.

BOOSTED INSECTICIDAL SOAP

Commercial insecticidal soap is more effective than anything you can make from dish detergent, and won't harm tender plant tissues. The soap mixture is most effective when "boosted" with rubbing alcohol (isopropyl alcohol), which removes the waxy cuticle covering from soft-bodied insects like aphids, whiteflies and leaf hoppers. This allows the soap to do its job effectively, but it won't have as much effect on hard-bodied insects like earwigs and Japanese beetles.

2 cups (500 mL) prepared commercial insecticidal soap
1 tbsp (15 mL) rubbing (isopropyl) alcohol

Mix up commercial insecticidal soap according to product instructions and put it into a clearly labeled spray bottle. Add the rubbing alcohol and mix. Spray affected plants thoroughly.

ANTI-ANTS SPRAY

Ants dislike citrus oils and will abandon their nests to avoid them, or you can rely on the sweetened borax paste (see below), which the ants will carry back to the nest. Simply flooding with a hose also works well because ants can't swim and a torrent of water will disrupt the nest and send them scattering.

3 pieces of citrus fruit (oranges, grapefruits or lemons)
3 cups (750 mL) boiling water

Use a citrus zester or sharp paring knife to remove just the thin outer peel from the citrus fruit. Put the peels into a bowl and pour the boiling water over them. Leave to cool. Use the cooled citrus infusion to splash onto unwanted ant nests in lawns or garden beds.

ANTI-ANTS PASTE

Ants will go for this sweetened paste which will poison their nest when they carry it back. Borax soap is available as a laundry product in supermarkets.

1 tbsp (15 mL) borax soap
Molasses or honey

Mix the borax soap with enough molasses or honey to form a paste. Put small dabs of the paste on pieces of waxed paper and leave them close to unwanted anthills. This will also interest bees and wasps, so wait until night to eventually remove the paste.

DISEASE SPRAYS

Fungus diseases are caused by microscopic spores that land on leaf tissue, where they take root. Eventually brown spots, streaks or blotches indicate the infection, but by that time it's well established.

To prevent fungus diseases like black spot on roses from getting started, the preventative spray must be used in advance of hot and humid weather, as a preventative measure.

PREVENTATIVE BLACK-SPOT SPRAY

1 tsp (5 mL) baking soda
4 cups (1 l) water
a few drops of liquid soap

Mix the baking soda with the water and add a few drops of liquid soap as a sticking agent. Use the spray every 7 to 10 days on rose foliage, starting in midsummer.

pruning

Pruning is a puzzle to most gardeners, and with good reason. Every plant has a genetic plan for its final mature size, and pruning isn't on the agenda. When gardening shears or pruners cut into living wood, buds lower down on the branch are activated to replace the lost wood. It's no wonder so many efforts to control plant size with

MAKING THE CUT

CUTTING wood on a 45° angle allows moisture to drain easily off the cut tip. Although you have cut only one twig or branch, two buds further down the stem will be activated, replacing the cut wood at a 2-for-1 ratio. That's why pruning to reduce size often produces a plant of greater size than you started with. Selecting a plant with potential dimensions to fit the space available is less stressful (for both you and the plant) and more successful.

pruning are frustrated by explosions of new growth. It would be much easier to select plants with potential mature size to fit into the available space. Check a good gardening book or carefully read nursery catalogues to find the potential size of most shrubs and trees and select one that fits your space. If shrubs in the garden are too big for their location, continued pruning efforts only cause disfigurement without solving any problems. Common plants like forsythia, spirea, lilac and dogwood come in various sizes and are inexpensive to purchase. Just dig out the old one and purchase the appropriately sized plant for the space.

The best reason for pruning shrubs and trees is to correct storm damage. Accumulations of ice and snow on branches amount to enormous weights that can crack and shatter wood. The ragged tears left are invitations to insect and disease infestations, and these are the first pruning concern for gardeners. It's important to call a professional arborist for any work that you can't reach from the ground with an extension-pole pruner. Gardeners have no business going up in trees where they risk their own limbs, but extension-pole pruners have a reach of 10–18 feet (3–5.5 m) and you can become adept at minor cutting and sawing repairs. The important work is to

cleanly remove any hanging branches, leaving behind a smooth cut with as little inner wood exposed as possible. Sealant products for pruning cuts are not needed and can cause serious decay by interfering with the wood's own callusing process.

Gardeners can find some success with pruning to invigorate sparse or tired shrubs by cutting out weak and spindly wood in early spring before buds break. Decreasing the length of all strong branches or canes by one-half at this time will result in energy being driven into the remaining buds when the weather warms. These super-charged buds will have more than their share of spring vigor, and you can enhance the burst of new growth with a generous mulch of compost or rotted manure over their roots.

Large and overgrown shrubs often have so many canes that their interior foliage dies from lack of light. To renovate a big shrub and trigger the growth of strong new wood, cut out one-third of the oldest canes each year, severing them as close to the base as you can get. You'll possibly need big loppers or even a pruning saw for this operation. Spreading compost or rotted manure generously over the roots will contribute to the plant's energy for wood production. After three years, you'll have a renewed plant.

Successfully pruning flowering shrubs is a matter of careful timing. Shortly after flowering in the present season, woody plants form the flower buds for the next year. If you want to reduce the size of the plant, it must be done immediately after the blossoms are finished. Waiting several weeks will likely cause you to remove next year's flower buds as you prune. Spring-flowering shrubs that bloom on old wood, such as lilac, forsythia, quince, flowering almond and daphne, should be pruned within three weeks after they finish flowering. Later-blooming shrubs that bloom on new wood, like spirea, hydrangea and rose of Sharon, should also be pruned after flowering, and that means in autumn or very early the following spring, before buds break.

right: Creative pruning involves finding the true line of a tree. Removing secondary wood—the thin twigs that carry leaves—helps to expose the architecture of Japanese maples.

HOW TO PRUNE A TREE

Pruning is not an annual rite of spring. Most trees seldom need pruning, but occasionally wood removal is necessary and useful to improve the tree's health and extend its life. Wind and ice damage can injure tree wood, leaving entry points for insects and disease. These must be removed cleanly, exposing as little interior wood as possible. Structural weight imbalances (A), crossed or rubbing branches (B) and low-hanging boughs (C) are also problems that can be solved by judicious and conservative pruning.

Some trees receive large amounts of nitrogen fertilizer when surrounding lawn areas are fed. They grow many twiggy branches (D) carrying excessive foliage that shades the interior of the tree. The shaded interior results in foliage loss, twig dieback and decreased air circulation—a favorable environment for fungus pathogens. Removing excess twiggy growth opens up the tree interior letting in light and air for healthy growth.

The best approach is to begin with a careful evaluation of the tree's growth pattern, preferably when the branches are bare and it's easier to see the full structure, including the interior. Remove dead or storm-damaged wood as well as crossed or rubbing branches. Consider if the tree is reasonably balanced, with near equal branch weight on all sides.

Most importantly, however, *never* cut the tree's top leader branch (E). The leader sets the form for the tree, and if you interfere with it, you will trigger alternate growth that may be harder to control and also less aesthetically pleasing.

How to Remove a Tree Limb with a Jump-Cut

When removing a limb from a tree, it's important to do as little damage as possible to the bark, which protects the important cambium layer just beneath. If the cambium is exposed, the growth and development of the tree may be seriously affected for the worse. The jump-cut method guards against the weight of a cut branch ripping a strip of bark from the tree trunk as it falls.

1. First, to split the bark, make a shallow undercut (1) on the branch at a place behind the planned cut.

2. Then make the severing cut (2) at a point 4–6 inches (10–15 cm) further out on the limb. If the limb should suddenly fall while being severed, the first shallow undercut you made will prevent bark from ripping a strip off the trunk.

3. With the heaviest portion of the limb down, make a third cut (3) to remove the remaining stub. Allow a slight protrusion, called the collar, to remain where the limb sprang from the trunk. Cutting the stub flush with the trunk will expose too much inner wood and can seriously damage the tree.

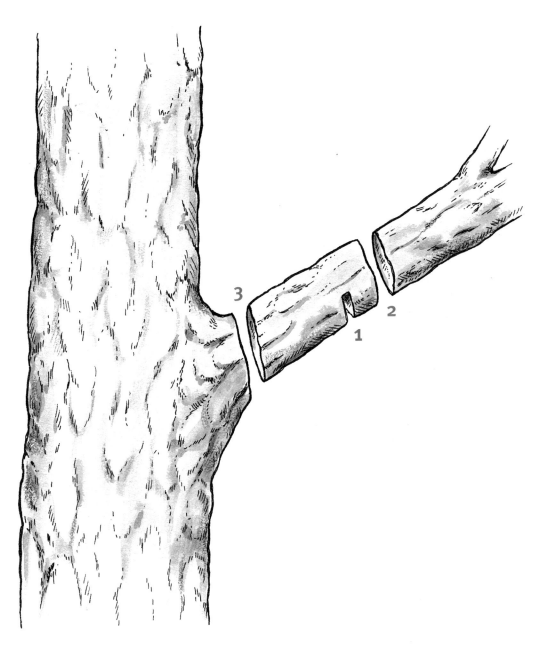

How to Prune Flowering Shrubs

Timing is an important guideline when pruning flowering shrubs. When a flowering shrub finishes blooming, buds for next year's flowers begin forming below the dead flowers. It is important when pruning that you do not cut off these dormant buds or you will be removing next season's blooms. Pruning should always be carried out judiciously and thoughtfully. Deadheading flowering shrubs to produce more blooms—on both spring- and summer-flowering shrubs—is done in a similar manner.

Spring-flowering Shrubs

Shrubs that bloom in spring carry their flowers on "old wood"—wood that has grown during the previous season. A spring-flowering shrub like this lilac blooms in May and within six weeks it sets invisible flower buds for the following year. Therefore major pruning must be done quickly after blooming is over in spring—ideally within two weeks—or there is danger of cutting off the newly set buds that will become next year's flowers.

These spring-flowering shrubs can be pruned soon after flowering:
• Serviceberries, shadblow (*Amelanchier*)
• Azalea • Flowering quince (*Chaenomeles*)
• Cornelian cherry (*Cornus kousa*) • Deutzia
• Forsythia • Lilac (*Syringa*) • Mock orange (*Philadelphus*) • Bridalwreath spirea (*Spirea vanhouttei*) • Viburnum

Summer-flowering Shrubs

Shrubs that bloom in mid to late summer carry their flowers on "new wood"—wood that grew in the same season as the flowers. It can be pruned any time after blooming ends, either in autumn or very early the following spring but before new growth is initiated. If you prune too late the next spring, you risk cutting off newly set buds that will become that summer's flowers.

These summer-flowering shrubs can be pruned before spring growth begins:
• Bottlebrush buckeye (*Aesculus parviflora*)
• Smokebush (*Cotinus coggygria*) • Rose of Sharon (*Hibiscus syriacus*) • Hydrangea • Goldflower (*Hypericum*) • Japanese kerria (*Kerria japonica*)
• Cinquefoil (*Potentilla fruticosa*) • Elderberry (*Sambucus*) • False spirea (*Sorbaria sorbifolia*)
• Bumalda spirea (*Spirea* x *bumalda*)

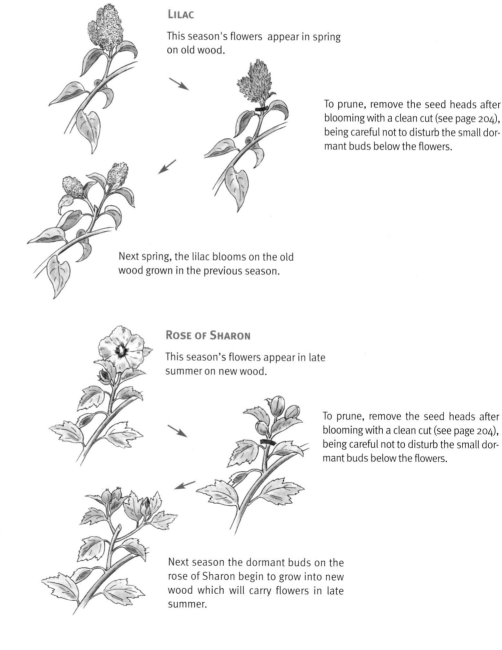

Lilac
This season's flowers appear in spring on old wood.

To prune, remove the seed heads after blooming with a clean cut (see page 204), being careful not to disturb the small dormant buds below the flowers.

Next spring, the lilac blooms on the old wood grown in the previous season.

Rose of Sharon
This season's flowers appear in late summer on new wood.

To prune, remove the seed heads after blooming with a clean cut (see page 204), being careful not to disturb the small dormant buds below the flowers.

Next season the dormant buds on the rose of Sharon begin to grow into new wood which will carry flowers in late summer.

HOW TO RENOVATE AN OVERGROWN SHRUB

You'll likely recognize when a shrub has become overgrown. It takes on a rangy, leggy shape, foliage appears more in some areas than others, and blossoms, if any, also show inconsistently. Renovating a shrub kickstarts the plant, forcing its energy to be invested back into what it does best: producing foliage and blossoms and achieving its mature natural shape and size.

Shrubs can be renovated by removing one-third of the old wood each year, over three years. In early spring of the first year, remove a third of the oldest wood as close as possible to where it springs from the crown of the plant. This will stimulate the shrub to put out new and vigorous cane growth from the crown. The second year, the new canes have grown in and another third of the oldest canes can be removed. This stimulates new canes to appear again. The third year, the new canes from the previous two years are growing strongly and the remaining canes of oldest wood can be removed, if need be.

Year 1 Early in spring, prune out one-third of the oldest wood as close as possible to the crown of the shrub.

Year 2 Next spring new canes will have sprung from the crown as a result of the previous year's cuts. You can now remove a further one-third of the shrub's oldest canes, again as near to the crown as possible.

Year 3 In the third spring the shrub will be growing strong new canes to replace those cut last spring. You can now cut the remaining canes of oldest wood, if you wish. By next season, the shrub will be revitalized with all new and vigorous growth.

TEN BEST FLOWERING SHRUBS AND WHEN TO PRUNE THEM

Successfully pruning flowering shrubs is not as complicated as it may appear, but it is a matter of careful timing. The key is to remember that in all cases, woody shrubs should be pruned soon after flowering, "soon" being relative. If this rule is followed, nature's routines of flowering on old or new wood take care of themselves (see pages 204–209).

If your flowering shrub has a diminishing number of blooms and is crowded and overgrown, turn to the previous page to learn how to renovate the plant and rejuvenate its blooming.

BUTTERFLY BUSH *Buddleia* species and hybrids HW 4–20 ft (1.2–6 m) –10°F (–23°C) Often slow to leaf out. Prune in late spring or early summer and cut out only dead wood that hasn't sprouted. Butterfly bush is marginally hardy in the north and often will die back to the crown, sending up entirely new canes each spring.

DEUTZIA *Deutzia* species and hybrids HW 3–10 ft (1–3 m) –20°F (–29°C) Prune immediately after flowering, shortening branches as necessary to maintain shape. Every third year, remove a few older canes from the base to prevent congestion and excessive shading of the interior.

LILAC *Syringa* species and hybrids HW 4–16 ft (1.2–4.8 m) –50°F (–46°C) Prune immediately after flowering, removing flower heads that can be reached and thinning out sucker growth. If the shrub is very tall and leggy, leave two or three of the thickest suckers to help renew the lower structure. Long branches can be cut back to an outward-facing, vigorous twig.

RHODODENDRON *Rhododendron* species and hybrids HW 2–20 ft (0.6–6 m) –20°F (–29°C) Prune immediately after flowering, carefully removing the seed capsules from branch tips. Do not attempt to shape the shrub by shortening branches. Remove old and leggy branches at the base to induce new and vigorous wood growth from the crown.

Forsythia *Forsythia* species and hybrids HW 5–10 ft (1.5–3 m) –30°F (–34°C) Every year, remove a few older branches at the base to prevent dense growth and keep shrub in "see-through" condition and allowing the canes to assume their full length. If forsythia is grown in a sunny location it can be cut back to the crown when necessary. If the shrub is entirely too large for its location, dig it out and replace it with a smaller variety of forsythia.

Rose of Sharon *Hibiscus syriacus* H 10 ft (3 m) W 8 ft (2.4 m) –20°F (–29°C) Wait until the wood has sprouted new leaves in late spring before pruning. In early June, cut back all winter-killed wood that has failed to sprout.

Hills of Snow Hydrangea *Hydrangea arborescens* 'Annabelle' HW 3–5 ft (1–1.5 m) –30°F (–34°C) This shrub with large globular clusters of white flowers blooms on new wood and can be cut back to the crown in early spring. Other hydrangeas, such as Pee Gee (*H. paniculata*), oakleaf (*H. quercifolia*) and bigleaf or Hortensia (*H. macrophylla*), all bloom on old wood. After leaves have opened in spring, remove only dead branches and thin out congested interiors where necessary.

Rose *Rosa* species and hybrids HW 3–30 ft (1–9 m) –50°C (–46°F) Shrub, hybrid tea and floribunda roses: In early spring, when buds are swollen but before they leaf out, remove dead wood, broken or damaged canes, and living wood less than ¾ in (2 cm) in diameter. Climbing roses: Remove dead, damaged and spindly wood and the oldest canes with little vigor. Try to bend and secure young canes in a horizontal arc to force many additional blooming buds to break.

Spirea *Spiraea* species and hybrids HW 1½–10 ft (0.5–3 m) –30°F (–34°C) Prune tall "Bridalwreath" spireas (*S. nipponica*, *S. canescens*, *S.* x *vanhouttei*) right after blooming to two-thirds of their height and thin excessive canes from the crown. For low-growing *bumalda* shrubs under 3 ft (0.9 m), cut back branches by one-half in spring before buds break. Those in a sunny location can be cut to the crown in early spring.

Wisteria *Wisteria* species and hybrids H 28 ft (8.5 m) or more –10°C (–23°F) In late winter, cut back the previous season's new tendril growth to leave 6-in (15 cm) stubs with three to five buds all along the older main wood. Cutting wisteria back hard in winter will often induce flowering in spring. Excessive tendril growth can also be removed again in summer.

caring for hard surfaces

Wood is the construction material that changes most rapidly and profoundly. Because of its porous nature, wood absorbs water readily in all seasons. In warm weather, fungus organisms are able to penetrate wood grain in dry and wet circumstances, beginning the irremediable process of rot. The best way to forestall or prevent wood from rotting is to apply a coat of water-resistant preservative every two years. Where snow lies on a wood deck floor, the preservative may need to be applied more frequently.

Asphalt is a strong surface requiring little care. A topcoat of black sealant applied every year will help to fill small cracks and delay their development into deeper fissures. Precast cement cobblestones and pavers can also be sealed with a clear coating to help prevent deep penetration of ice. Any dry-laid stone surface is eventually loosened as snow and rain erosion carry sand away, causing pieces to "float" and allowing frost to begin heaving them up. Sweeping fine jointing sand across surfaces of manufactured pavers or natural stone will fill gaps in the joints and hold the stones tightly in place.

Stone surfaces in shady wet locations with poor air circulation may be colonized by algae. This green coating over the surface of the stone is very slippery and a serious safety hazard. The species of moss that grows in cracks between stones is harmless and ornamental, and some gardeners make efforts to encourage its growth. But green coatings across the surface of the stone must be promptly removed. If the algae aren't too well established, you can spray them with a solution of eight parts water to two parts liquid chlorine bleach. Be careful not to get this mixture on moss in the cracks or ornamental plants nearby—they won't appreciate it. If the algae persists, you'll need to scrub it off with a stiff wire brush.

If you go to the trouble and expense of installing hard surfaces in your landscape, you should keep them clean, free of damaging elements and safe to use. Keep shaded areas free of slippery algae (see right) and keep all hard surfaces used by people ice-free by using coarse sand or a road-salt substitute—salt will eventually cause pitting and permanent damage.

winter protection

Winter conditions can be tough on plants, even when they're growing well within their hardiness zone. Plants in exposed locations bear the brunt of desiccating winds that also lower air temperature. Where wind is a certainty in winter, it's a good idea to put more delicate plants near walls for some protection. Or consider placing them on the warmer side of taller plants that will filter the wind. A few strategically placed conifers will help to make a windbreak for an exposed corner, and bushy plants like yew and cedar are ideal for building in a bit of protection.

Tall cedars are particularly vulnerable to filling with heavy snow that splays their branches outward. It's worth going out into the storm with a broom to brush off accumulated snow and ice. But you can prevent the problem in late autumn by gently tying them round with jute twine, threading the twine through the interior branches to give them support and hold their shape together.

Roses shouldn't be pruned until spring, but climbers and some tall plants may have long canes that need securing. To prevent breakage and wind damage, tie the canes to a fence, trellis or even a stake so they won't whip around in the

The roots of newly planted perennials haven't got a firm grip in the soil and can be heaved out by the action of frost. Prevent this by laying thick mulch over them in late autumn. Use shredded or very small leaves 2 inches (5 cm) deep. Remove in earliest spring to allow the soil to begin warming.

winter wind. Other tall plants and young trees may also need additional stakes to ensure they remain upright and stationary.

The foliage of broadleaf evergreen shrubs like rhododendrons and euonymus can be burned by wind and strong winter sun. Anti-desiccant sprays are benign organic preparations that can be sprayed on from a ready-to-use bottle, coating each leaf and protecting its tissues from desiccation. (The spray also works well on Christmas trees, keeping their needles from drying out in your living room.) Anti-desiccants should be applied to broadleaf evergreens in the garden in late autumn when day temperatures are still just above freezing.

Very few plants require wrapping if they are reliably hardy within your climate zone. But if an evergreen plant hasn't been in the ground long, it may not be able to keep its tissues hydrated when exposed to wind or late winter sun. It's best not to completely enclose a plant, but you can insert stakes around it and attach a burlap barrier to help shade the foliage and break the wind. Place the stakes so that the burlap won't be touching the plant, and staple or pin the fabric in place. Diaper pins work well to wrap and secure the burlap around each stake.

last words: a comfortable seat

People landscape their gardens for different reasons. Some gardens are so rough and uninviting they can't be used without major structural intervention. They're too hot or too shady, the ground is uneven and pot-holed, and the soil is chronically saturated. Others are pleasant settings, but lack the interest and detail of a stimulating environment. They're too flat or too narrow, there aren't enough plants, and everything is open to the public view.

Using landscaping skills you can make these challenging spaces into garden retreats. Once you gain some experience and confidence in planning and construction, you can go a long way toward making any garden a welcoming environment. But keep asking yourself how far you want to go. Sometimes the baby gets thrown out with the bath water as heavy equipment rumbles in to shake, rattle and roll right over the natural world. Should the garden be as lavishly upholstered as your living room? Do you want the fences wired for sound? Is this still a garden, or is it an extension of interior living space? Would you rather be indoors?

Aggressive landscaping projects that entirely replace a familiar setting can sometimes go too far. It's not always necessary to rip out every corner, and most gardens have features well worth preserving. Retaining plants with sentimental associations expresses your "ownership" of the project, and your desire to have the

garden remain a personal place. The point of landscaping is to enhance the natural terrain and provide us with a comfortable seat under the best tree in the yard. The challenge of every landscaping project, big or small, is to find a balance between the natural character of the garden and imposed structural changes making it more useful.

The gardener's role in landscaping is to order the small universe of the backyard. Investing your time and efforts in the garden brings a hands-on knowledge of the spirit of the place. You'll know its valuable assets and the short-comings you intend to change. Planning a patio, building a pathway and making a planting bed are projects that bring the reward of personal satisfaction. If the work is beyond your own capabilities, that's when to ask a professional landscaper to get the job done.

Not every project in the garden is large. Sometimes the most satisfying changes are small and contained within an afternoon's work. What matters most is that you find reward even in the small corners, working with plants, wood and stone. The best-made garden rests on subtle construction techniques and is formed with materials of the earth. Lilacs, not chlorine, perfume the air. And the gardener's influence is everywhere—in the massing of groundcovers, the hedge of flowering shrubs and the comfortable seat under a tree with character and distinction.

the home gardener's reference library

Reading influences experience, and experience guides our choices in reading. Gardeners read about how to make plants grow, or how to accomplish a skill, and then they go out and do it. These are authors with valuable and useful information for gardeners.

Adam, Judith. *The New City Gardener: Natural Techniques and Necessary Skills for a Successful Urban Garden.* Firefly Books Ltd., 1999

Bennett, Jennifer. *Dry-Land Gardening: A Xeriscaping Guide for Dry-Summer, Cold-Winter Climates.* Firefly Books Ltd., 1998

Cox, Jeff. *Landscaping with Nature: Using Nature's Designs to Plan Your Yard.* Rodale Press, 1991

Dirr, Michael A. *Dirr's Hardy Trees and Shrubs: An Illustrated Encyclopedia.* Timber Press, 1997

Druitt, Liz, and G. Michael Shoup. *Landscaping with Antique Roses.* Taunton Press, 1992

Fisher, Kathleen. *Taylor's Guide to Shrubs: How to Select and Grow More than 400 Ornamental and Useful Shrubs for Privacy, Ground Covers, and Foundation Plantings.* Houghton Mifflin Company, 2001

Hayward, Gordon. *Garden Paths: Inspiring Designs and Practical Projects.* Firefly Books, 1993

Hill, Lewis, and Nancy Hill. *The Lawn & Garden Owner's Manual: What to Do and When to Do It.* Storey Communications, 2000

Paterson, Allen. *Designing a Garden: A Guide to Planning and Planting through the Seasons.* Camden House Publishing, 1992

Roach, Margaret. *The Natural Lawn and Alternatives.* Brooklyn Botanic Garden, 1993

Roth, Susan A. *The Four-Season Landscape: Easy-Care Plants and Plans for Year-Round Color.* Rodale Press, 1994

Schenk, George. *The Complete Shade Gardener.* Houghton Mifflin Company, 1985

Silva, Jeff. *Building a Healthy Lawn: A Safe and Natural Approach.* Storey Communications, 1988

Stell, Elizabeth P. *Secrets to Great Soil: A Grower's Guide to Composting, Mulching, and Creating Healthy Fertile Soil for Your Garden and Lawn.* Storey Publishing, 1997

Taylor, Norman. *Taylor's Guide to Trees: A Complete Guide to Gardening with Trees.* Houghton Mifflin Company, 1987

Whitner, Jan Kowalczewski. *Stonescaping: A Guide to Using Stone in Your Garden.* Garden Way Publishing, 1992

index

photo credits

PUBLISHER'S ACKNOWLEDGMENT

Firefly Books thanks **Humber Nurseries Ltd.**, "Ontario's Largest Garden Centre & Butterfly Conservatory," in Brampton, Ontario, for graciously allowing us the use of their property as well as plant materials and garden accessories for photography purposes.

PHOTOGRAPHY CREDITS

Front cover photo by **Andreas Trauttmansdorff**. Author photo by **Mark Mainguy**. **Adam Gibbs Photography** back cover tl, c; 2; 9; 11l; 34; 36; 40tc; 50; 77; 81tl; 89; 94tl, br; 100-01; 108-09; 125; 128bl; 136bl; 144; 162tl; 163tl, br; 164tr, bl; 165tl, bc; 179-80; 185br; 191bc; 200tl; 211br. **Karen Bussolini** back cover tr; 11cl, cr; 15tr; 17bl; 38c; 45bl; 46l, cr; 56; 58br; 60; 88; 99; 110l; 114br; 124; 131; 135; 150tl; 154; 187; 196; 210br; (Design: James David) 46cl; (Design: Dickson DeMarche Landscape Architects) 10; 14br; 16tr; 84-85; (Design: Juanita Flagg) 12; 13; 87; (Design: Wayne Renard) 95; (Design: Johnsen Landscapes and Pools) 28; (Design: Randolf Marshall, Landscape Architect) 71; (Design: Susan Muszala) 68br. **Frank Del Vecchio** back cover b; 14tl; 16bl; 17c; 19; 21; 22; 24br; 25; 26; 31tr; 35; 37; 38r; 39r; 58tl; 61tr; 68tl; 82-83; 86l; 90tl, bl; 92; 110r; 114tl; 115tr, bc; 118tr; 134; 139l; 178; 189bl; 212. **Alan & Linda Detrick** 40bc; 105; 106bl; 107bl; 113; 132tl; 183tr; 185bc; 191tc; 197; 200bl, br; 201; 202tl, tr, bl; (Design: Andrea Buckingham) 8; (Design: Michael Levine) 40tl; 41; 46r; (Design: Ardie Runkel) 93. **Garden Image**/Ian Adams 118bl; 123tr; 129tr; 183bc; 184tr; /**Christine Beck** 133tc; /**Mark Bolton** 137tc; 194tl; /**Alan & Linda Detrick** 130; 214; /**Therese d'Monte** 191tr; /**Michael Dodge** 185tc; /**Andrew Drake** 86r; 156; 213; /**Wally Eberhardt** 91tc; /**Tony Giammarino** 14bc; 141; 211bl; /**John Glover** 11r; 163bc; 190tr; 210bl; /**Mike Grandmaison** 188br; /**Dency Kane** 137bc; 163bl; /**Ernst Kucklich** 114bl; 194tr; 199; 215; /**Carole Ottesen** 126tr; 127bc; 182bl; 190bl; /**Rich Pomerantz** 166tl; 193tl; /**Phillip Roullard** 102; /**Peter Symcox** 146; 190tl; /**Gerald Tang** 137br; 183bl; /**Connie Toops** 147; /**Nance Trueworthy** 161; /**Martien Vinkersteijn** 136tl; 151tr; 152; 189tl. **Garden Matters**/**John Feltwell** 90br; 119bl; 123tc; 132bl; 137tr; 182tr; 191bl. **GardenPhotos.com**/**Graham Rice** 86c; 91tr; 128tr; /**judywhite** 31bl; 61bl; 80tl, tr, br; 81bc; 106br; 118tl; 122tl; 123bl, br; 126tl; 132tr; 133tr; 136br; 137bl; 151bl; 162br; 185bl; 191tl, br; 195br; 205; 211tl, tr. **Garden Picture Library**/**Philippe Bonduel** 91tl; /**Mark Bolton** 165br; /**Eric Crichton** 150bl; 169tl, br; /**John Glover** 119bc; 195bc; 210bl; 211bc; /**Georgia Glynn-Smith** 198tl; /**Sunniva Harte** 15bl; 168tr; 193tr; /**Neil Holmes** 184br; /**Lamontagne** 133tl; 168tl; /**A.I. Lord** 169tr; /**Zara McCalmont** 153; **Mayer/LeScanff** 121; 127tl; **John Neubauer** 181; /**Jerry Pavia** 188bl; /**Howard Rice** 54; 81tc; 91br; 151tl; 163tc; 185tr; 189tc; 211tc; /**Gary Rogers** 150tr; /**Ellen Rooney** 117tr; /**J. S. Sira** 117tl; 127br; 188tl; 189br; /**Friedrick Strauss** 167tl; /**Juliette Wade** 81bl; 193br; /**Stuart Webster** 39l; /**Didier Willery** 107bc; 151bc; 166tr; /**Steven Wooster** 165tr; 167bc. **Greer Gardens/Harold Greer** 81br; 91bc; 106tl; 107tc, br; 115tl; 116bl, br; 119tl, tc; 122br; 123bc; 127bl; 128br; 129tc; 132br; 133bl; 136tr; 150br; 167br; 168bl; 169tc; 192tl, br; 194bl, br; 195tc. **Holt Studios/Willem Harinck** 155; 198br. **Horticultural Photography** 38l; 115bl, br; 116tr; 117tc, bl; 119br; 122tr, bl; 126bl, br; 128tl; 129tl, bl, bc; 133bc, br; 148-49; 162bl; 163tr; 182br; 183tc; 184bl; 189bc; 192bl; 195tl; /**Muriel Orans** 40br. **Jardin botanique de Montréal** 81tr; 90tr; 106tr; 107tl; 117bc, br; 118br; 119tr; 123tl; 127tr; 129br; 137tl; 151tc; 164tl, br; 165bl; 166br; 167tc, tr, bl; 169bl, bc; 182tl; 183tl; 184tl; 192tr; 193bl, bc; 195tr; 210tr. **Andrew Leyerle** 24bl; 39c. **Positive Images/Karen Bussolini** 165tc; /**Jerry Howard** 193tc; /**Lee Lockwood** 80bl; /**Ben Phillips** 91bl; 115tc; 151br; 162tr; 168br; 183br; 185tl; 200cl; /**Diane Pratt** 190br; /**Ann Reilly** 116tl; 188tr; /**Pam Spaulding** 107tr; 114tr; 189tr; 210tl. **Connie Toops** 32; 45tr; 127tc; 166bl; 170; 195bl. **Mark Turner** 139r. **Wild & Natural/Bill Beatty** 202br.

ILLUSTRATION CREDITS

Sarah Jane English 29; 32; 33; 52-53; 62-65; 69; 72-73; 76; 78-79; 96-97, 121; 144-45; 171-77; 204; 206-09. **Frank Del Vecchio** 43. **Terry Shoffner** 18; 30; 57; 59; 66-67; 70; 74-75; 98; 103-4; 111; 120; 142-43.